THREE YEAR PICNIC

*An American Woman's Life
Inside Japanese Prison Camps in
The Philippines During WWII*

Evelyn Whitfield

PREMIERE EDITIONS INTERNATIONAL, INC.
CORVALLIS, OREGON

ABOUT THE COVER:

The background rendering is from a 1930's postcard depicting beautiful Burnham Green in Baguio, The Philippines. The picturesque scene was a day's journey by car from a remote gold mining camp in the northern part of Luzon where the author and her husband were living when evacuated. The Japanese inscription translates as "permission denied"—or simply "no." This message was stamped on most of the internees' petitions.

THREE YEAR PICNIC

An American Woman's Life
Inside Japanese Prison Camps in
The Philippines During WWII

Evelyn Whitfield

P PREMIERE EDITIONS INTERNATIONAL, INC.
CORVALLIS, OREGON

All photographs, drawings, correspondence, documents, media clippings and memorabilia used as illustration are from the private files of the author, except as noted.

PREMIERE EDITIONS INTERNATIONAL, INC.
2397 N. W. Kings Blvd., #311, Corvallis, OR 97330
Telephone (541) 752-4239 — FAX (541) 752-4463
E-MAIL: *publish@premiere-editions.com*

VISIT OUR WEB SITE:
http://www.premiere-editions.com

EDITORS:	Irene L. Gresick
	Beatrice Stauss
DESIGNERS:	Lynn Bell
	Donna Reyes
ILLUSTRATOR:	Nancy Allworth
PHOTO EDITOR:	E. Theresa Rolow
BACK COVER PHOTOGRAPHER:	Ray Westbrook

ISBN: 0-9633818-8-1
Library of Congress Catalog Card Number: 97-75384
Printed in the United States of America

for
Lauri

The Lord is the strength of my life; of whom shall I be afraid?

Though an host should encamp against me, my heart shall not fear: though war should rise against me, in this will I be confident.

— Psalms 27: 1, 3

EVELYN WHITFIELD, BATONG BUHAY, THE PHILIPPINES, 1939

ACKNOWLEDGMENTS

With warm gratitude, I acknowledge helping hands along the way — my close friends, and all the members of my extended family; former students who have heard me speak publicly; my church and academic friends and acquaintances; and my new associates in this professional field — what a support group!

I am indebted to my publisher, Irene Gresick, who has been my guide, protector, friend, and instructor in this new realm of presenting my writing to the world. My niece Nancy Allworth's gifted hands sketched as I described various scenes; her heart is deep into this production, and her excellent illustrations add immeasurably to this book. Beatrice Stauss spent many hours meticulously scanning every sentence and page for the little foxes of typos, syntax errors, and depth of clarity. Lynn Bell and Theresa Rolow enhanced our work with sharp eyes for detail and skilled hands at computer graphics. Donna Reyes envisioned the front cover. I am grateful for her compelling design, and for Ray Westbrook's color portrait that appears on the back cover.

My daughter Laurel Josephine Watkins and her daughter Kimberly Kindred were part of the planning. My two other granddaughters, Kelia and Jennifer Kindred, have always been there to assist me in my physical needs in this sometimes strenuous enterprise.

Other caring people offered personal artifacts and memorabilia to augment our illustrations. They include Norm Yates's rare stamps, Robert Mason's currency and Mike Ryan's coconut knife.

EVELYN WHITFIELD, POLO CLUB, MANILA, 1938

CONTENTS

Norman Whitfield, Polo Club, Manila, 1938

~PART THREE~
HOLMES

THE MOUNTAIN PROVINCE, THE PHILIPPINES

~PART FOUR~
BILIBID

~PART FIVE~
RESCUE

~PART SIX~
POLLY'S SCRAPBOOK

China

Taiwan

Luzon Strait

Luzon

Vietnam

South
China
Sea

Luzon Sea

Philippine
Sea

Sibuyen
Sea

Philippine Trench

Bohol Sea

Sulu Sea

Balabac Strait

Moro Gulf

Mindanao
Sea

Borneo

Celebes Sea

New Guinea

Indonesia

PROLOGUE

Let me tell you a little of what it was like to live in the Philippines before the Japanese invasion of 1941. This lushly beautiful country, scattered around among thousands of islands, populated by a wonderfully diverse people, partly tropical and formed by volcanoes in the sea, was governed by the United States in a benevolent paternalistic manner for many years. The U.S. did not go in to conquer the Philippine Islands, but came into possession of them through victory in the Spanish-American War of 1898. Then our government set about Americanizing its new possession.

We built roads, hospitals, and schools. We taught and enforced sanitation, immunization, and the English language. We introduced modern techniques of agriculture, mining, and commerce. We penetrated the primitive mountain regions where headhunting was still customary, negritos shot poisoned arrows, and Moros stood sullenly by the roadside, sometimes throwing rocks at American cars. We fought and greatly diminished fevers, small pox, tuberculosis, dysentery, and water-borne diseases. We tried to prepare this country for the democracy it would someday attain.

The Filipinos were largely of Malaysian ancestry, but there were many tribes and dialects. The headhunters in the north of Luzon, called Igorots, were pagan, and very different physically from the low-landers — stockier — said to be descended from the Mongolians. The Moros of Mindanao and Zamboanga were Muslim, and the most colorful of all Filipinos. Probably two-thirds of the Filipinos, however, were Christian, with Catholic predominant, the heritage from their Spanish conquerors.

Americans and Europeans were everywhere, and almost always the "boss." They were running the great sugar mills of the Southern Islands; they were running the logging operations that pulled out beautiful hardwoods for export; they grew the pineapples, coconuts, and hemp; they supervised and in many cases owned the gold, copper, and base metal mines. They taught in the schools, and they were missionaries of every denomination.

The Filipinos grew the food, did all the manual labor, worked in our homes as house servants, provided the public markets, created the beauty (wonderful fabrics, jewelry, clothing), and in general, made life very easy for the white bosses and their families. They are a beautiful people, with exquisite light mahogany skin, dark eyes, black satin hair, and usually slender build. I came to love them, many individually, all *en masse*, and through the years also developed admiration and respect.

For me and my husband Norman, it was a "best of all worlds" situation in those halcyon days. As young marrieds, our life was social, gay and adventurous. In the cities, work was carried on in almost European fashion, with long, unhurried lunch breaks. When we lived in Manila, Norman and I both came home during the noon hour — rested, bathed and changed, and lunched before returning to work. In the mines and forests, it was quite different. The men worked very hard, for long hours, with little time off. On one of Norman's jobs, he had only Christmas Day off during one whole year, and that was given grudgingly. There was little for the women to do, and many were idle, which seemed frivolous to me. Brought up in a small Oregon town, where everyone was expected to be useful, I chafed at the lack of purposeful activity, and usually tried to find work. I also spent many wonderful hours gardening.

People have asked me many times how Norman and I happened to be in the Philippine Islands in 1941, when things were in such turmoil in the Far East. Some of you might remember that jobs were scarce here in those depression days, so when we got out of college (we had been engaged for three years), Norman decided to go elsewhere for work — and his parents were living in the Philippine Islands. Furthermore, there was a gold rush of sorts out there. So he worked his way out on an ocean liner, hopped off in Manila, and made his way up into the mountains to join his father in the lumber business, supplying timbers to the gold mines. Norman was a logging engineer, so this was a good occupation for him.

A year later, accompanied by Polly Whitfield (my mother-in-law to be), I went out to join him, traveling on a Danish cargo ship. Norman and I were married in Manila, which was glamorous and beautiful then, but we lived up in the mountains most of our years there. We loved it—it seemed adventurous and free, and we were young. Eventually, in 1939, we were living in the far north end of the Island of Luzon, in the mountains, at a gold mining camp nearly inaccessible by car, almost completely isolated. It was beautiful, and with three servants to make my life easy, I had time to work in my lovely garden, filled with orchids, gardenias and hibiscus—and to follow Norman around in the mountains.

But in December of 1941, everything in the world changed, of course. The first we knew of it was the radio news of the bombing of Pearl Harbor—and suddenly the 8,000 miles between us and my family in Corvallis, Oregon, seemed a great distance. The Japanese planes came low over our mountain mining camp, and we were almost immediately ordered by the Philippine government, a commonwealth of the United States of America, to evacuate—and this is where my book begins.

—Evelyn Whitfield

EVELYN WHITFIELD, LUSOD, THE PHILIPPINES, 1938

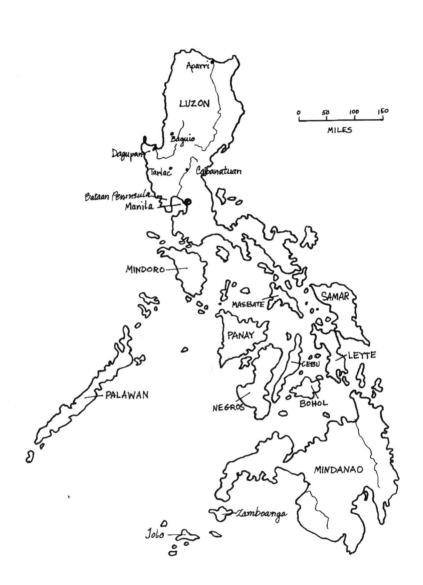

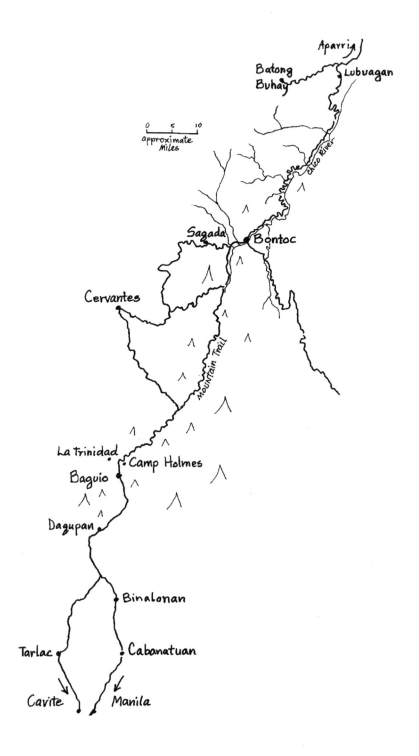

~ PART ONE ~
BEFORE THE INVASION

OUR HOME AT BATONG BUHAY, THE PHILIPPINES, 1941

Chapter 1:
IT CAN'T HAPPEN TO US!

The perfect early morning stillness held even the tall pines in its enchantment; no breath of a breeze stirred their glistening needles to a sigh. Not a trace of mist remained from the miracle of another dawn just passed. The heavens were peaceful and nature wrapped in shimmering beauty there where mountains, sky and forest were a symphony of blue and purple as far as eye could reach.

Thin spirals of smoke rose straight above the five little unpainted houses half-hidden among the trees on the steep, rough mountain-side. I reflected for a moment that it seemed even quieter than usual this morning. Because our radio had quit the night before, we had missed the early news and band music broadcast. My husband, Norman, had gone up the hill to his sawmill. The black and white kitten and I were musing over the flower arrangements for the day.

The date was December 8, 1941 — still December 7th on the other side of the International Dateline. We were at Batong Buhay, an isolated gold mining camp far north of Baguio on the island of Luzon in the Philippines.

My little neighbor Mary called several times before her voice penetrated to me through the depths of my fragrant reverie — and the news she shouted was beyond any believing. Such things didn't happen on a golden December morning, not in this world — but the world had changed while we slept.

The women of the mining camp and the few men who hadn't gone off to their work before the news of the attack on Pearl Harbor was broadcast were soon huddled around the radio in the mess house, protesting and cursing, but beginning to credit what we heard. I sent a shakily scrawled note up the mountain to Norman, and the men at the mine office were told.

Their first action was to post lookouts on the highest points, for planes from the North would fly over us on their way to Baguio and Manila. Already Manila had been bombed — now word of bombing at Baguio. A great fleet of Japanese ships was said to be in the Philippine waters. Our planes and pilots were destroyed together on the ground at Fort Stotsenberg. Thundering across the air waves came the reports as the toll mounted, appalling, tragic, heart-scarring. Even the announcers were so distraught that they spoke sometimes huskily, sometimes fairly shouting, often tangling their words and sentences.

We were suddenly conscious of being thousands of miles from home. There was a rage at the ruthless marauder who had put the torch to the tinder and deliberately started the unquenchable flames of war. We were homesick, and already had a foretaste of nostalgia for life as it had been to that hour and would never be again. The sunshiny days of our youth seemed suddenly gone. Yet we had a great faith, and that faith remained with us through the next almost forty months of trial — we were sure we would be rescued, the Americans would come, God was on our side. This faith gave us the backbone that never bent in a submissive bow to our conquerors. We believed in the righteous invincibility of our country.

Our actions for the next three days were as erratic as our thinking, but in one opinion were we all agreed — that we were safer right where we were than anywhere else in the Islands. When the servants threatened to bolt, we spoke to them seriously and kindly of our complete security, believing in it ourselves.

Only one road gave access to the Camp — a hair-raising narrow one. It was often closed by slides, so it would be no trick at all, we thought, for us to permanently block it — if we needed to — with a stick or two of dynamite. The homes, mess, Camp store and hospital had ample food and supplies for months ahead, and if worse should come to worst, we were confident that we could easily "take to the hills" and remain hidden and protected indefinitely. The hill people, the Igorots, were friendly to us.

So, from the depths of our innocent assurance, we laid careful plans, and even sent a ham radiogram to a dear family friend in Manila, offering her the hospitality and sanctuary of our "safe isolation."

There were five young couples of us, a few bachelors, and two small children. Baguio, the nearest city, was a long day's journey to the south over perilous mountain roads. We had been having a wonderful life, carefree and far from the rest of the world. Now we were stunned — but still confident.

I sewed constantly on new blackout draperies, so that we could dispense with the nightly choice of pinning up all the extra blankets and sheets and tarpaulins over doorways and windows. In the evenings, we gathered at one house or another, and in the stuffy dimness talked endlessly, pausing only to listen to new broadcasts. Then we would disperse to our own homes and keep on indefatigably with our feverish weighing, guessing, planning.

On the morning of the third day, I bustled about the kitchen, hurrying to get through and on with the sewing, pausing briefly now and then to study the effect of the one finished panel hanging a little askew. Norman came in, and a glance at his face told me the news he was bringing was bad. It was.

We had been completely wrong. Instead of being a secure hideaway, our Camp was a dangerous trap, directly in the path of Japanese troops now making an unexpected landing a little to the north of us, at Aparri. They would surely invade our whole region. A Philippine government official had just telephoned our manager, demanding the immediate evacuation of all American and British women and children to Baguio, stating firmly that all the mountain roads were to be blown in a matter of hours.

Chapter 2:
EVACUATION

Some words acquire real meaning only through experience. "Evacuation" to me had always vaguely meant peasants streaming down a road deep with dust or thick with mud, their poor belongings on ox-carts or their own humble backs, their faces dull with hopelessness. It certainly had not meant *me*, snatching a suitcase from a closet shelf, confusedly throwing in dresses and no belts, mismated shoes, passport, birth certificate, a handful of sterling silver teaspoons (we were just starting a set, so I must have thought it important to save them), and my newest nylons; trying to be calm enough to quiet my demoralized servants and get them ready to leave with me; deciding at the last minute to take the kitten.

I never dreamed it could mean stopping my routine preparation of a casserole of macaroni and cheese for lunch, walking out of our home almost empty-handed, leaving it just as it was in its early-morning disarray, never to see it or anything in it again.

It came to mean, with experience, the shriek of a telephone, a man's voice speaking sharply. "Within an hour— only the women and children—watch for planes!" and always, "Last chance! The Japanese are on their way. The roads will be blown!"

The picture is sharp-etched, indelible in my memory. It was a somber, rainy mid-morning when we left Batong Buhay, our mountain mining camp; the start from Balatoc Mining Camp ten days later was made in the chill darkness just before daybreak; the harrowing departure from Bilibid Prison past flames and street-fighting and snipers came at nine-thirty at night. The settings and times could differ, but the pattern of evacuation seemed tryingly repetitious:

women, with their children, standing around while the men, brusque with worry, load the trucks first with the odd assortment of luggage; unsteady goodbyes and choked admonitions to "Take care of yourself, honey!" while hearts fill with terror and loss at the separation; the one inevitable case of hysteria or abandoned weeping that meets with such cold disapproval from the other evacuees.

Evacuations always seem to take forever. The trips are hot (or cold), uncomfortable, dangerous. Now and again the ominous roar is heard, the trucks grind to a jarring halt while the word goes flying: "Get into the ditch!" The first time everyone dutifully holds a pencil between his teeth, remembers the cotton plugs for his ears, and hugs the ground until the planes are gone. We all knew about Sue Duncan who, with her baby son in her arms, ran out with the others to stare at the planes that first morning. No one then suspected that they could be other than our own, until those deadly bombs came hurtling to the earth. Blonde, pretty Mrs. Duncan had just time to fling her baby to the ground and cover him with her own body. Later, in the Baguio prison camp, she had learned to get around on her one leg and crutches, her triumph and reward the sturdy little lad, who after his months of suffering, grew to walk and run like the other kids.

But when we were doing our scuttling act from this town to that, we knew only that the young mother had lost her leg, and her baby had been injured, and no one knew yet whether either would live; and all because they had looked up at planes. The stark reality of the danger had been brought home to us, and helped us to deny ourselves that little peek that was so hard to resist.

Lying prone in a roadside ditch was so unfamiliar an act to us that in spite of the grave aspects, most of us were inclined to feel foolish about it, especially when the smaller children gleefully made it a game. The planes overhead were always too high to identify, if they came into view at all, and we probably couldn't have identified them, in our inexperience, had they been lower. So, for the first few times, knees did shake ignominiously (and secretly) for minutes after the alarm had passed.

One man was always sent along with each group of women as guard and chaperon, and I retain a vivid image of our guardian on that first trip down the Mountain Trail. He was a distinguished-looking British geologist, black-bearded and sun-helmeted, and with a gun across his bare knees, he appeared a very bulwark of protection. After one look at the beard, and a comprehensive glance at us that noted our bright kerchiefs tied peasant-wise over our hair, our dust-streaked faces and odd-shaped bundles, a stern little Philippine Constabulary officer halted us just outside of Baguio, and demanded to know what, or who, we were. Rather taken aback, we said, "Americans and British," but he looked very skeptical and finally burst out, "You look like Portuguese to me!"

The nights were so bad. The first one we spent at a wayside rest house, with nothing more upsetting than the bedbugs and my playful kitten to contend against, yet sleep would not come, and we were on our way down the Mountain Trail, in deep fog and without lights, by three in the morning. The next night our shelter was an unoccupied native hut that proved to harbor a million ravenous fleas left behind by some long-gone dog.

That long trip down to Baguio had been fraught with indecision and setbacks from the beginning. Road washouts made the first lap too slow, necessitating an extra night along the way.

But we breakfasted on fresh strawberries at Mount Data Lodge the following morning. The Swedish consul and his family joined us, exclaiming ruefully that they were just on their way up to our mine, where the Consul, a very handsome and charming man, had hoped to find sanctuary for his pretty American wife and two small sons for the duration. So they turned with us back down the hazardous road they had just traveled.

We were more than half the way from Mount Data to Baguio when a tall, red-headed stranger waved his arms at us in the middle of the highway, and excitedly warned us that Baguio at that moment was being evacuated because of the bombing, so that it was senseless for us to proceed. He offered us the additional information that some of the Baguio people were even now at a sawmill camp close by, and that we might find room there.

The Consul and Dr. Skerl, our protector, saw the rest of us safely headed toward the sawmill camp, then took one car and went on down to Baguio to investigate. They returned at night with the report that only a few people had left the city, and they felt it was as safe as any place. We spent the night at the sawmill camp, with the fleas whose viciousness one could never forget.

Days and nights seemed a blur of riding, jouncing, and rebellion at being forced to run away. At the end of the trip we were stiff, filthy, hungry, and utterly tired, and at a loss about our next move. With the bombers over the cities, no place offered any security or rest.

In Baguio, I first called my friends Marge and Larry, at the Balatoc Gold Mining Camp. They gave me a lovely, solicitous welcome, along with my kitten, who promptly scratched the baby. I sent my two devoted little house girls on down to the lowlands, to their families, and never heard from them again.

Much to my relief and delight, Norman arrived unexpectedly on Sunday, and we planned that we would stay with our friends for Christmas, and then perhaps we could decide on a course of action. He had ripped three of our priceless Amorsolo paintings from their frames, and rolled them up to fit into his duffle bag, his only luggage—so we had some paintings and sterling spoons, anyway. Before he left Batong Buhay, he had dumped the gold bricks that had already been milled down the deepest shaft, and as he left, on foot, he had been followed by armed Igorots, from the But-But tribe, and he never knew whether they were protecting him or had nefarious motives, but he was never harmed. He caught a ride somewhere along the Mountain Trail and arrived in Baguio after a three or four day trek.

We had barely settled in with our friends, whose tiny daughter Laurie Lynne was our godchild, when the next telephone call came. The nightmare caravan moved on, gathering more and more into its wretched procession and bringing Norman and me to another, harder parting. Christmas came and went in an air raid shelter with scarcely a word to note its passing. Again, only the women and children, with a few men for guards, including Larry, were given transportation on the crammed school buses.

Along the way from Baguio to Manila, we pulled off the road a dozen times to watch our troops go by. Slim, laughing boys held up their fingers in the victory sign to us from their tanks and trucks as they rolled onward to their destruction at San Fernando. We felt such a thrill of pride and security in them, and were probably no more ignorant of the ghastly futility of their fighting that battle ahead than they were.

And all the while, hope remained alive in us that the real evacuation might still be possible, that great fortified ships would come for us, and we would sail away some night from the dusty, nerve-shattering hell that war was making of our lovely islands.

Chapter 3:
BOMBS BURSTING IN AIR

The bombing of Manila by the Japanese in December of 1941 never seemed to me so awe-inspiring as the accounts of the European and British, especially London, raids. Our own demolition explosions and fires at Cavite, Fort Wm. McKinley, and Pandacan, were far more spectacular to see. But we were sickeningly aware that Cavite was actually a duplicate Pearl Harbor; that the harbor and the river were glutted with wrecks and bodies; that many of the raging fires and those crumpled walls we could see from our borrowed apartment were the result of those bombs. Reluctantly we sought shelter during the raids, hating the very thought of cowering from the enemy, and always wishing there were something we could *do.*

Strange situations arose while the startling wail of the siren shrilled at us to take cover. Dignity was hard to maintain when I found myself assigned to a crouching position under a counter in a drug store, the glamorous Botica Boie, where we had always gone for ice cream sodas, watching the gorgeous Spanish girls giggle and drink their whipped-cream topped hot chocolate. I was aware of the huge glass ball of colored water swinging eerily overhead, and an aged Filipina shared my niche, counting her beads feverishly. My friend Erna, who lived uncomfortably near an air field, could find no better shelter, so she told me, than under the bed. So during a raid, there she and her dog and the cook would lie, my friend saying over and over to herself the Scientific Statement of Being (from Mary Baker Eddy's book, *Science And Health With Key to the Scriptures*), the dog growling restively, and the cook naming her saints.

My long hair was a trial to me in the heat, and the task of keeping it combed and up, in the hectic rush of raids and alarms, quickly decided me that life without it would be much simpler. So I made my appointment at a nearby beauty shop, and submitted to the artistic fussing of one Hans over my "hairstyle." Then bombs fell devastatingly in the Walled City and on the Port Area, and planes roared low overhead. I spent three memorable hours sitting on the floor, my back to the wall along with the other customers, surrounded and canopied by mirrors and skylights, with some of the waving gadgets still on my head.

The owner of the shop, an Austrian with pro-Nazi leanings, suavely served us syrupy coffee and tiny crackers and Roquefort cheese about noon, so we all, operators and clients, munched and supped companionably over the movie magazines we pretended to look at, wishing we were almost anywhere else where there might be a bit less glass around. When the all-clear sounded, I paid my bill, said an abrupt thanks, and darted out the door and down the street, amused at amazement of others, with my hair still in tight and multitudinous pincurls. The only clear idea I had at that moment was to get back to the apartment before the next raid started. Through the following months when I gave my short curly hair its customary brief combing, I sometimes wondered just what type of coiffure the hair stylist had intended for me.

On a Sunday morning, I sat for an extra hour, when church services were over, awaiting the end of a raid. The church was a small frame building, but no alarm or uneasiness reflected in any of the serene faces there, as we sang *a cappella* all the old familiar hymns while we waited out the bombers.

The frequency of night raids caused us to work out an efficient routine. Before we went to bed each night, the handy rubberized bag was filled with diapers; nursing bottles of water were prepared; two baby blankets laid beside the bag; and a collection of small cushions was all neatly organized for hasty exits. When the siren sounded, two adults picked up the babies and the rest the equipment. Then away we scurried down to the third floor where we and the other tenants arranged ourselves in the stairwell around the elevator shaft, comforted somewhat in the knowledge that at least we were "safe" in the heart of this modern concrete and steel earthquake-proof building. When the raid ended, we could ride back up to our ninth floor, but during a raid no one used the elevator. The temptation to stay up topside to watch at least one raid was so strong that it had to be put down each time anew.

Sometimes, as on Christmas Eve, it seemed as though the raiders were deliberately tantalizing us. They came again and again, all through the day and night, and no one dared attempt a cooling bath. It was impossible even to prepare or eat a meal. Yet that night no bombs were dropped. For hours on end we heard their droning rise and subside — and that was our Christmas.

One night, when we tuned in on the radio to hear Station KGEI, San Francisco, we heard a news reporter telling the world "Manila is surrounded by a wall of fire!" And there we sat, watching the great flames of the Pandacan oil fires, Cavite Naval Yard and City, Fort McKinley supply dumps; and the docks and Walled City still burning from the afternoon's raid. We could see the whole circle from our high position, and the malevolent glare reflected against every window. I was thinking, as I listened and watched, of my family at home, and my heart felt as though it would never stop hurting in the understanding of the grief and anxiety they would be suffering as they listened, too, to such broadcasts.

Those days, people seemed close to tears, although no one would have admitted the depth of his feeling, if he could find expression for it. Families, even there in the Islands, were scattered to the winds, without communication; it was like trying to find a trail in the jungle to locate those from whom you had become separated. By this time, neither Norman nor I had the slightest idea where the other one was, and this was always at the top of my mind. I kept thinking he might have gone back up into the hills he knew so well to join the guerillas. I didn't know at that time that he longed to do just that, but was afraid that somehow it might endanger me.

And so the new order seemed to be senseless destruction of life and happiness and beauty, and the heart and mind grew numb with trying to accustom oneself.

Chapter 4:
OPEN CITY

From our balcony we witnessed a beaten, crippled American city being torn to pieces by vandals. Manila seemed to *us* at that time an American city, even though the names were Spanish and the people Filipino. While it was a Filipino metropolis, many of its residents were striving then for Americanism. We always considered it not a native city, but like our own, and humanly, we found its bitter tribulation the more poignant because of that.

None of us had a clear idea of what "open city" really meant, other than that by declaring Manila "open" the Government hoped to save it from further destruction, and to protect the populace against any more bombing. We tried to assume an air of relief, but it was a bitter disappointment to us that even our attempt at defense was to be withdrawn, and I think we all experienced a secret feeling of humiliation and forsakenness.

The very evening that the announcement was made, we heard newscaster Ignacio Javier's cultured, disdainful voice assuring us on the local news broadcast that our forces were hurling back the hundreds of thousands of "beardless boys" whom the Japanese were now "reduced" to using for invasion troops on the beach at Antimonan. Rumors poured in on every breeze—great convoys were speeding to the Philippines from home; fantastic armadas of planes were close and would soon fill the air, making short work of the overrated Japanese navy and air force; our submarines were cutting the enemy fleet to pieces even now in the Philippine waters. Reinforcements—rescue—were always so close!

In Manila, though, we knew we were alone and utterly defenseless for the time being. Manila was indefensible, they had said; now that word described us. As the armed forces withdrew from the city, lawlessness blew like a typhoon through the broad avenues and narrow alleys — wrecking, looting, fighting, carousing. From the great warehouses on the docks flowed a river of corruption, the looters who carried off everything they could and destroyed what they couldn't.

Down the famed promenade of Dewey Boulevard along the Bay front thronged thousands of men, women, and children, straining under their loads of food, clothing, household furnishings, Red Cross goods — then somewhere ridding themselves of the load, streaming back again to the source. They rode in carromatas, on bicycles, in cars, or they ran. A man would bend beneath a half of beef from the Cold Stores *bodega*, or warehouse, knowing that the meat wouldn't last forty-eight hours in the tropic heat out of the freezing unit. We were aghast at the heedless waste. His wife would pant in his wake bearing a lovely Oriental rug from the Luzon Brokerage warehouse.

To complete the sordid spectacle, in the big hotel area near us the Boulevard was lined with buyers for the loot, accessories to the crime screeching, "I will buy! I will buy! How much you want, huh?" Most of these buyers were refugees from Europe and Asia who had taken sanctuary by the thousands in the Islands during the last year or two, and from the day of their humble, timid arrival, had been slowly but shrewdly working their way into control of the small retail mercantile business of Manila. Occasionally one would see some desperate American dart into the melee to retrieve, if he could, something he recognized as his own.

Every corner grocery and native *tienda*, every shop from the incense-thick Bombay stores to the modern American department stores downtown, was fair meat to the loot-crazed mob. Windows and doors were hastily barricaded; frantic shopkeepers did what they could to guard their stocks. Clusters of American men stood around in front of the hotels arguing the possibility of restoring and maintaining some kind of order, without arms or authority to do either. Native police seemed nowhere in evidence. We saw dozens of buildings violated without hindrance.

We had all been warned by radio to stay off the streets, of course, but our search for food went on in spite of mobs and closed stores. In our apartment, one day, we found that we had nothing left in our cupboard but one pound of lima beans, to serve six adults and two babies. So Larry and I— I because I had lived in Manila, Larry because he was big and strong and smart—pushed through surly masses on the streets to get to the Red Cross; we appealed to the YMCA, and to a big hotel nearby, offering anything they wanted for some canned milk, at least. But money in our hands couldn't buy food in Manila those days.

The last straw was the bombing on the Pasig River. We had ceased to worry about planes, and when the bombs dropped that day, destroying buildings along the bank as well as the ships they were meant for, we lost even that slight sense of security. We were shocked that the Japanese would stoop to prey on that most vulnerable of all places, an open city. We had no way of knowing then that the ships there gave them a technical excuse for thus violating international law. Of all the bombing that was done in the Islands, this had the most shattering effect on all of us.

Quezon City

City Limit

San Juan R.

Tondo

Santo Tomas University

Bilibid Prison

Pasig R.

Intramuros

Malacanan Palace

Docks

Paco

Santa Ana

Ermita

Dewey Blvd.

Malate

Manila Bay

City of Manila

0   1
miles

Chapter 5:
NEW FLAG OVER MANILA

Early in January 1942, suspense was so thick it hung in the air like a pall. Our American flag had vanished from the roof of the High Commissioner's office and residence building. Without fanfare, it was gone; the pole stood stark and waiting. We waited.

Then they came—in trucks filled with soldiers, and in beautiful American cars confiscated for the grand entrance, the Japanese swept down Dewey Boulevard, preceded by their banner of the Rising Sun. Manila was that day officially occupied. Again we disregarded warnings and flocked to the street to watch as they came into the city, to mock quietly among ourselves their symbol that immediately fluttered from the top of that bare pole and from every pole in sight, henceforth known to us as the "fried egg."

Filipino faces were typically expressionless at the drama enacted for their special benefit, but not ours. We rather arrogantly considered it all very stagey (the shoe being on the wrong foot); we were nonetheless a thoroughly miserable and homesick group, standing there and scoffing away the last fleeting moments of our freedom.

Then it was ended. The conquering heroes quickly herded us off the streets and into our homes or hotels, and the radio began its incessant bleating of proclamations and orders: "Stay in your houses. Black-out strictly enforced. Curfew for everyone at dark. Registration to be announced. The forces of His Imperial Majesty of Japan to be respected and obeyed. The enemy [us] has been vanquished and we are the conquerors [and they were] come to gloriously liberate the enslaved Filipino." And so on. The streets were empty of civilians, and we watched in fascination from our high windows the posting of hundreds of guards about the buildings and along the streets.

We were not accustomed to the appearance of the uniformed Japanese, and were not admiring, then or ever during the years to follow. Perhaps it's difficult to see grace in one's captors.

The moon over the Philippine Islands was full that first week in January. Its brilliance picked out in silvered clarity the total scene through the night, giving us no relief. In the white hours we sat waiting, watching, sleeping little and lightly. The second night of the occupation, hoarse shouts filled our small corridor and heavy fists pounded on our locked door. Japanese soldiers were there, and they were drunk. They had with them a cringing Filipino interpreter who was very nearly speechless. Insistent that we were violating the blackout, they had to be shown how the moon reflected from the glass doors on the balcony before they withdrew in ugly humor, leaving us nauseated with shock.

Rifle shots rang out continuously in the streets, day and night, and the guttural sounding shouts never ceased, but we could never see where the excitement or disturbance was nor what it was about. We had been warned by our departing government to destroy all intoxicating liquors, but the warning must not have been completely observed, for drunkenness seemed rampant among the soldiers.

~ PART TWO ~
SANTO TOMAS

Chapter 6:
AND THE GATES CLOSE

One of the tenants of the building was a lovely Spanish girl, the wife of an American Standard Oil career man in the Islands. Her elder sister was married to a German, which gave her more freedom to come and go than other Europeans, but both sisters were ardently anti-Japanese, with all the emotional vigor of their Latin blood. When they discovered our food predicament, the elder one offered to see what she could do for us, although we were strangers to her, and there was a real risk, even then, in being too obviously sympathetic to Americans. At her insistence, we pooled our cash and gave it to her, and on the seventh day of the New Year, she and two servants came fairly bounding into the apartment, laden with food—vegetables, canned milk, meat, even two live squawking chickens. We almost wept our gratitude and threw ourselves into an orgy of cooking. Our luncheon menu included a tuna fish salad, hot biscuits, potatoes, and sausages. The table was set, and we were gloating with anticipation, but we never ate. On that day, before noon, the call came.

All morning we had been watching and wondering as little groups of white people were marched past, literally at the points of guns. The occupants of the Bay View Hotel, across the street from us, had sat since breakfast time in the shadeless, throbbing heat in front of the building, each with a bundle or suitcase, surrounded by guards. By telephone, we had received a guarded warning that we might be moved somewhere soon; that the district next to us had been cleared out two days ago.

Suddenly, at eleven o'clock, our apartment building seemed filled with Japanese. All the occupants were assembled, and lined up (in an unrecognized portent of a thousand future line ups) in the apartment of the manager. There we were listed by name, age, sex, and occupation by an official-appearing Nipponese civilian in immaculate whites. Guards stood about, bayonets ready for the first sign of insubordination from this menacing group of women, children, elderly people—with four or five young husbands intent only on causing no trouble for their families.

The questioning ended, we were instructed to return to our apartments, pack food, clothing, and bedding for "three days," and to be ready in half an hour when we would be taken "to a certain place." Everything in those war days was shrouded in great secrecy. The men's belongings must be packed separately. This latter order sounded ominous to us, for we never ceased to live with the fear that they would take all the young men away. I longed for Norman, and caught myself thinking in a panic that now he might never be able to find me. I still had no idea where he was, making it impossible even to try to send a message tracing my steps this far. I took a moment to put in a cautious telephone call to the dear friend who had loaned me the apartment, but could only say that we were leaving at once. Then a soldier lunged in, looking for cigarettes, and motioned for us to leave.

In the entrance of the building, guards pawed through our suitcases, grumbling loudly at those who stretched the prescribed limits a bit, searching rather clumsily, but thoroughly, for flashlights, cameras and film, knives, even scissors. Then, and in later searchings, the soldiers displayed a childish curiosity about our personal effects, often examining closely with much excited talk among themselves some foreign toilet article or gadget, especially anything basically feminine. I had hurriedly entrusted our precious colored movie film to the pretty Spaniard, telling her not to let it get her into trouble, but to save it if she could. I left our camera in the apartment, in the darkest corner of the highest cupboard, not really believing that I would see it again, but not pleased at the idea of some Japanese soldier enjoying it!

The searching was slow and tedious, but finally we were loaded into the vehicles—women and children into a bus, men into a truck. The bus jerked away in one direction, the truck in another, and we crossed our fingers against our fears.

We kept up a continual chatter of light banter in our bus, while our escorts glared blankly. Repartee centered about the fine points of being evacuated and cautious innuendos concerning our hosts. A few women, in spite of themselves, were obviously pale from envisioning a sickening future of machine-gunning, mass rape, or unthought-of horrors; certainly none of us had the slightest conception of what to expect. We were aware of the Filipinos, many openly weeping, who massed along the streets to watch our convoy into captivity.

But the women's chins were up, and scornful determination fiercely bristled in the atmosphere, while the laughter and talk flowed on, somewhat too shrill. Once, during the lengthy years of internment that followed, a certain commandant of the Santo Tomas prison camp expressed his puzzlement to one of our Central Committee members when he said, "I do not understand the American women. They are in a prison, their country is already defeated, they have nothing. Yet they laugh, they sing, they are always working at preparing food. How is this?" The pattern was set at the beginning. Tears and fears were not to be condoned; one does not weaken.

Our bus took us to Santo Tomas, an ancient Spanish university, and there we beheld an amazing spectacle. Sitting on the grass of the campus, beneath the lovely old trees, strolling down the graveled path, picnicking from cans and boxes, were hundreds of people. Many waved to us, and here and there a friend would call out. This looked anything but sinister. It might have been a large club picnic, except for one incongruous, back-to-the-real-world factor— the omnipresent Japanese bayonets gleaming amid the pastels and whites of smart frocks and suits.

We stopped in the plaza in front of the main building of the University and actually let out whoops of relief to see the men of our group standing there waiting for us. Larry immediately hurried forward to help Marge and the baby, but a soldier pushed him roughly and snarled unintelligibly, but obviously enough, to get back over where he was. Larry's white face was a mask of fury for an unguarded moment, and the spectators all looked ill. For the first time, we were actually seeing an American "pushed around" by the Japanese, and we didn't like it. There was nothing to do about it, either, but take it, and wait.

After lining us up and checking us off, the Japanese designated a guide for us and motioned us to take our bags and follow him. Canned goods are heavy, and Marge and I had almost filled my suitcase with what the Spanish woman had brought us, especially the baby food. Without masculine muscle, the bag was nearly immovable, but when I pantomimed that I'd like some assistance, the rebuff was contemptuous. So I gave the whole thing up and left the suitcase there in the plaza. Up to the third floor we climbed, then along a long corridor, and down a flight of stairs to a room already bulging with women and babies, bedding and clothes and food. Blankets were spread all over the floor, and upturned chairs and school desks utilized for mosquito net props; other desks had been pushed together for beds. Marge and I cleared a space in front of the door inside the room, marking out our spot by laying a sheet on the floor, and a suitcase and knitting bag at the ends. There had been neither pad nor mosquito net in the borrowed apartment (too high for mosquitoes) for us to appropriate.

Then we hurried outside, where I tackled that loathsome suitcase again under the unmoved stare of the guards. By pushing and shoving, I had maneuvered it across half the plaza, when straight out of the cinema a hero stepped forward. Without a glance at the soldiers, a broad-chested fiery-topped giant of a man strode to my side, announced loudly, "I'll help you, sister! Where do you want this to go?" He picked up my bag and marched into the building, unscathed.

Breathless with gratitude and admiration, and trying to keep ahead of his huge strides, I led him carefully up to the third floor, down the long dismal corridor, down the flight of stairs to the right room, with some pride—to find that he looked quite red in the face as he demanded, "What kind of a game was that? Just why in hell did you take me up to the third floor and then back to the second floor?" I had no answer. That was the way the guide had showed us to our room, and I didn't know there was any other way to get there. All the thrill was quite gone from my dramatic rescue, and my thank-you was meek.

Outside again I joined one of the buzzing little groups and for the rest of the afternoon we conjectured and wondered. Conversation was guarded in tone but grim enough in content. The hungry ones took time out to eat late in the afternoon, deleting extravagantly from their food supplies bread, unheated Vienna sausages or corned beef, and juicy slices of golden papaya. We gave a sad and fleeting thought to chilled crisp salad and hot buttered biscuits, but seemed to have no appetite for what was available. Someone made coffee, but put milk into it, which spoiled it for me.

Along the outside of the fence which surrounded the campus Filipinos milled about, peering through at us with an intermingling of incredulity, curiosity, sympathy, and fear. Among them were old family servants and long-time employees of American business concerns, uncertain now of their own futures and feelings. They sadly assured their former employers later that they felt very much like forsaken children. Within a few hours they found one concrete thing to do, and threw themselves into the task wholeheartedly. They brought food, clothing, cots, mosquito nets, pillows, dishes, cooking utensils, anything they could retrieve or think of. For the next few days these articles passed through the fence, over it, and under it; we who were from out of town stood on the sidelines wishing desperately to see one familiar face out there, so that we, too, could send for a few of the things we needed.

Finally the mobs of eager Americans on the inside and clamoring Filipinos on the outside were dispersed abruptly by the Japanese, who objected far more to the sympathetic loyalty of the Filipinos for Americans than to the supplies being brought into Santo Tomas.

At five o'clock we were sent inside, into the sweltering, filthy, infested, crowded corridors and rooms. Everyone moved about constantly. Babies wept inconsolably through the long night for their own comfortable cribs. The weak little showers in the antiquated bathrooms were never off. The provident few who had been able to bring pads or blankets or cots stretched out for troubled dozing, but our first experience with trying to find a comfortable position on a concrete floor discouraged us. Mosquitoes descended on us in vicious swarms. Bedbugs scurried from walls and chairs and feasted on us if we sat down for a few moments. We dared not undress for the night.

Marge and I took turns carrying Laurie Lynne up and down the halls until she would at last drop off to sleep. Then we would carefully lay her down on the sheet, but every time she would at once turn over, bumping her poor little head on the hard floor, and waken screaming with terror. Someone came to our rescue with a mosquito net for us, and once, then, we crawled under with the baby, and tried to soothe her to drowsiness as we held her between us. But she took this for play time and her giggles and delighted, wordless chattering roused those who were trying to sleep, as she bounced first on her mother and then on me in hilarious glee. We retreated again to walking her up and down the corridor. Endless night.

Guards in heavy boots clumped through the halls and rooms all night long, turning on lights, walking on the makeshift beds, talking loudly among themselves—I truly think they were not sure what they were supposed to be doing with all these women and children. Once, a few nights later, when I had found a box to sleep on, I was resting under the net. A guard approached. With real horror in my heart, I felt his hands fumbling with the net. I feigned sleep with every nerve shrieking. Then he turned away, and I realized with a queer shock that my little-boy pajamas on loan from a friend, curly short hair, and petite stature had misled him into thinking I was a child. He paused, then tucked in the mosquito net! For all our years in the Islands, we had lived among Japanese, and knew them to be extraordinarily gentle and loving with children. I found it blessedly reassuring to discover that even these soldiers, trained to hate us and ready— on command—to destroy us individually or *en masse*, could still show love and tenderness.

We knew, that first night, that we were now prisoners indeed—Americans without freedom. Had we known then that our captivity would endure for more than three years, under steadily deteriorating conditions, it would have been an unbearable prospect.

Chapter 7:
LIVING SPACE

We soon realized that the "three days" previously mentioned by the Japanese was not to be taken literally. We always maintained our temporary status, nevertheless. People looked two weeks, three months, or even a year ahead, but that was the outside limit of pessimism.

It was obvious, however, that no matter what our length of stay, certain concerns were of immediate and vital nature. Never wholly satisfied and often hungry, life became a scramble for food, and that remained our preoccupation. Quartered in dirty buildings in a hot climate, under conditions ideal for plague and epidemic, cleanliness became a fetish and sanitation a battle cry from the first day. But the one issue that caused more clashing of personalities, more disruption of friendly relations, and a disproportionate share of the unavoidably irksome rules, established itself at the beginning as "living space." [Wasn't that why Japan began the war in the first place?]

A Central Committee of internees was formed, and they drew up a plan. Protection for women and the small children as the first consideration, the plan was to have men's and women's rooms alternating throughout the building. It was immediately perceived that this was neither convenient nor practical. When we noticed that the Japanese soldiers had not yet registered interest in the women, and meant no harm to the children, the plan was changed.

The men were then segregated to one side of the building, and the women to the other. Then the whole second floor was given over to women, and the men moved up to the third floor. Eventually, the men moved into the other large building, occupied for the first few weeks by a few nuns.

I recognized my blessing in finding a spot, the second day, in one of the laboratory classrooms, for we had a sink in the room, and a Bunsen burner, both treasures! Regulations were firmly drawn at once that only the occupants of the room were allowed to use the sink. Battles were waged even within the room about what might or might not be washed at the sink—face and hands, yes—feet and underwear, no! Brushing teeth was allowed, but rules varied on dishwashing. It was generally conceded of prime convenience, albeit unsanitary, and as the lines at the public sinks and laundry troughs grew longer and longer, and the people wearier, the dishes were washed in the room sinks, and almost everything else was, too. That was later, however; at first, the standards were high and decisions firm.

In a most business-like manner, men marched in and out of the rooms measuring and figuring, and establishing impartial quotas, which unfailingly brought wails of protest from the occupants. Each newcomer found herself unwelcome, not wanted! In the third week, I found sitting disconsolately on a battered brown suitcase in the doorway of my room a middle-aged woman, who snapped as I approached her, "There's not a bit of use in your telling me to get out. I've been refused by three monitors, and I'm going to stay here!"

We had just had a small exodus of missionaries from our room that day, so I could reply graciously that we'd be happy to have her move in. She looked so surprised, and before I could explain such unprecedented generosity, tears welled up in her eyes and streamed down her weathered face. "I just felt I couldn't bear it if I got pushed out again," she said huskily. "My husband's sick, my sheets were stolen, and I didn't want to come in here in the first place, y'know, but the Japanese would have us in."

Mrs. Hawkins became such a staunch friend to me, and I was always so glad we'd had room for her, for her cryptic speech and wonderful accent were the joy of my life for the next two years. She had a career in Santo Tomas prison camp, too, did my acerbic English friend. Every afternoon, come typhoon or Camp inspection, she fixed a spot of tea on the Bunsen burner, that invaluable relic in our room of lab days, for her crotchety little arthritic husband. Pathetically, sometimes, she was reduced to warming up the vile brew furnished us by our hosts, and stewed to ruination in the Central Kitchen. As the Americans secured their coffee by hook or crook almost to the end, so the British did their tea.

(A few days before I left Santo Tomas two years later, Mrs. Hawkins formally served tea and odd little sponge cakes to me and a friend, in her neat tiny shanty, with a small home-made table set, and precious sugar special for the occasion.)

Once, when a new influx of internees brought an increased quota to rooms already insufferably packed, our little room held an organized rebellion. We felt that "the measurers" were not getting a true picture of conditions when they saw the room as it was in its daytime orderliness. So we put our mosquito nets down in night position and arranged everything as though we were ready for bed. Then, with each woman in her place, we called in the head of the Room Space Committee to see for himself that "the room is perfectly airless when the nets are down; some of the women can't even get down the aisles between the beds, and it simply wouldn't be humane to put anyone else in here!"

But neither our best expressions of indignation—nor our most charming smiles and wittiest arguments—achieved a thing. Hundreds of women were still to be housed, and house them we did, with from fourteen to ninety women to a room. Each woman was allotted her bed space, a foot-wide aisle, and room for a suitcase or shelf at the end. She was blessed if she were thin and had few possessions. The fat and wealthy were accursed and never settled. Eventually, time and prison life took care of the latter.

It was difficult to not encroach on your neighbor's territory, but it was the crime of crimes to do so. Two friends might go in together on a shelf, and occasionally even push their beds together under one net to obtain extra aisle space. In the eagerness for the unattainable luxury of privacy, however, most of us sought and kept every inch of space allotted and countenanced no trespassing. The careless one was never out of trouble, as her bed edged over a bit, or she forgot for a moment and left her tin cans on someone else's bit of shelf.

Marceil never made it. Vivacious, French, an artist, and her own person, her bed was just a shade wider, her clothes far more numerous, her hobbies and occupations more cluttered in nature than those of other women, and her Gallic thrift would let her part with nothing for the sake of peace. So she lapped over, on both sides, and it was like living with a time bomb in the room. She hummed and whistled, chattered and sang while the ladies fumed. With gay abandon, she loved those who loved and admired her, and fought for her comfort like a furious kitten when selfish protests seemed to endanger it. The problem was never settled. When appealed to with love or pathos, she was chastened and meek, and bunched her belongings on top of her bed for that day. When exasperation reached its peak, and in an uncharitable moment she was threatened with expulsion from the room, she displayed the whole gamut of emotion from laughter to tears.

[Three weeks after liberation, before we were evacuated from the Islands, I visited Santo Tomas and found Marceil crooning busily over her delicate pastel of a child while her clothes swung gaily over the bed at the right and her suitcases leaned against the one on the left, and all the ladies still fuming.]

I think the men weren't bothered so much with the rearranging complex. But ah, the ladies—seldom a day would pass that one didn't confidentially present to the elected room monitor a brand-new idea for complete rearrangement of the entire room to the greatest advantage of all! The sorely-tried monitors, their backs to the wall, attempted every remotely feasible scheme, and beds were moved back and forth, this way and that, cross-wise, back again. No confirmed housewife can resist furniture moving, and we were all housewives. Only when the work crew finally stalled on changing the arrangement of the mosquito net wires did the general bed-shuffling subside—within limits. Spaces were traded about among the women themselves to the end. Our room was especially unadaptable. It was narrow, with only two windows, at the end, and there were two large, awkward pillars in the center. Cots were arranged down each side with heads to the walls, and between the pillars in the center were fitted in snugly four more, running parallel of the room. It was a really touching sight to see the women who, in the beginning were still a bit heavy, having to turn sideways to get down the strips of aisle. It was funny and grim to observe two ladies, trying to make up their cots at the same time, playing an annoying and involuntary game of bumps-a-daisy.

It was not, by any stretch of imagination, amusing to waken during the dark lonely hour just before daybreak, to find oneself lying in sodden dampness, the sheet a twisted rope limp about your feet, your very being crying out for fresh air to cleanse away the smell of hot, sleeping human-ity. The soft shuffle of straw chenilas (the loose, heelless slippers worn by everyone in the tropics) never ceased through the nights. One after another of the five hundred women in our section slipped from her bed, oozed down the shrouded aisles and out into the airier corridor to breathe again. Every drawn breath in the room would seem to be audible; some were, of course, undeniably so, for the snor-ers lay with us, their snorts the bane of the night.

Into the bleak starkness of those unenchanting classroom dormitories a tireless effort was made to bring some beauty, some nicety to show we hadn't lost our faith and hope, to alleviate the painful memory of beautiful homes and gracious living. [As we stood four deep in a single cold shower or awaited our turn for the wispy mop, one young British woman used to delight me by stating firmly, "We mustn't ever lower our standards, y'know."]

Some beds were covered with counterpanes. Our little private cupboards or shelves were curtained with remnants of printed material or the last presentable panel of a skirt.

The artists among us created clever sketches, crayon or watercolor scenes to put up around the room. Jars of greenery or hibiscus blossoms were set about on tables and shelves. Doors were replaced with curtains for more air and light. Bulletins were symmetrically arranged on the boards, with often a sketch or two for decoration. Ours had a cross-stitch motto at the top, contributed by a member, with the legend, "What is Home Without a Mother?"

Neatness and order were compulsory. All rooms had rigid rules concerning beds being made early in the morning, floors swept, clothes put away or hung up, cans out of sight. Those women who had always been immaculate were as nearly that now as their best efforts could make them, and they suffered most. The untidy were untidy, and suffered less. Most of us tried to keep clean, tried to create an air of comfort.

The battle with vermin and tropical pests was unending. We managed to obtain mouse traps, which helped. We killed scorpions and bedbugs upon sight, battled lice and mosquitoes; our devotion to sanitation was total.

But as the hundreds became thousands, and the rooms seemed near to bursting, one by one with exasperating reluctance, the Japanese would release the vacant rooms in the buildings. Each addition to our living space was a major triumph for the internees. Each request was met by many refusals before the final consent brought some relief to the straining space problem for a little while.

Those empty, closed-off rooms caused a foment of discontent among us as we squeezed closer and closer. So did the isolated building known as the "Padres' Building," never opened to the prisoners, but occupied in spacious grandeur (we thought) by a handful of priests connected to the University. We could never decide at the time whether they were actually imprisoned there, as we were in the other buildings, or had some freedom, although we did know that they still received pupils from the outside. Often at dusk we watched, unabashed at our rudeness, as they sat down at a long table to dine, served by servants and presenting a tableau of all the lost pleasures and luxurious habits of our lives "before." We were conscious of a "little match girl" complex growing from that nightly spectacle, but it gave us a vicarious pleasure just to look, anyway.

During the day, the priests rode their bicycles on their building's flat roof. Sometimes they rode around and around, with only their heads visible to us, moving smoothly with a weirdly disembodied look above the rim of the wall. All their public activities afforded us interest, and the wonderful choral concerts near Christmas and Easter won our admiration, but still we felt the sting of those empty halls and rooms, so near and yet so totally unattainable.

Chapter 8:
VISITING FIREMEN

If the Japanese conquerors of the Philippine Islands retain an indelible impression of American and British women (I think they didn't like us much at that time anyway), it was that we were always either soundly asleep in the daytime or with our heads unaccountably under our beds with only our posteriors in view. Such a picture should be haunting enough to satisfy the most vindictive of us.

We soon realized that we were going to be inspected by every ranking officer who landed on Luzon. Driven by curiosity, perhaps, they swarmed through the internment camps, always looking very official and only technically interested, of course. Escorted by the smooth-haired little Commandant of Camp Santo Tomas and an interpreter, and surrounded by a retinue, with great clanking of swords and shuffling of polished boots, they marched through the corridors, talking among themselves, glancing right and left as they progressed. Usually an official announcement would be made to the Camp that an important general was to honor us with an inspection that afternoon, and that we must be sure to stand and bow. Many times the general did not arrive at all, or was very late. We had been required, of course, to give the internment camp a pre-inspection extra polish.

Word would speed ahead of the visitation when it did finally arrive through the gates, and where a moment before the halls and rooms had teemed with life, the unceasing flow of conversation resounding through the buildings, only silent, empty space remained. We women lay on our beds, and when the now-familiar footsteps sounded down the corridors, buried our heads in pretended sleep. If caught on our feet, we promptly needed some unextractable but important object under the bed, so of course couldn't see the visitors peering through the door. Bow, we did not.

Somewhere half way along through the dragging years came a lull in disciplinary matters, as though the Japanese had given up hope that we could be regimented and conformed to their standards of correct conduct for prisoners. During those few months, we no longer bothered to pretend; we coldly continued our occupations, remained seated and simply ignored the pompous processions.

It was during this period that I one day sat knitting in the corridor in front of my room, and noted without really transferring my attention that we were again undergoing an official scrutiny. But this was not a good time for sightseeing, for as usual in the early afternoon, the halls were nearly vacant, and most of the women were resting in their rooms. All the door curtains were pulled shut and fastened for privacy.

Thus it was only a scattered, unsleepy few of us who saw one curious officer (who must have been feeling really cheated) drag a heavy chair across the corridor, climb up on it, and peer over the curtain into the room next to mine. A Committee member happened to be along that day, and his expression at that moment was such a mixture of helplessly amused disgust. Our composure already shaky with the overwhelming desire to laugh at the performance of this officer of His Imperial Majesty, we few spectators were quite undone. The Committee member told us later that all along the way that afternoon he'd had trouble with this group, who insisted that they wanted to inspect the rooms. When he explained to them over and over that this was the siesta hour, and the ladies would all be asleep and probably not decently attired for inspection, they were disgruntled, and one of them, at least, was unconvinced!

Our captors were obsessed on the subject of our manners. It was explained to them that the bow was not our customary manner of greeting even our friends, so that it was not necessarily a sign of deliberate discourtesy that we didn't bow to the guards, commandants, and visitors. I don't believe the Committee, though, went into the viewpoint that we would consider the bow submissive and thus unacceptable. There came a time when the Japanese made it a serious offense not to do so, and non-bowers were punished. The whole matter, essentially so petty in the grave years of war, became a symbol to us and to them. We would go to almost any length to avoid meeting face to face, within bowing distance, any Japanese. Even the children absorbed the general attitude, and more than once were found tormenting a guard by mischievously encountering him on each of his short trips back and forth along his stretch of wall, bowing to him elaborately each time so that he must return the courtesy.

One of our Commandants gave us an illustrated lecture on the proper method of bowing—hands at side, bending the body forward from the hips, low and stiff. It's a gentle little custom, ancient and expected, easy to accept in peacetime. It must have seemed inexplicable to them that we would not bow!

Viewed from an impartial standpoint, the re-education of our Camp staff should have been a source of satisfaction to us. Few of the officials stayed long in the Camps without relaxing their early hostile vigilance, and eventually declaring frankly that we were neither so arrogant nor so uncultured as they had been led to believe; that, in fact, we were quite likable, and after the war was ended, when we were no longer forced to be inimical, they would like to renew the acquaintances they had made among us.

Kodaki made a long speech expressing this feeling of his, but froze our response to this friendliness by blandly declaring that we, as a people, were really very nice and he liked us—but our government was the enemy of mankind, through no fault of ours, and must not be tolerated. [It was in this same speech that one commandant, Kodaki, who was quite fluent in English, gave us a clue to our future in their hands. This was after the middle of 1943, and the Japanese felt pretty confident, still, of their success. The repatriation ship was gone, we were being treated with relative decency, and Kodaki beamed brightly behind his heavy spectacles as he made the revealing remark, "While we are victorious, we can afford to be magnanimous!"]

Some of the Commandants acquired the habit of wandering alone around the Camp, pausing to chat at any sign of courteous receptiveness from a prisoner. Kodaki, particularly, and his second in command, Koroda, really sought to make friends among us, but this always seemed dangerous to us, and most of the internees made only guarded responses.

But for all of the Commandants, such an attitude of tolerance vanished during the presence of official visitors. Prisoners to be coldly viewed we became and remained, then, until the last gleaming limousine flying a swastika or a rising sun had swept out the front gate.

Chapter 9:
NIGHT ALARM

The supper lines were long since finished, cans and enamel plates washed and tucked under the beds ready for the rush to breakfast, and since dark had fallen in its sudden tropical "now it's day, now it's night" way, curfew was in force and we all were inside of the buildings or in the inner patios. Under each dim light was a bridge foursome, laying out the cards on anything with a flat surface, and vying with would-be readers for a share of the poor illumination. We had been getting our bearings during those first few weeks, and people were a little less restless, more willing to find diversion other than incessant conversation on the subject of getting out.

The moon was not yet up, and the still-grassy patio was filled with people sitting close together on woven mats, or strolling about in the dark, and murmurous with talk, punctuated by the constant slapping at mosquitoes.

Suddenly, with no second of warning, out of the night came blinding flashes of light above us, followed by ear-shattering explosions we instantly recognized as anti-aircraft fire. Wild excitement gripped us—there, that was bombing! We knew that sound well enough. A shout went up even as we automatically sought shelter at the sound of gunfire. "It's a raid! It's our planes! They're here! It's begun!" People prayed, shouted, hugged each other, instantly convinced we were about to be rescued.

It lasted but a few seconds, and all evening long we scarcely breathed in our jubilant anticipation, but nothing more happened, and there was no word of explanation to us from the Commandant. It was hard to settle down for the night, and the building rustled with restlessness until daylight.

Even this, though, was <u>proof</u>. We knew without being told this time that Manila was bombed last night. We said over and over "<u>That</u> was no rumor." And sometime late in the day, the story came into Camp of the plane or planes that slipped past the lookouts and surprise-bombed Manila. We made a great thing of the strange incident, and attached vast significance to it for months to come, so eager were we in our grasping at straws.

[I read the other side of the story in Colonel Robert Scott's stirring *Damned to Glory*, but I am glad that none of us knew then that our Philippine Air Force, which did the bombing that night, was composed of three "hay-wired" B-17s.]

Keyed up over this bombing as we were, we began to organize ourselves against the time when "things begin to break." In each room, an air raid warden was appointed to keep order and see that people didn't get close to the windows, run outside the building, or do any premature celebrating. With my duties as Room 23's warden well in mind and responsibility weighing upon my shoulders, I went all out to take care of my ladies when the next alarm fairly threw us out of our beds a few weeks later. "Keep away from the windows! Don't turn on the light!" I shouted as I charged down the aisle toward my post at the doorway—and halfway there nearly fell to my knees as the building shook and terrifyingly creaked in the grip of the second big tremor. Then the realization came to us that this was an earthquake, not an air raid. Accustomed as we were to quakes there in the Islands, this one gave us a cold thrill, for it was severe. Minor tremors went on all through the night, but only the first few were of that intensity.

This type of attack we definitely didn't like, yet the Camp was chuckling the next morning at the story about the alarmed big fellow who had bounded from the third floor of the men's building down the stairs and outside before he remembered that he was stark naked.

Chapter 10:
AND NOW BATAAN

No wall of steel and sawali, no barriers of censorship, no bayoneted garrison could keep us from living the Battle of Bataan. Night found us huddled, half shivering in our thin gowns, at every Westward-looking window, straining our eyes for the sight of those far off flashes and our ears for the muffled rumble of big guns. Those least evidences of American military activity were the bread of our lives, the gleam of hope.

Bataan came to be a magic word at Santo Tomas. Stories from the front gate spread through the Camp like living flames to bolster our spirits. There was the young guard who told one of our American gatemen, "Goodbye. Tomorrow I go to Bataan, and we do not return from that battle." There were the trucks of Japanese bodies, we were told, that sped past in convoys from the battlefield; and there was a terrible stench on evening breezes of bodies being burned in the great incinerator in Manila. There were grapevine communiques received and believed by us from the Filipinos outside.

We lived in ignorance of the grim truth about the intermittence of those flashes and rumbles. No word of non-reinforcement, starvation, fever, and dearth of ammunition reached us. We had no realization of the terrible last stand defense our armed forces were making, gave no credence to Japanese reports of their victorious progress in the battle. We leaned heavily on our faith in the "invincible strongholds" of Mariveles and Corregidor.

Then the gates swung open and swallowed one day a haggard little family who had just come from Bataan. Parts of their story and appalling predictions became Camp conversation almost before they had registered and become *bona fide* Camp members. The first rumor raised a storm of controversy, with the staunch hearers chafing and branding both story and narrators as hysterical. Others, reluctantly accepting eye-witness report, prepared to believe that Bataan could fall. We waited for more complete reports in a depressive atmosphere of nervousness.

The young couple, who had two small children, had been instructed by the Japanese not to talk and were reluctant with details; they were also ill and incredibly weary, but bit by bit the full story reached us.

They had been sometimes behind the American lines, sometimes actually surrounded by the Japanese, driven from one hiding place to another; fugitives from a holocaust, spending hunted months on miserable rations, never safe, never daring to relax for a moment. At last, when the answer was too clearly written for them to fail to read the truth, they found a way to give themselves up to be brought to the prison camp, and it seemed sanctuary to them. They insisted that our forces were on the verge of unavoidable surrender— that nothing could save them now, and that the conditions on that Bataan battlefield were horrible beyond telling.

It was only a few days after they came in that their ominous warning was fully confirmed. Over the wall, in waves, came the news of the Fall of Bataan. Posters everywhere in Manila proclaimed the Japanese victory. There would be no more flashes, no more trucks; only Corregidor remained to us now, and even we realized that couldn't be for long. We could think or talk of nothing else, but still were determined that we would conceal our fears and heartaches from the enemy. Almost unanimous approval was given the decision to go on with the stage entertainment scheduled for that evening as though nothing had happened, and we crowded into the patio and hung from the windows to see it, applauding and laughing—whistling our best whistles, into the sinister, deserted darkness.

Weeks later, the army nurses from Bataan and Corregidor were brought into Camp. We were cleared out of the foyer of the Main Building, and guards stood around while the nurses, looking impossibly tired, dressed in soldiers' khaki clothing, empty-handed, were assembled there for an hour. Although we hung over the staircase to watch, grief-stricken at what we saw, we had no chance to mingle with them. The Japanese demanded their complete isolation from the civilians, so they were housed in the Santa Catalina building just across the street on the north side of the Camp. The road was hastily closed off to make a passage between their dormitory and the Camp, with a heavily-guarded gate.

Food, clothing, games, books, even cigarettes and cosmetics and toilet articles were collected quickly from the meager supplies of the deeply stirred internees and delivered to the nurses somehow. Their meals were prepared in our Central Kitchen and carted over to them. Some messages between their quarters and Camp got through inevitably, but all communication was officially forbidden.

The Commandant suddenly lifted the ban when they felt, apparently, that any news the women might tell would no longer be current. The nurses were released from their exile, and were of us and with us, soon absorbed into the Camp, taking on the job of running the hospital—just another group of prisoners.

They brought us the whole Bataan epic at last, and answered a thousand questions concerning those who fought there. They graphically described for us that heroic, impossible struggle, and tore our hearts out with their descriptions of the sacrifice made on that battlefield that our country might gain the time it must have. Loss and bitterness came with their reports, and we honored them for their bravery and the grueling, devastating experience under fire they had survived.

Chapter 11:
THE NEWS

We took the Fall hard, and after Corregidor was gone, too, it would seem that there was no further cause for optimism. But such was not the reaction of the Camp in general. We grieved over the infamous Death March, and were struck down again and again by the reports that filtered in from the grim concentration camps where survivors of the Battle suffered and died in terrible numbers from privation, dysentery, fever, and abuse.

But "over the wall" we continued to get our news via the efficient bamboo telegraph system. It was all good news! Even reports of local guerrilla activities in the Philippines were ballooned into effective organized resistance of great forces led by Americans. What little bad news came in was either disregarded entirely or shrugged off as inconsequential, and anyone who persistently repeated items not encouraging was in danger of being disliked!

It was a strange, unconscious conspiracy between the tellers and hearers that distorted the defeats, withdrawals, and delays, comprising the truth of our part in the first year of the war in the Pacific into a fantastic blaze of glory dreamed up by those incurably credulous, exiled, seemingly abandoned Americans in the Philippine prison camps. In part, it was due to an unavoidable misunderstanding by the Filipinos who listened to radio broadcasts, and then made such reasonable errors in their transcriptions as substituting "Davao," a name they knew, for "Rabaul," of which they (and many of us) had never heard. Thus we heard almost daily of the bombings of Davao, and it lifted our hearts to feel that the Philippines had not been forgotten, and we said among ourselves, was not that a logical place to begin the counteroffensive in our Islands? This was in 1942!

Characteristically, Filipinos go out of their way to please, and they were then most reluctant to be the deliverer of unpleasing tidings. So to this, too, we can attribute some of the predominance of good news; they graciously told us what they thought we would most like to hear. And we did not want to hear bad news. We didn't, and would not believe it when we did hear it. Since we were really ignorant of the true state of unpreparedness with which our country was then struggling, it seemed impossible that it could take more than a few months at the most for us to regain what we had lost and beat the tired, poverty-stricken and war-ill enemy to his knees.

We quoted the staggering production figures from those thin, closely-typed sheets, and the Chinese English-language newspaper that was sometimes smuggled in, which euphemistically termed our gallant, lonely air force there "an umbrella over China." We wore to trite threadbareness our prejudiced philosophy concerning the weakness of any nation which produced "mere automatons" as soldiers, and had to steal blueprints and patents to build its navy, planes, and guns.

In May, 1943, eleven hundred persons who had been released by the Japanese to live in Manila, (elderly people, invalids, a few mothers with very small children, and some others who "worked the system") were re-interned, and for the first time we heard and recognized as truth what had really happened in the Coral Seas, at Guadalcanal, Wake, Midway, and elsewhere in the Pacific. By then, though, the real news actually had taken a turn for the better, for Tunisia had fallen, and we had at last established ourselves in the South Pacific. So the bitter went down with the sweet, and we continued believing subsequent good reports and rejecting the bad.

While some of these people had listened irregularly to the news, risking their very lives in the mere possession of the forbidden radio, they also had been the victims, to some extent, of our own U.S. propaganda, and they were excitingly optimistic then regarding the time it would take MacArthur to "come back," as he had promised.

There were some wonderful tales brought in by these returnees from the outside. I sat with a group one night, for instance, and heard a friend tell about the mestizo boy who came to see him at his home. The boy said he was forced by the Japanese to run a fruit barge along the Inter-Island route. On his most recent trip, he said, as he was piloting his clumsy craft across a stretch of open water, a U.S. submarine suddenly emerged near him, and after peremptorily ordering him to pull up beside the submarine, the American captain boarded the barge. The boy was, of course, flying the Japanese flag, so the American was about to take him prisoner, but after a little conversation, he decided the boy was still loyal to his own and our country. He did, however, insist upon buying all the fruit, and paid for it in American dollars. The boy cried, "But sir, I cannot spend this kind of money in Manila! The Japanese would want to know where it came from, and they would kill me for a SPY. Sir, this will make great trouble for me."

"Oh, well," replied the officer, with a laugh, "hang on to it for a few weeks, and then you'll all be using it again!" The American then departed, taking the emblem of the rising sun with him as a souvenir. We did love that story.

And then there was the Filipino captain of the *Mayon*, formerly a small luxury cruise ship for Inter-Island tourists, during the war ferrying between Manila and Hong Kong. His ship was lying in Hong Kong Harbor recently, the captain told a re-internee, when suddenly out of nowhere, as swiftly as death, bombers with the American symbol swooped down over the Bay, dropped their bombs, and flung themselves back up into the sky before the anti-aircraft batteries could fire a shot. He gloated that the damage had been colossal to Japanese shipping, and that not one of those planes had suffered. We loved that one, too, and chose to believe it no matter what.

Rapturously we decided that these were the first authentic signs and that from now on we could expect deliverance at almost any moment. Even the genteel little woman whom I did not at first recognize without the "transformation" she had always worn, and who said in speaking of the recent death of her husband, "So you see, I've lost my hair, my home, and my husband!" in that order, was positive in her prediction of quick relief now.

The Japanese were trying, about that time, so we heard, to make an epic movie of their conquering of Bataan. In their ambition to reconstruct every glorious incident, they attempted to use some of the American war prisoners. They had them again march down that infamous, tragic way, and sought to make the crossing of a certain bridge particularly dramatic. In the Camp, as we listened to this tale, we were incensed at this perceived cruelty, but as the story went on, we found one part to be grateful for. The Filipinos along the way, instead of rising to the occasion as the Japanese had hoped with stones, and jeers, crowded as close to the prisoners as they dared, calling out encouragement and their warm friendliness, surreptitiously passing them money, cigarettes, food—anything they had. Film was ruined and the Japanese raged. Time and again they beat off the natives with violence, but anywhere that they tried to film their pictures in the open, the story was the same. Is there documentation for this tale? I don't know, but to us it was believable.

Chapter 12:
LONELY HEARTS

How could it be possible, I recall wondering with compassion, for the people in that human mass, with no moment of aloneness during any of the twenty-four hours, to give such a heart-catching impression of loneliness? Everyone appeared so avid for friendship, affectionate companionship, someone to share with.

I recognized that many were without attachments when they came into the Camp. There were young wives who for months did not know where their husbands were, and when they did know, were wretched in the knowledge, picturing to themselves in somber detail the difficult adjustments to widowhood and trying to be brave and uncomplaining.

Hundreds of stranded refugees from China and India, classified by us as transients, since they didn't belong to the Islands, were strangers to all of us and even to each other. They had no friends, no money, and some had been abandoned without even their most personal possessions, put ashore and left there by ships' captains of neutral or enemy nations. Most of these were British nationals, caught in Manila *en route* from China to Australia.

Undreamed-of numbers of "old-timers"drifted in from their forty years or so of voluntary exile in the provinces, relics of Spanish-American War days. They had been forced, now, to leave their native families on the outside, and lived in anti-social distrust of all except their own peers, and for the most part, in perpetual, petulant disapproval of everything about the Camp. They could not conform, despised our Committee, disregarded the most elementary rules of sanitation and personal hygiene, and lobbied ill-naturedly and persistently for permission to bring in their native families. They formed the most patience-trying group in Camp, but the sight of those bitter old men, alone, angry and getting thinner every day because they could not, or would not, take care of themselves, made me sick with pity.

People soon grouped themselves congenially and for convenience, with anywhere from two to forty, pooling their food, work, and equipment. Most of the larger groups, usually the employees of big companies before the war, broke up within a few months, when conflicting opinions and the inevitable unequal division of work brought disharmony. But the units of two, three, and four seemed to work out to mutual advantage, and many maintained their original arrangements until the breaking up of the Camp. It might be three men, or two mixed couples, or two older women, or a family of three with an adopted stray—many and varied were the groupings, and some were conspicuous for either their oddity or aptness.

Sometimes these marriages of convenience developed sentimentally; occasionally one would break up in cold dislike. Deep, long-lasting friendships were made that had such foundations they have endured—the foundations of perfect understanding of each other's problems and pleasures, of mutual need, and of being together when each was at his worst or his best. Romance, illicit or smiled upon, grew and flourished. Partnerships that began in innocent friendship between a lonely woman who needed a man's strength and a lonely man who wanted a woman's companionship (and housekeeping abilities, probably), could easily lose their first platonic quality in the emotional atmosphere of Camp.

There was a <u>temporary</u>, disoriented feeling in our lives. Everyone had some of that sensation of being suspended in mid-air. We didn't have the wartime slang, so had never heard "out of this world," but it expresses exactly our mood. It brought ruin and trouble to the runaway few who came to believe that there was no tomorrow—that what they did or were, in the Camp, had no bearing on the rest of their lives.

In that heterogeneous mob we were American and British nationals, including quite a number of Canadians, with other nationalities represented by only one, or a dozen, or a hundred persons. But protected by the passports of American and British husbands or fathers were also Chinese, German, French, Portuguese, Russian, Filipino, Spanish, Assyrian, Czech, Polish, Italian, South American, Dutch, Belgian, and mixtures thereof. They were the foreign wives or children of American soldiers or businessmen or British representatives in the Orient, where mixed families were very common. There was a Native American woman and her little tribe; there were American citizens of all colors and kinds. Spanish was almost as prevalently spoken as English; Russian, Tagalog (the native dialect made official for the Philippines by President Manuel Quezon before the war), French, and a dozen other languages could be heard all through the Camp. English, the language of the Camp, was accented piquantly in cosmopolitan variety.

The same diversity prevailed in the social and economic status of this population. White residents of the Orient fell pretty generally into a few groups: representatives and employees of the big "Stateside" or European corporations; city business men, doctors and dentists, lawyers, accountants, missionaries, scientists, educators, government employees (diplomatic corps were not interned at Santo Tomas after the first few weeks), engineers, miners, and loggers.

There were few laborers, for the work of the white man in the Far East at that time was almost entirely either professional or supervisory. Spicing that undramatic, pretty conservative mixture, though, was a liberal, polyglot sprinkling of China Coast, bedraggled entertainers, beachcombers and exiles —some of them from the very dregs of humanity— found more colorfully then in the Orient than perhaps anywhere else in the world.

This was the group which supplied us with most of our "characters." There were two black-haired, flashing-eyed, swarthy Portuguese women from Macao, for instance, known as "Toots" and "Shanghai Lil," who were tough in the fullest significance of that word. These two, time and again, argued to the point of blows, their fights becoming so rough and bloody that even husky men hesitated to try separating them. Toots was finally expelled from the Camp by the Japanese for her incorrigible pugnacity; months later, a chastened and sad figure, she was readmitted, but her escapades had ceased. What happened in Manila City to change her so completely was not known, but it must have been a hard and pitiful lesson.

Equally notorious was the sharp-faced gambler who, before the Camp authorities finally put a stop to his activities by confining him to our in-Camp jail, plucked the amateur poker players clean, instituted and profited by several merchandising rackets, and altogether found even a concentration camp a fertile field for his felonious talents.

In a different class altogether, but fascinating, was the tall, heavy-bodied woman who wore her coarse black hair in a single braid down her back. She drifted through her existence with a detached, blank, lusterless and drawn face, seldom speaking, growing daily more ragged, never quite clean, an enigma even there among the unusual. Rumor had it that she was the castoff daughter of a wealthy American family, paid to stay out of the country. But every day I saw her, she was stalking alone in her gloomy world, doing nothing, saying nothing, hopefully unaware of some of the cruel conjecturing that went on about her.

In every room at least one of these "different" personalities could be found—in one, a kleptomaniac; in another, a drug addict, or a prostitute (there were said to be fifty of these on our floor, but who it was that counted them I never heard!). They kept life in a turmoil sometimes for their roommates. In our room, the gentle white-haired wife of an eminent sugar chemist, First Reader in our Manila Christian Science church, social and civic affairs leader before the war, was distressed by the actions of her exotic *mestiza* next-bed-neighbor who was, with ingenuity and success, alienating the affections of an American girl's husband. It was a bit of a shock to us to learn that the quiet, curly-haired girl in our room, so wholesome in her appearance, with a sprinkling of little freckles across her pretty nose, was the manager and part-owner of two of the most notorious houses of prostitution in Manila, and was in the Camp only because she preferred staying there to dealing personally with the Japanese.

Strange alliances grew out of this propinquity of conventional society and the uninhibited. A few men who had been known and respected in the community for years succumbed to the skilled beguiling of young women who were different from their accustomed group. Here and there one would see a woman who had never lived a domestic type of life settle down to dishwashing and vegetable-peeling as though born to it.

Drinking, gambling, stealing, prostitution, and even treachery there was, of course, for this was a little city in itself, and in any city, those elements are present. We had more than our share of it, perhaps. But the good people went right on being good, and if in their seeking surcease from the stultifying conditions of imprisonment a few of them strayed, it was at least typical of the times—the same thing was happening at home and being blamed on the war. Each current sensation replaced yesterday's, and would itself be forgotten in tomorrow's. To many people, one of the most important criteria of character during that time was the willingness to work!

Chapter 13:
THE ANNEX

It was the shabbiest little building, and its long covered runways and worn porches gave it an awkward, home-made look. Its foyer was cluttered with cots and chairs, and the earthy-smelling dark corridor beyond seemed always full of drying clothes. But it had no long stairs to climb, and no high windows out of which a toddler could tumble, so the Annex had been reserved for mothers with small children.

During the daylight hours, that building literally rocked and vibrated with the strenuousness connected with extreme youth. Mothers with chronically harried expressions bustled back and forth constantly, chasing down missing offspring, snatching a free hour to do the laundry, cleaning and tidying their little nooks, each containing the mother's cot and a crib or two, and then immediately having it to do over again.

At certain hours there were almost regimented processions: of mothers, clutching clean, squirming little bodies wrapped in ragged towels *en route* from the sinks to their cubicles; of fathers, taking their small sons or daughters out for awhile so that the mothers could get something done; of shrieking, skipping, punching, tussling youngsters sent out to play. One of the funniest and most typical sights in Camp was the morning parade of young women pausing to chat a moment on their way to the bathroom to empty the children's potties. They would stand there, so unconcerned about surroundings or the amusement of anyone passing by, each expertly balancing the little receptacle while she asked for the latest rumors.

Among the "how do they do it" everyday miracles was the fresh, starchy clean appearance of most of the small children. Somehow, those busy, harassed mothers turned out their little girls in dainty sun-suits or frocks, ironed to the last ruffle, in those first years. Colors became faded, and lace wore off, and little rents appeared; small shoes became scuffed and eventually were outgrown, but the children started the day as clean as ever at home. Hundreds of cunning blonde or black curly heads were as neatly pigtailed or adorned in ribbons as those of the fairy-tale children one used to see along the Boulevard with their Chinese amahs. Grubby little hands and knees were scrubbed just as frequently and thoroughly, too. Small boys followed the example of their fathers and big brothers and went through the day shirtless while their skin turned golden in the sun. Their hair was kept short in man-fashion, and smelled as sweet as summer hay.

Mothers shed bitter tears, with real cause, for their children—for the struggle to keep them clean, happy, fed, safe, and well was a crushing burden.

Many a one has told me that lifting her warm, sleep-heavy child from his immaculate crib, she would find every morning the little telltale spots of blood indicating that bed-bugs had been there, too. Children were given three meals a day, of the best food the kitchen could offer, yet the vitamin-conscious American women would worry at the lacks; even the minimum bone-building and tooth-making requirements were far from being fulfilled, of course. In the back of her mind, too, each mother had always the aching, haunting fear that this experience might mark her baby, might keep him from growing up into a normal, wholesome person.

Connected with the Annex was a diet kitchen for the little ones, where expert dieticians marshaled their whole knowledge to provide from the niggardly stocks available the nearest possible answer to a balanced and nourishing diet. As food provided by the Japanese decreased in quality and quantity, an unwritten law was observed in the Camps that whatever there was of special nutritional value (such as the fishy-tasting, orange-yolked duck eggs, or the few baskets of bananas) was to be reserved for the children. For the first two years, they seemed to remain as lively as ever, but most of them took on a lean, wiry appearance, and eventually many seemed to stop growing. That was especially true of the ten to fourteen age group.

What volumes could be written about these concentration camp babes! There were those who were brought into the Camps before the age of memory, who reached their third and fourth birthdays knowing nothing of houses, private bathrooms, new clothes and toy departments. To them, the United States or England or Canada would be as a storybook land filled with doting grandparents, green lawns to play on, and ice cream cones—and they would go there as soon as the American soldiers came.

Those of primary school age had a way, just at first, of asking troubling questions; they remembered a different way of living, and didn't care so much for this one. It was difficult to teach them patience, to explain without frightening.

All ages displayed one characteristic that was peculiar to the circumstances: they developed a poise far beyond their years. Constant association with people of all ages and types and nationalities, spending their formative years against a background of war and fear and deprivation, being so early initiated into acceptance that most of their little desires could not be indulged, produced in them self-reliance, adaptability, even self-discipline.

They showed little evidence of the nerve-strain which never left their parents; they didn't complicate their lives with worry or regrets or fears for the future. They were very aware of the difference between the Japanese and us, but were friendly toward the guards. Only occasionally did one show signs of dislike, and almost never of fear. They developed precocious vocabularies, the result of their being so much in the company of adults who spent so much of their time in conversation.

These were the children of democracy. They slept, ate, and played with youngsters whose heritages ran the gamut in race and tongue, religion and occupation, social status and material position, all on one level now. Their conversing acquaintances numbered old men, missionaries, ex-criminals, Japanese guards, and the privileged from Manila society. They chatted easily with anyone in the vicinity, and could identify many "friends" whom their parents would never recognize. With cosmopolitan nonchalance, they acquired words and phrases from different languages and incorporated them gracefully into casual use.

The porch at the north end of the Annex soon became known as the whipping post, for it was there that irate mothers, to avoid annoying their neighbors, dragged their wailing offspring to administer corporal punishment. It was a long way to go, and if the child could do some good fast thinking on his feet, he had a fair chance of talking his way out before they could get there. But through any day, a goodly number of small bottoms reddened under the stinging spankings their owners had somehow earned. Mothers soon discovered that keeping their children unspoiled as to material desires was a small project compared with keeping their conduct controlled and disciplined. They roamed the Camp in packs, combining their fertile imaginations to achieve an infinite variety of mischief—picking up colloquialisms from some of their strange companions that were hair-raising to their parents; day by day straining the worn apron strings.

Marge, whose tiny daughter was as dainty as an apple blossom, bemoaned to me that the very first song her baby learned was "Bobby is a stinker, Bobby is a stinker"—the old familiar childhood chant. Laurie Lynne, endowed with a limpid gaze from azure-blue eyes, sunny blonde curls and an adventurous disposition, came to be known throughout the Camp. Long before her steps were steady, she made her way alone to the third floor of the Main Building on a tour of exploration, while search parties scoured the Campus for her. She was a born collector, and bore her trophies proudly to her mother, who then spent embarrassing hours trying to find the owners of the shoes, lipsticks, and drinking cups her daughter had "found" in the rooms up and down the Annex corridor. She slipped away from the supervised playground to call on her friends in shanties, safe from discovery in the mazes of Shanty Town or Glamourville, and sure of a cookie or piece of *poto* (rice bread).

Bits of Americana too apt to pass by emanated from the Annex—like the small boy, goaded by a bossy big sister, who finally shouted at her, "Aw, lemme alone! This is a free country, isn't it?" And there was Beth, the flaxen-headed five-year-old daughter of a mining man, who was asked, "Are you a missionary?" and replied staunchly, "No! I'm an American." Tiny tots centered their play ideas about daily life familiar to them—standing in line, roll call, room cleaning, bedbug killing! I can hear the agitated voice of the young British mother calling to her child on the teeter-totter, where she was singing at the top of her voice, "Seesaw, Marjorie Daw, can't you go any faster?" The mother called to correct such a corruption of her beloved British language: "Fawster, Hilary, fawster!"

Only a very few babies were born after the first year in Camp, for the Japanese had placed an unequivocal ban on marital relations, the lack of privacy enforcing their rule probably more effectively than their threats. The first Commandant's ludicrous inspiration to set up an "Affection Tent" had been hastily vetoed by the Central Committee and chuckled over by the internees. During the second year, however, they discovered through petitions for outside hospitalization that there were several pregnancies in the Camp, and left us gasping with an order that the prospective fathers were to be jailed, some for thirty and some for sixty days; and that the mothers would spend the remainder of their confinements at the Hospicion de San Jose, outside the Camp, isolated from their husbands and friends. Although a certain amount of facetious commenting on the situation could be heard, the unfortunate couples really had the sympathy of most of us, which apparently was not the effect the Commandant had hoped for.

Further discipline along this line was averted by a reversal of the Japanese policy the third year when family life again became legal! Even then, there were not many additions to the Camp population. Vitality was running very low, and general health poor. Most people felt that it was neither fair nor sensible to have children under the conditions there. The future was looking ever more uncertain, for as the American forces drew closer to the Philippines, the temper of our captors grew correspondingly more capricious, their "magnanimity" noticeably waning. There was nothing to prevent the venting of their animosity and frustration on the trapped, defenseless prisoners.

[Those Annex babies, in their clean little sun-suits, some knitted from string, toes cut out of too-short shoes, undernourished and accustomed only to privation, gave thousands of American soldiers what they were seeking in February, 1945—a reason to win the war they were fighting. They found themselves individually considered a combination of God, Santa Claus, and all the heroes of history. They had been talked about, dreamed of, and expected for thirty-seven months, and when they arrived, they received such a welcome from even the three-year-olds as no man could ever expect on earth. Those children were so conditioned to love our rescuers that they threw themselves almost violently at any uniformed figure in a very ecstasy of greeting, and the GI's loved it.]

Chapter 14:
CHRISTMAS

A long about September 1942, at the end of the first rainy season, we were beginning to wonder what could be done about Christmas. We blithe optimists wouldn't concede that we'd still be in there then, but admitted that we should make some kind of preparations, just in case. Fully a fourth of Santo Tomas's population was children, and the whole Camp keenly felt its responsibility to them. For awhile, there was only desultory planning. Then certain groups of men would disappear for hours of the day; a mysterious workshop above the museum gave forth sounds of saw and hammer and the smell of paint behind locked doors. Knitting needles began to work their way through masses of pastel wools; bits of bright cotton materials littered the corridors. Committees were formed, and the propagandists went to work.

During the months of November and December, hardly a person in the Camp was not working on some consuming project. Handles of worn-out toothbrushes, small blocks of wood, pieces of cardboard, tin cans, and every scrap of cloth, yarn and string were greedily seized upon and soon started on its way to whatever it was to become. The most familiar sound was the scraping of sandpaper on wood, as cigar boxes, bamboo, and strips of native hardwoods were smoothed and polished to gleaming beauty. Pillows were looted of their kapok or feathers for stuffing hundreds of droll ducklings, pandas, kittens, dogs, horses, and dolls; irreplaceable cloth was cut up into thousands of tiny squares and then laboriously sewn back together again. Artists were hard at work and secretive; there was a wonderful air of mystery and fun.

Out of all this sacrificing, scraping, inventing and contriving came such a Christmas! Love could do no more. Christmas morning, as the crowds gathered around a big tree put up at the Annex, dazzlingly laden with home-made, charming decorations, a wonderful Santa Claus made a triumphal entry with great ado. Santa enraptured the children who were not totally terrified, bounced around and around, greeting as many as he could, then jovially distributed the presents. This was a huge task, and he had to have many helpers, for not one child had been overlooked or left out. Fashioned of wood and painted with the child-beloved red, yellow, and blue, were kiddie-cars, scooters, wheelbarrows, trucks, and doll beds. Each little bed was occupied by a winsome, gaily-dressed and lovable, though slightly lumpy, rag baby covered with a dainty piece-quilt and perhaps embroidered sheets. There were sweets to eat, too, even watery ice cream; and Christmas carols to sing, and laughter, and a stage entertainment—a play for the little ones. Nothing was lacking that Christmas. Some of the children also had tiny trees and extra presents from their parents and friends. It seemed wonderful, incredible. And poignant beyond any description.

All the week before Christmas there were entertainments for the Camp. Children and adults together staged a religious pageant, resplendent with costumes and even scenery. [My gold taffeta housecoat, packed because I loved it, and utterly impractical, its heavy cording the happy, permanent home for bedbugs, finally came into its own as a royal gown for a thrilled young actress.] There were almost daily special church services, and musical programs by the Camp choruses, and a stage show. Every room was decorated, parties were planned among friends and within rooms; a wholesome sense of unity stimulated an unfamiliar vivacity and half-forgotten gaiety.

Presents were exchanged among the adults, too-exquisite cribbage boards, intricately inlaid with different native hardwoods and lustrous from polishing; hand-worked handkerchiefs, plastic costume jewelry from those old toothbrush handles; boxes, with carved monograms or quilted linings, gaily-painted tins for storing food, or generous smartlooking ash trays cut from tins, shaped and painted; a jar of homemade mango chutney; a box of candied pomelo peel. Everything was hand made and the product of ingenuity and hard work. Almost everything was cleverly done, and some of the gifts were works of art. Marceil, the French artist in my room, gave me an exquisitely designed French cookbook she had created.

It was inevitable that the Japanese would use this Camp celebration for a propaganda opportunity. They took reels of film of the stacks of children's presents, the tree, the Santa, the people laughing and relaxed. It was quite natural that they might even take the credit for this display of their magnanimity. Some internees were bitter about this, but it was not likely to become an international issue.

Gifts of food poured into the prison camp from friends, Filipino former employees, and service groups. The Japanese were prevailed upon to make it a visiting day, the first, and the only one I can remember, so all the late morning and most of the afternoon hundreds—maybe thousands—of people milled about on the front Campus seeking their friends who might have come in. Reunions were marked with a pathetic eagerness to make the most of every fleeting moment. This was a time when the loneliness of those who didn't have their families with them, who didn't have friends from the outside, who couldn't see those they longed for, made for aching hearts.

Beneath the deep feeling of gratitude, and pride in something well done, and pleasure in a day when perturbing worries had been somewhat laid aside, lay a strain of disbelief. How could it be that we were there, that this were really so? Since we were, and it was, how could we have been so lighthearted and easy for a day? It was a "puzzlement," but it was Christmas.

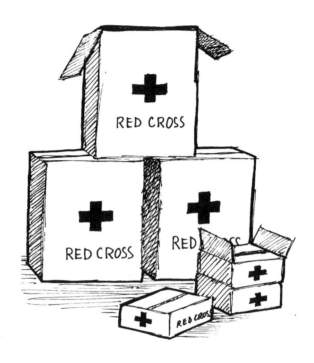

Chapter 15:
BLESSED TO RECEIVE

K nowing their own country so well, the Americans were the most confident members of the Camp that some kind of relief would soon reach us through the International Red Cross. So we readily believed and counted on every rumor of shiploads of flour, canned stuffs, medical supplies and clothing being unloaded for the use of our internment camps. The food quite early on was so dreadful and inadequate as it came from the Central Kitchen to the food line that serious malnutrition was setting in, and depression was widespread. The Japanese made no apology for this, replying to protests that all the rice, meat, and vegetables were needed for their armed forces, which was probably quite correct. We supplemented with anything we could find or acquire, and there were highs and lows. When food was allowed in over the wall, we were much better off. When that was stopped, the situation soon became crucial.

It only gradually dawned upon us, after repeated disappointments, that the Red Cross was helpless in the face of Japanese refusals to promise safe conduct for any vessels. It was uncertain if such shipments would ever actually come to us. We comforted ourselves that our countrymen would never give up trying.

This confidence saved our pride at that first Christmas, when the first food kits thrillingly did arrive, were actually distributed to us, and found to be British! That few pounds of tinned food did wonders for Camp morale, and it was known that there was another kit soon to follow; so we began hoping that it would become a regular thing.

There was a bit of teasing gloating on the part of the Britishers, of course. While we surely were not finicky about our food in those days, it is a fact that some of the contents of the package were more relished by the British than by the Americans. But ah, it was food—good, clean, tasty food, and our gratitude was uncritical. Even the tins themselves were put to use immediately after they were emptied. The little squarish corned-beef cans made toothbrush and soap holders; the small flat ones that had contained the precious white sugar were naturals for ash trays; the cartons were used for storage, and the packing for starting fires in that nearly fuelless country.

There was much debating about whether we should dig right in and enjoy the food now, or hoard it against the thinner time which was certain to come; some followed one course and some the other. Certain people were known to have consumed most of theirs in the first forty-eight hours. Most put them away and used them gradually—a few hoarded with smug self-discipline.

Everyone delightedly ate with clear conscience the perishables—cheese, crackers, raisins (biscuits and plums to the Brits) and chocolate bars. Many people were obsessed by the fear that having in a weak moment allowed us to have the food packages, the Japanese could still have a change of heart and confiscate them for themselves.

Within a month, a second kit was distributed, also British; this time from Canada, and containing some real treasures. There was a can of Canadian bacon, full of clean, white fat; maple leaf butter, American and Canadian cigarettes, toilet soap. (*Wonderful* to have soap!) There were not enough of these packages to go around, so they were allotted one to every two persons. It was difficult to divide them, for they contained only one can of most of the items, and some of the foods were much more desirable than the others. Couples or families with an even number of members had no real problems, but the odd-numbered groups and single individuals mulled long and hard with their selected partners to get an equitable distribution—butter to one, perhaps, and bacon to the others; one would take the marmalade, and the other the cheese. Chocolate bars, cartons of prunes, cigarettes and soap were measured into halves exactly, while the items least in demand (such as creamed rice and curried lamb—both too similar to our Camp food to arouse any enthusiasm) were left to the last to piece out inequalities.

In addition to this head-scratching over dividing the kits, much thought and care was put into trading which sprang up simultaneously with the unpacking of the boxes. Non-smokers did a thriving business, and felt they really had a great advantage, for they were easily able to trade their cigarettes from this kit for food. Typically British delicacies such as the curries, marmalade, puddings and tea were offered by the Americans for the corned beef, butter, or deviled meat (the latter was expected to be similar to our canned spiced meats, but proved to be like them only in texture, and very bland). The cheese was fit for the taste of a gourmet, and it was nearly impossible to find anyone who would trade his off for anything. Butter was equally prized—and the bacon and white sugar.

This trading was a wonder to see and hear. Every bargain was a hard one, for the value of each item was established on the strength of the traders' desires. It kept the Santo Tomas prison camp occupied and buzzing with excitement for days, and the little tins and packages were seen changing hands everywhere for as long as a month later.

Our pleasure in receiving this precious food was not complete until we had it by our bamboo telegraph that the military prisoners at Cabanatuan and Bilibid had also received theirs. We didn't hear until much later that the other civilian camps, at Baguio, Davao, and Bacolod, missed out entirely on these two shipments. It still is a mystery that they should have been so cheated, for their need was at least as great as ours in Manila. The Davao and Bacolod prisoners were eventually brought to Manila, but too late to share in the two packages.

This seemed the end of it, for a long year passed before anything was heard of further relief. The Britishers had it on us, at that point. But we knew as surely as anything that the United States would move heaven and earth to contribute if there were a possibility of the goods arriving where they were meant to go. So we weren't surprised, but were delighted and relieved, in November of 1943, when we were told that a large shipment of food, clothing, medical supplies was *en route* to us from home on the return trip of the August repatriation ship. The cargo had been transferred from the *Gripsholm* to the *Tia Maru*, where the repatriates made the switch between ships.

Rumors flew thick and fast as to the exact contents of the shipment, and also as to what was happening to it. It was known to be accompanied by a representative of the International Red Cross; some had him correctly a Swiss, but the most interesting version was that he was an expatriate member of the Japanese Imperial family, and virtually a hostage aboard ship!

Our stories weren't too fantastic, at that. This man had been sent with the goods to verify their safe arrival and proper distribution to internees and military prisoners in the Philippines. Yet when the ship arrived in Manila, he was taken directly to the Manila Hotel, and kept there as nearly incommunicado as possible until he could be returned to the ship; to the best of our knowledge, he never saw any of the camps, nor any of the cargo again; certain it was that none of us ever saw him.

The gloom-spreaders agitatedly told a tragic tale that the whole cargo had been unloaded and left at Shanghai, or that some of it had been left there and the rest was on the way to Japan!

But it did arrive! Men from our Camp were called upon to help with the storage of enormous boxes in a warehouse in Manila. The boxes were marked as clothing, medical supplies, shoes, and so on. There were also thousands of food cartons weighing about fifty pounds each. Our men helped separate the supplies for Baguio, Cabanatuan, Bilibid, Santo Tomas, and the new Camp at Los Baños. All of this was exciting, but we held our breaths yet, wondering if the Japanese would actually allow us to receive these wonderful things that surely they themselves needed and wanted. So the weeks dragged on into December 1943, with many false starts and stories, and it was not until the twentieth that the trucks drove in with their fabulous loads.

To all of us, the scene that followed was the ugliest in the history of the Santo Tomas prison camp except the pre-execution beating of three Australian escapees. Thousands of cartons of food were unloaded and were placed on the plaza, and then before our incredulous and heartsick eyes, Japanese soldiers proceeded to rip open packages, destroying with their bayonets every can and packet in the boxes. Mothers whose babies scarcely knew the flavor of milk watched in frantic grief while cans of powdered milk were hacked open and dirty fingers explored, then spilled, the ivory powder onto the grass; men turned away with violence written in their faces as can after can of meat, butter, jam, coffee, sugar, was ruthlessly destroyed.

This, then, was the answer to our hopes. We could see it, but we could never have it. And in a world of starvation, a way to relief could be what we in our anguish conceived to be madness. Hysteria mounted dangerously, and there was hatred in the air; hands were white-knuckled and clenched, and children clung to their parents in terror at the atmosphere of despair they couldn't help but see.

But before the soldiers had made much more than a beginning, the Central Committee took action. Pale with anger, the chairman and others stalked into the Commandant's office without even the formality of knocking, and in scathing words, told him exactly what the world would be thinking of Japan, and what we thought of him. They said, in effect, "You have lost face this day already, and if you don't stop that wicked action out there on the plaza, Japan will be despised wherever men talk together down through the ages!"

The Commandant was visibly impressed and humiliated, even, and with many apologies and denials that he had been at all aware of what was transpiring fifty feet from his office, gave a sharp order, which was all that was needed to halt the debacle.

So they stopped, but it took awhile for the anger and distrust to loosen enough for us to at last turn with rejoicing to the sight of those wonderful packages. We were amused, in fact, that all of the Old Gold cigarettes were being confiscated because of a small propaganda blurb on the package. The cigarettes were stripped of their outside wrapper, then eventually delivered, too.

The lines began to form, small boys with their Christmas wheelbarrows and wagons or any conveyance available volunteering their services to women and older people, or to fathers who had more than one carton to manage, for a few centavos or gratis, delivering the big tan boxes to the owners' rooms or shanties. We each had received a number, in groups of five hundred, in a well-planned system, and the distribution was achieved with dispatch and efficiency, and with, of course, tremendous cheer!

Within a few hours, every bed was laden with the contents of a kit, and delighted exclamations rang through the buildings. A more perfectly balanced selection could not have been made. This seemed a great quantity of food, after two years of meager Camp rations. Most of it was Army pack. The very rations that our soldiers were already tiring of were nectar and ambrosia to us. Now the provident ones really had something to store up for the wet weather ahead, and the improvident, or famished, had a field day of abandoned eating. Coffee parties flourished, smokers turned the air blue, children ate and smeared chocolate on beaming faces.

Along with the food came the desperately needed medical and dental supplies. After two years of fighting disease with little more than isolation and sanitation for weapons, the arrival of quinine, sulpha drugs, insulin, digitalis, various preventive serums, vitamins, sedatives, and digestive aids was hailed as a bonanza by our little in-camp hospital and the crew of volunteer doctors and nurses. [This hospital was probably one of the best-staffed institutions in the world at the moment, with almost the entire Rockefeller Foundation medical and research people who had been evacuated from China to the Islands. But they, and the other Camp medical people, had felt severely handicapped by their total lack of supplies.]

Clothing there was, too, and shoes for everyone with normal-sized feet. [No size fours, so I stayed with my native *bakias.*] Soap, razor blades, tooth powder, cold cream (unscented—important, for thereby hangs a later tale), toilet paper—all the things we think we can't possibly get along without until we do it, but so gratefully appreciate when we have them again. And there were bath towels, and sheets, and for the mountain camp at Baguio, there were warm sweaters and even blankets.

Among the clothing received, each woman fell heir to a "play suit," with a skirt over the shorts. They were all the same, except for little variations in the prints or colors, but more than ever before, the Camp took on a look of being an "institution" when these new outfits blossomed out. Stocky or emaciated, tall or short, old or young, few ladies could resist the newness, and the wholeness, of this generally unbecoming outfit, just as the men, one and all, donned the khaki shorts they received. These shorts, of greenish, stiff material water repellent to the point where they could hardly be washed, were queer-looking garments with a striking flared effect, nearly knee-length on all but the very tallest. How we laughed, but how we enjoyed having something fresh and new—and nobody looked any worse than anyone else, so that wasn't a problem.

So the new shoes squeaked through the corridors; untattered towels and sheets fluttered from the old clotheslines, jealously guarded by their owners; the garbage cans once more had something in them. [The only disparaging remark I ever overheard regarding the American kit was a mild British comment that "Really, there's quite a difference between the quality of packaging of the American and British food, don't you think? They have used so much cardboard and inferior metal, while ours was put up in the same excellent tin as ever." It was obvious enough, even then, we thought, why this was so, for in every cardboard package was the inscription, "War Time Economy Package." But we didn't feel the point worth arguing.]

It is undeniable truth that this third and last Red Cross shipment must have saved hundreds of lives in the Camps. The majority of prisoners carefully budgeted all the imperishable foodstuffs, and managed to make them last through the last, longest, hardest time. On many a day, when famine stalked grimly through the corridors, and servings had become so insignificant that they seemed about to cease altogether, a forkful of canned ham and eggs, or a third of a glass of milk, or even a cup of weak coffee made from the powder we had saved could stave off the hunger cramps. Vitamin capsules distributed to individuals were exhausted before the real emergency set in, but the surplus was carefully doled out to the worst cases, and seemed to help. When the watery mess that masqueraded as supper seemed too nauseous to swallow, but swallow it one did, it was easier for the cube of fine white sugar that we allowed ourselves for dessert.

Our hymn of gratitude can never be sung long or loud enough to express the depth of feeling we had over those little cans and boxes, that great carton of relief. This would have been a more woeful tale without them.

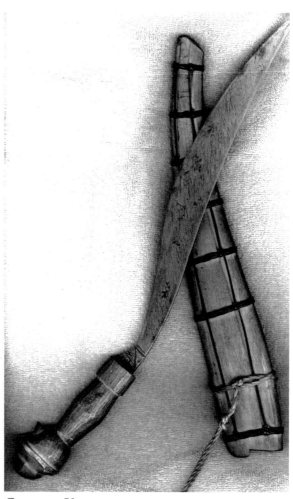

COCONUT KNIFE

Chapter 16:
BETRAYAL

To those who have had to depend greatly on their fellow men, treachery is a dreadful word. It revealed itself in different ways in those prison camps; the seriousness of the consequences varied, but the principle was the same.

Early in the first year, we were warned repeatedly by our Central Committee and other leaders to be cautious in our actions and speech, for not everyone was to be trusted. So unaccustomed are the guileless Americans and British to distrusting anyone, this wise counsel was not always remembered. When the finger of suspicion singled out this or that person as a traitor, we were inclined to scoff and call the talk "spy stuff."

News stories were indiscriminately discussed, the Japanese were heartily described in a language colorful and profane, and few people thought about being discreet. Then the lesson was learned in a sudden hurry when several men were summoned to the Japanese office and told in understandable terms what their fate would be if they didn't cease their disrespectful remarks about our captors. They detested being referred to as "Japs," particularly "yellow-bellied" ones, it seemed!

At about the same time, we discovered that the Japanese also knew exactly how much we knew about the news (which was certainly not much), and that meant but one thing—that there were indeed listening posts among us. A few individuals soon found themselves being placed in Coventry, but even then we couldn't be sure they were all spotted, and voices were lowered and company more carefully selected when forbidden subjects were being discussed.

The most tragic case of betrayal occurred toward the end of the first year, when a man with a criminal record, whose intransigent wickedness could not be tolerated any longer by the Camp personnel was threatened by our Central Committee with being turned over to the Japanese. He had resisted all attempts at punishment by the Camp, and was felt to be a menace. But in a fury at the threat, he went to the Commandant himself, and gave to the enemy a list of names of army and navy men in the Camp.

These men had always been in danger of detection; it is more than probable that the Japanese knew all about them, but were not sufficiently interested to round them up and ship them off to the military camps. I had a friend among them, a veteran of World War I. He was a Naval Reserve officer, and at the outbreak of the war in the Philippines, reported for active duty at Cavite, where he went through fire and disaster. When we were all captured, he came into the Camp with his family under his real status of a civilian employee of an American corporation. He was always a fine, clear-thinking, hardworking citizen of the Camp, one of our leaders. His story was that of many of the group.

When the traitor's damaging job was finished, the Commandant apparently felt that the presence of these men could not longer be ignored, so to save some face, a great issue was made of it; hundreds of people were questioned, and eventually all of those on that list were removed. They were taken without advance warning, or opportunity to collect even a few clothes and to say goodbye to their families. As punishment for not originally revealing their military status, they were imprisoned for two or three months at notorious Fort Santiago, with no communication at all with those they had left behind at Santo Tomas. Then their families were informed that the men were being transferred to a military prison camp. A few clothes, toilet articles, and a small amount of money, might be sent them. Underground messages later reached us from the men saying that the clothes and some of the other possessions had reached them, but that much had been confiscated along the way to Cabanatuan.

The end of this story is as grim as the beginning. Most of the men are gone—some died of starvation and mistreatment; some went down on ships on the way to Japan, as my friend did. The traitor who murdered them died violently at Cabanatuan, where he had been sent with those he betrayed. This was a scarring and hurting experience; I shared a close friendship with my friend's wife and sister and children, and knew their special anguish.

The most frequent form of disloyalty, and in the overall picture there were really only a few who did any of this, was the buying of privileges from the Japanese, either with money, friendliness or tattle. Out of a total of thousands of prisoners, perhaps not fifty could be accused of such dealings, and they must have been opportunists who would have scrupled at nothing in normal life.

An astonishing rash of such stupidity broke out through the Camp over the choice of repatriates in 1943. Nearly all of the sailing list was wholly legitimate and approved, with diabetics, heart cases, some elderly persons, some Rockefeller Foundation people; but with them went men and women both who had literally bought and paid for that priceless privilege.

The Camp was thoroughly aroused over it, to the extreme that representations were even made to the Japanese. Koroda, a guard, referred it up to Kodaki, who with something of a smirk, insisted that the list came out of Washington, and only a few extra places, left vacant by internees who refused the chance to go, had been filled by the Japanese with some who had not been so inimical. A clever, sardonic cartoon circulated around the Camp showing cripples and white-headed prisoners on the shore, waving goodbye to muscular, husky repatriates boarding the ship. (This was the only repatriation ship during the entire war, so far as I ever heard.)

Concerning most of us rather more personally were the people who took advantage of positions of trust to add a bit of down to their own nests. Everyone knew who they were, of course, for nothing could be very secret in that unprivate life. It was at least aggravating to know that a few members of the kitchen crew, for instance, had larger and better meals (not much), and in a few instances even ran a little side-line business with Camp rations, when there was never too much and usually not enough to go around. Inevitably, in some instances, some reputations were quite ruined.

Prélude
C-SHARP MINOR

S. RACHMANINOFF. Op. 3, Nº :

Chapter 17:
THE GRACIOUS HOUR

When God created the tropics, He lavished rich gifts upon them: a climate meant for ease of living; a riotous wealth of color; a grace shown in slender, swaying palms and the curved mystery of orchid blossoms.   •

In this Eden, there are some flaws, however. There are impenetrable jungles, and through those jungles some of our people endured miserable treks under guard. There are unfriendly creatures—tiny stinging ants, deadly reptiles, disease carrying mosquitoes. White men wilt in the humid heat of the day, and natives in the tropics sometimes seem to fall behind the procession of civilized progress through sheer languor.

Yet the beauty of these lands can hold one enthralled. When, at the close of a grinding day of sweat and dust, drudgery and privation, we left the buildings and disposed our chairs about the plaza and front lawns, we entered for awhile into what seemed heaven. Soft, cooling breezes stirred the heavy air, and we could close our little bamboo fans and lay them aside for an hour. Then the sun began its swift descent beyond the horizon, and the vivid sunset colors lighted the world with a shimmering glow. Nothing short of a divine genius could catch or record those sunsets on canvas or in words. Sometimes, for a few lovely moments, the great billows of clouds would be deep rose against the azure sky, then slowly ripen to peach and coral, and into purest gold. If the day had been even remotely sensitive to distant storms, crimson, purple, turquoise, and green flamed breathtakingly against the livid background. Month after month, we watched the wonderful sight with rapture. No enclosing walls could shut it out. Day after day we came to count more on the peace and rest we found at that hour, when war and hatred were relegated to their proper place in unreality, and only loveliness remained. It was like a great symphony—the lost chord—a prophetical view of the new heaven and earth.

Before the last glow had quite faded from the lowest clouds, darkness had fallen, and in a few moments a star or two would appear, then their myriads burst forth in white brilliance.

We had music, too. A camp broadcasting system was installed, and splendid record collections donated, so that all through the evening we could listen quietly or not, as we chose, to programs which included everything from Schubert to Fats Waller, complete opera scores, symphonic classics, country music, and Walt Disney background music. Programs were arranged with the hope of suiting everyone; even patriotic selections such as "American Ballad" and "Washington Post" eventually began appearing at discreet intervals.

To sit there, perhaps chatting a bit, idle and relaxed, listening with full or desultory attention to the music, watching the sun go down in glory and the great pale moon rising from behind the palms and acacias, feeling the sweet coolness as the sultry heat retreated; delighting in the twinkling gaiety of fireflies which would sometimes light in your hair or on your arm—it was to live again. Literally, we were no more free, no less under surveillance, yet the tenseness dissolved during those evening hours.

Oddly, the moment this soothing little interlude was finished, just before nine o'clock, and the music ceased with the traditional goodnight lullaby—that moment, the mood of gentleness was shed, chairs banged closed, people swarmed briskly into the buildings, pushing through the crowded foyer, voices high again, eyes strained and alert, nerves tight. But the sanity of that evening quiet was like a lifesaver, nevertheless, and must have made the difference between seeing it through, or not surviving. The other camps had no such breathing spell, and I can never account for this evidence of Kodaki's permissiveness, unless he thought it kept him from having more trouble with us.

Chapter 18:
LITTLE THINGS

A chair, a new toothbrush, a pottery plate, real toilet paper from the Red Cross, bamboo knitting needles, a twenty-five word message from home—little things, but what they meant to us was beyond expression. It has been my experience that my fellow man can rise to quite inspired heights when the occasion demands; that he has a hidden store of fortitude and humor and compassion which may lie unsuspected until it is called for. Through one major trial after another, I have seen him calm, courageous, selfless, someone to be proud of, an unsung hero.

But my hero found it more difficult to maintain his forbearance, sense of humor, and unselfishness through years of dreary days filled with thankless labor, doing without, enduring endless association with *many* people.

I have seen a quiet, apparently serene woman suddenly break, collapsing in hysteria, at having to wait too long in a sluggish bathroom line. A friend of mine, a dear and gentle family person, endured everything nobly until his skin broke out in an itching rash, then he had a complete, dangerous nervous breakdown. One of the floor monitors met every problem with calm decision and truly unlimited patience until our vital drinking fountain was found to be choked with tea leaves; then she blew up!

A quiet school teacher and the socialite owner of one of Manila's most exclusive dress shops convulsed the Camp by throwing rolls of bathroom tissue at each other in strident rage over a matter so unimportant that the cause of that memorable quarrel was quite forgotten even in the telling.

Harder to bear than hunger, for me, was the incessant chatter, the curiosity about each other's personal life, the gossip and anger. An old family friend approached me at the foot of the stairs one day, his face white with what I discovered immediately to be fury, and told me I was befriending a bad woman. This man loved my family, and I think was fond of me, but at that moment, the anger pent up inside of himself was finding an outlet—and I was stunned.

Sometimes a blow-up would occur over an act of thoughtlessness, like the tea leaves in the fountain, or a window left open and a bed dampened by a sudden shower. Tensions would sometimes develop between individuals that could affect a whole room. Some tiny irritation or frustration might cause an explosion that actual hardship or suffering could never set off. Men who never mentioned their stabbing pains from serious hernias carried on their too-heavy jobs uncomplainingly, but might criticize unfairly and even crossly our hard-working Central Committee over a difference of opinion.

For it was small things piling one on top of the other that made up our days and nights of waiting. And it was small things, too, that brought some comfort and some enjoyment into those days. For months after we were imprisoned, we had no place to sit. We spread *petates*, the woven mats that in the Philippines serve every purpose from rugs to walls, on the grass outside and sprawled ungracefully and uncomfortably, and in the buildings sat in the middle of our mattresses on the floor until our backs ached. Even after we had beds of some sort, we could only sit on the edge to visit or knit or read. The corridors were lined with an inadequate number of heavy, stiff wooden classroom chairs, innately uncomfortable and alive with bedbugs.

Thus the acquiring of a folding canvas deck chair became an event to be remembered. Aguinaldo, a successful Filipino merchant in Manila, owner of one of the largest department stores before the war, prevailed upon the Commandant to allow him to bring in some merchandise to sell to the prisoners, and the deck chairs were received with such gratitude and elation that he had soon brought in enough for everyone, I think. Now we could sit back in comfort to knit or read, or lounge on the plaza in the evening. They were sought after more than clothing or anything else Aguinaldo could bring in. Some people even carried them to the chow lines to sit in until the line began to move. They were placed in regimented rows, hundreds of them, before an entertainment, so that all seats were reserved. There are few things I could name that contributed so much to our relief as did our little folding chairs!

I also recall with pleasure the day I acquired a chipped pottery cup and plate to replace my tin can and enamel dish, and my feelings when I found a fork, bent and tarnished, but to me a treasure, as I had owned only a spoon. These things spelled luxury, and seemed to me to make everything taste better. I had particularly disliked the enamel plate— my crockery plate and cup were Spode to me.

My dear friend Marie, then in her sixties, who had owned a sumptuous estate and been served by a staff of at least fifteen servants before the war, who could entertain a hundred guests without borrowing so much as a teaspoon, who had servants born in her home, who had traveled the world over, proved herself a true aristocrat in the Camp by adapting herself without a murmur to this new, trying life. She treasured a large wooden cupboard that someone arranged for her to use for a bed (by turning it on its face) so that she would not have to sleep on the floor. Months later, when the carpentry shop undertook to supply wooden beds to all who needed them, she found herself sentimentally reluctant to part with the cupboard, in spite of its clumsiness and undeniably-active inhabitants.

It was the same in the matter of deeds. We had learned the hard way to expect little and appreciate much. The most touching thing that ever happened to me was a surprise birthday party given me by the women in my room that first year in the Camp. It didn't dawn a particularly happy day, for I awakened in an indulgence of self-pity, feeling that it was simply a rotten place to spend a birthday; thinking that no one even knew, since I was actually alone in the Camp, and determined that I'd certainly skip this one altogether. But stepping from the door to go down to breakfast,

I found my friend Larry waiting there with a "happy birthday" greeting. I felt better, warmed and cared about.

About noon, an angel in the form of a Red Cross nurse sought me out with my first word from Norman, timed to arrive on that particular day, and when I wept in relief and loneliness, my friends surrounded me to share it, too. At last I knew that he was in the Baguio internment camp, and even though we could not communicate (the nurse was taking her life in her hands to bring me the message), a burden I had carried for those three months was lifted.

That afternoon, when I went to teach my classes in our in-camp school, I found that even my students had noted the date somehow, and had incredibly obtained a pre-war box of scented bath powder for me—a delight from another world!

And finally, after a long lovely evening outside, I came back to the room to find gifts and even, miracle of miracles, a little cake and lemonade, and gay little speeches of affection from my roommates. There is no defense against love, and the hardest hearts melted when they realized that all around them was friendship to be had for the seeking, love waiting only for recognition. I knew that the warm hand of God had rested on my shoulder all day, assuring me I could never be alone.

"Can I help you?" "Let me do it for you." "I have more than I need—could you use this?" Little words, little sentences, but every time they were spoken they brought help and comfort, and I think most people said them more often during those times than ever before in their lives. You might never know the name of the man who turned your clumsy mattress over on the grass for you so that the other side could be sunned; you didn't stop for an introduction before you took someone's proffered aid in wringing out a sheet at the laundry troughs; you accepted the volunteered services offered and returned the favor without thinking about it, in a prevailing spirit of cooperation. Everyone needed help, everyone gave it.

WAR DEPARTMENT
SERVICES OF SUPPLY
OFFICE OF THE PROVOST MARSHAL GENERAL
WASHINGTON

March 12, 1943

Mrs. R. H. Whitfield,
    c/o Base Metals Mining Corporation,
       Field, British Columbia.

Dear Mrs. Whitfield:

      The Provost Marshal General has directed me to inform you that Mrs. L. E. Whitfield, formerly semi-officially reported as interned by Japan at Santo Tomas, Manila, is now officially reported as interned by Japan at Santo Tomas, Manila.

      If her name appears on further information received by this office, you will be notified.

                Sincerely yours,

                Howard F. Bresee,
                Colonel, C. M. P.,
                Chief, Information Branch.

Chapter 19:
THE HOMESTEADERS

It is quite unlikely that those first pioneering souls who erected a large canvas advertisement on four poles for shelter from the sun had any idea of establishing a new kind of home life for internees, but in that spot of hot shade the irrepressible shanty came into being.

Roofs developed walls and called for floors, and roof and walls and floor made a shanty, which demanded furniture, then decoration, then permanent dwellers. One shanty led to another, until there was a thicket of them, called Jungle Town, for its resemblance to the famous hobo cities in the United States. That inspired other settlements, with such names as Shanty Town, Glamourville, Froggy Bottoms, Intramuros (in one of the inner patios), with named streets, elected mayors, community utilities, and volunteer organized police protection.

They had a tough time of it, too, but survived and thrived through every trauma. At times they fell into disrepute with the Camp government; then again they'd run afoul of the Japanese. They were once totally banned by the Commandant, but by the time the ban was lifted, they had proven themselves important. For a little, they were regarded as mere shelters from sun, noise, and crowds, and a place to eat in semi-seclusion.

Then permission was granted for a few male members of established households to sleep in their shanty homes to guard the areas from both outside and inside night invasions. Filipinos from outside came over the wall, and Japanese guards and internee miscreants alike found good "scrounging" for some time in the unguarded shanties.

This immediately started a campaign to allow men with shanties to use them for sleeping quarters, to relieve the ever mounting congestion in the buildings. And toward the end, whole families moved into them, transferring their entire living to these fragile structures of bamboo and nipa, weathering heat and storms and mosquitoes for the privilege of living as families again.

The shanty contributed the most colorful chapters to the history of Santo Tomas. Each one that was built helped the whole Camp by lessening the crowds in the corridors and rooms. Shanty dwellers were less mentally tired, less nervous for being away from the buildings during the day. They had a new and wholesome interest, for most owners not only made the interiors of their tiny shacks as attractive as possible, but diligently landscaped the immediate surroundings, and stately banana trees, bougainvillea and cannas, hibiscus hedges and native vines, grew swiftly for even the amateur gardeners, and soon lined the Cornmeal Avenue, Beef Stew Boulevard, and Banana Lane roadsides with bloom. Before a year had passed, picturesque villages like movie versions of Filipino barrios covered most of the Campus area except the front, where they were forbidden. Even the two patios, inside the Main Building, long since worn smooth and bare of grass, were given over completely to homesteading, and were no longer available for romantic trysts.

Typically, the shanties lent themselves to disreputable uses as well as the solid respectability of home life, and abuses of the regulations time and again would threaten to cause a complete revocation of the privilege of anyone's owning and using any kind of a shanty. When he discovered that behind the closed windows Japanese rules were being disregarded, the Commandant demanded that all covering vines be torn down and all sides left open above a three-foot wall. Whenever the Camp incurred the Commandant's displeasure, for any reason, his first and direst threat was to seal the shanties. This using the shanties as a club over our heads set the Camp on its mettle, and police forces within the areas were organized and operated to enforce all rules and use all possible repressive measures on deliberate offenders. Once in awhile, for the good of all, it was necessary to forbid an individual to own or use a shanty, but this was difficult. There were a few instances where the whole shanty area was declared "off limits" to persistent lawbreakers.

When building first started, nipa, bamboo, and sawali, woven bamboo matting that has a thousand uses, were the materials most used, with an occasional "mansion" being erected with some solid lumber or a real roof. It was the work of only a few days for two or three men to complete a typical eight-by-ten or -twelve foot small-family house, or slightly larger duplex. In those pioneer days, the builders bought the nipa in bundles for the roof, from Filipinos on the outside, and laid it on the bamboo slats themselves. Bamboo poles were split for a clean, resilient flooring. Sawali was wrapped around and nailed on the supports to make walls. Windows were covered with flaps, held open by notched poles. All but a few of the shanties were on stilts, native-fashion.

As the utility of the shanties revealed itself more fully through use, the initial simplicity was quickly outgrown, and partitions elaborated the small interior into separate rooms — a kitchen alcove, a sitting and sleeping area — and often a separate bedroom was added later. Pull-down beds and tables, built-in benches and cupboards, and swing-out baby cribs were adroitly contrived for compactness.

Later, enterprising contractors instituted the importation of prefabricated shanties from Filipinos on the outside, and construction became simpler, if costlier. When it became more and more difficult to obtain materials, and inflation sent prices sky-rocketing to fantastic figures, shanties were bought and sold for hundreds, then thousands of pesos (invasion currency, usually borrowed money from outside), and at last became priceless when all sources were cut off. In August of the first year, the total cost of the shanty I shared for a short while with Marge and Larry was eighty-five pesos — forty-two dollars and fifty cents.

In one respect the shanties were wholly bad — they were not safe. As fragile as doll houses generally, many collapsed dismally in the big typhoon in November 1943, while others leaned tipsily or settled crookedly into the water-soaked soil. As the flood rose, shanty dwellers were forced to evacuate to the buildings, abandoning some of their little possessions for lack of space elsewhere and time to retrieve them. They crowded into rooms already full and slept in corridors for several nights before they could return "home" to clean up the muddy, odorous, pest-infested mess that was left. It was calamitous, and the losses were hard to bear, but back they moved, as quickly as the waters receded below the floor levels. During the high water, small but spectacular expeditions were made for salvage purposes by hardy souls who had to swim part of the way to their shanties, joined by adolescents who plunged with them into the filthy waters caused by the backing up of the sewer system, high tide, and typhoon precipitation.

And at the end, when mortar shells crashed through even the thick stone walls of the Main Building, the shanty areas offered no protection at all, and became a scene of tragedy and loss of life. Still the home owners clung to their make-believe sanctuaries, and there they stayed, some of them, long after the waiting years were ended and the war was over.

Chapter 20:
MONEY

For many months, the amount of food one ate depended to some extent on the amount of money one had, or could beg, borrow, or earn. Until the tides of war turned wholly against the Japanese and they began to really attentively create discomfort and hardship for their prisoners, we could nearly always buy, if we had the wherewithal.

Only a few individuals entered the Camp with any appreciable amount of cash, and those sums dwindled rather more rapidly than expected. It was the custom in the Far East to sign "chits," that convenient and expensive habit of easy, instant credit available everywhere. Because of this, we carried little cash. Before the war, an American or European could walk into almost any store in the Islands and sign for any purchase. Even the poorest laborers operated on the credit system.

So money was rather scarce the first year, and rates on loans ran as high as thirty-five percent. The invasion currency made its appearance within a few months, but realizing its worthlessness, Filipinos and prisoners alike avoided, so far as possible, using it or accepting it at first. When, however, it became evident that soon the Japanese would have control of all bona fide Philippine currency, people began to hoard it, and trade with the despised "Mickey Mouse" money. Coins of any denomination disappeared altogether, and we paid for our fruit and peanuts with crisp little one, five, ten, twenty, and fifty centavos notes. Interest rates on loans dropped sharply if the money received were in invasion currency, then ceased altogether. Eventually, loans that were made with Mickey Mouse money stipulated that they would be paid back in dollars, at a rate to the borrower's advantage. A hundred dollars would satisfy, perhaps, a thousand peso loan.

Another effect of this inflation was the enormous value placed on the hoarded real currency, either U.S. dollars or Philippine pesos backed by the U.S. treasury. When it ventured on the market at the last, passing cautiously through the hands that played with fire, certain underground dealers would pay ten-to-one or higher in the invasion money or merchandise. It was contraband—hot money—for the Japanese had long before called in all such currency, placing a heavy penalty for hoarding.

Private enterprises for earning money were at first rather frowned upon as not being in the communistic spirit some felt was appropriate. But initiative, lack of competition, and a seller's market made the first attempts so successful that before long, hundreds of internees were bartering or vending their hand-manufactured products, and all merchandising was organized and even licensed. A vendor's market was set up in one end of the long, covered dining shed, where shoddy displays included everything from marbles to soggy-looking cake. The Camp then opened its own nonprofit canteen and added a bakery goods counter and meat market during its heyday. An exchange center mushroomed from the hand-to-hand tradition to a full-fledged buy and sell business occupying the center of the mezzanine floor, with hoarded, hard-to-get items at phenomenal prices, protected by glass doors and presided over by volunteer salespeople.

Non-internee businesses, too, insidiously crept in and grew. Aguinaldo set up a small order department in the foyer of the Main Building and for a few months, internees could pay cash or even get credit "until the cessation of hostilities" for sleazy clothing, lawn chairs, and cheap toiletries, now nearly all Japanese-made. Pellicers, a Spanish company whose Manila store was still open, also gave credit and took orders; *sub rosa*, Mr. Pellicer cashed checks for prisoners with Philippine bank accounts. Filipinos were allowed in to sell vegetables, fruit, meat and other foods, and soon had a thriving market established within the Camp during the morning hours. Ready-to-eat lunches could be contracted for with restaurants and individuals in the city, and were sent in daily, to a very privileged few.

Each of these sources contributed but little food to the mass of prisoners, actually, but every loaf of rice bread, banana-leaf wrapped package of the yeasty rice loaf called *poto,* kilo of peanuts, hand of bananas, or luscious papaya brought into the Camp staved off the day of hunger a little longer. This was a time of comparative plenty, and during this time many far-sighted people tried to buy non-perishable food to store away. Unfortunately, most of what could be bought was not at all suitable for storing—even canned foods are suspect in the tropics after a while, and the goods we were buying had been in the Islands since before the war.

One woman in Room 25 down the hall bought a gallon can of pumpkin (the only thing available at the moment), and stored it under her bed. And there it exploded. She and her roommates were cleaning fermented pumpkin out of their beds, clothes, and hair for days!

None of this extra buying lasted very long. When it was cut off entirely, and even secret methods failed, and one hundred and fifty grams of cereal a day was the allotment for each prisoner, then we felt only gratitude for every *peseta* borrowed or earned and spent on food, whether it had been eaten then and added to our strength, or hoarded for the future, which had at last become the unpleasant present.

Most respected of all money-making methods was that of selling one's skill. Salable talents included carpentering, dressmaking, cooking, and baby-tending. Two or three scientifically inclined members undertook to produce lipsticks, not successfully, and tooth powder, quite distasteful. Groups of boys hired out to do "all-out" cleaning jobs on women's rooms. One man earned a good amount every day carrying women's mattresses outside for the necessary weekly sunning. An ex-furniture dealer went into the mattress debugging and repairing business. Husky girls rented their services to women who felt unable or unwilling to do their hour of bathroom duty each month. A Manila businessman dyed clothing on a charcoal stove; Marceil, the French artist in our room, painted children's portraits, or did lovely pastels of anyone.

Peanut brittle stands sold out their daily stock without difficulty, as the tantalizing odor of hot brown sugar tempted still-hungry internees in the early evening hours (much to the disapproval of the Camp dentist, who had enough to do without trying to mend the broken fillings and teeth of the peanut brittle eaters). One rather startling fact emerged somewhere along the line that the woman in our room who with her sons had been very successful with her peanut brittle sales was found to be a leper. She showed no evidence of this disease, and we were totally amazed to find ourselves in such close contact with it, and certainly realized we knew very little about leprosy. Most of us had a faint impression that it was highly contagious, stories of the *Bible*, *Father Damien*, and *Ben Hur* being our only sources of information. [Years later, after liberation, I learned that this lady was able to attain complete remission.]

Several women did laundry work for others. Beauty operators could cut, shampoo and wave hair without any special equipment, and had all they could do for awhile. One woman managed to get her permanent waving machine into Camp, and until the supply of waving fluid gave out, she made a very good thing of it.

Expert knitters could have all the orders they ever wanted, and were often signed up for six months ahead. This was one of the professions I chose, and in partnership with my dear and generous friend Florence, worked at it for many hours a day to earn what I needed to buy my daily bread and peanuts. First we used new wool that was brought into Camp; then crochet cotton, purchased from Aguinaldo; then and finally ordinary grocery twine (which was priced at nearly a hundred pesos a cone by November, 1943, and found only on the black market). We used anything knittable that could be obtained by unraveling old knitted garments. One older man brought us a disreputable red sweater from his college days. We unraveled it, split the yarn, and knit him a fine new sweater. We always made our charges on the orders in proportion to what had to be paid for the materials, plus the time required for producing the finished product; and the price increased, of course, with the inflated values of everything else.

Most of our trade was in socks, for men, women and children. Twine that was too heavy or coarse was split by a tedious process, and the ply that we used was soft and durable. If we contracted to do the splitting, too, we had to make an extra charge for it. That part of the job was usually done outside during the evenings. String panties for the ladies and for small children were much in demand, and polo shirts for men became popular as clothes wore out.

In spite of the number of women who were good knitters, only a few could maintain the pace required for the commercial scale. It was ruinous to the eyes, and under the rush of orders, a nerve-wracking business, but it provided us with a small steady income. We could afford to be particular in our choice of customers, since there were always more orders than we could take. Florence and I became very adept at knitting in the dark, especially on the socks, which helped out production, as the Camp was always under blackout.

I had another occupation, too, that brought me some money. I became a pro-tem secretary for a British shipowner who wanted desperately to reconstruct as many of his records as he could, and who dictated to me sometimes for hours on end. I learned that when he said "dollars one million," I was to write one million dollars; zed was the letter "zee," and "Clark" was pronounced "Clock." This was very good experience for me, and I enjoyed doing the work, which lasted a long time.

All essential services were, of course, volunteer and free. Doctors, dentists, nurses, dieticians, carpenters, teachers, cooks, sanitation squads, plumbers, handymen, seamstresses, Camp officials, and welfare workers—all worked long and hard, against innumerable obstacles, as part of their perceived duty. Special tutoring could be hired, outside of regular schooling, in many subjects, but was never very much in demand, as the curriculum offered by the school was satisfying in its scope and quality. I taught typing, short-hand, and business—my teaching field. There were no text-books, so my memory was all important, and I feel quite sure that this was true for most subjects. The entire educa-tional staff of all Island schools was available, and school was a major priority.

It was probably possible to live without any money at all, and no doubt there were many who did just that. But having a little money, even part of the time, made such a big difference in one's welfare and attitude that going far into debt became a way of life. Eventually, there would be noth-ing to buy, and when those times arrived, this became a great leveler. Many of the debts may not have been repaid, were forgotten, forgiven, or the principals didn't survive. But the invasion currency they were made in became a tawdry sou-venir, displayed along with a soiled flag and rifle in shop windows throughout the land.

Chapter 21:
THE PEOPLE

When the Japanese began working through Manila by districts to round up their enemies, the first to go were of course those near the Bay area. On the fourth of January, 1942, they emptied the Leonard Wood Hotel and its surroundings, and those four hundred persons had a nightmare two days at an old opera house known as Villamor Hall while the Japanese military and Nazi advisers tried to decide what to do with the prisoners once they had them. The "four hundred" were the charter members of Santo Tomas, entering there on the 6th of January. From then on, every day saw additional communities unloaded *en masse* at the gate. Outlying districts were untouched for several days, and it was weeks before the city was "completed."

Those who lived in the suburban areas had, therefore, a better chance to organize their packing, and from the first, they outshone the rest of us in appearance. There was a difference, too, in the temper of the pick-up squads, and on their whims depended how far one could go in saving much or nothing at all. I knew a man who was taken just as he was, and not allowed to retrieve even his upper dental plate from the bathroom shelf. On the other hand, several households were notified two or three days in advance when to be ready and came in with trunks and furniture.

To describe how the average Santo Tomasites, those who arrived in Camp with a bedroll and one suitcase, dressed and looked, is simple enough.

The men quickly adopted certain styles and clung to them. At first, it seemed as though most of them were going to be stubborn in the matter of beards; an early ugly stubble began to develop into beardish proportions, while the women clamored their complaints to no avail, for it was obviously a point of pride. Husbands informed their wives that "razor blades will be impossible to get, so I might as well get it started now as later on." But the hot season with its clinging dust and prickly heat began to take the matter in hand, and most of the bushy disguises came off. The supply of razor blades did hold out—the men ingeniously kept them sharp by pressing them round and round inside of a glass, for example. There were not many men who shaved every day, but most could not stand to let it go more than two days. The few beards that endured became masterpieces—especially the wavy black ones, and a few that glinted silver and white; there was one outstanding red-gold bush that gave its owner the look of great vitality!

To reduce the need to launder, and save wear and tear on clothing, the average man promptly shed his shirt, and it was with difficulty that he was persuaded to wear it even to meals —and almost always he left it unbuttoned. Long pants were simply cut off, in many cases, to make shorts. Some men took to wearing wooden bakias (native sandals, like beach shoes) while working, to save their shoes, but men's bakias were awkward and very noisy, so most of the men didn't care for them. A few of the braver, or rasher, of them went barefooted, disregarding the dangers and discomforts of tropical soil. So, for daily wear, a man's outfit might be a pair of shorts, string socks, and worn shoes. When he wanted to dress up, he might don the long white trousers he wore into the Camp, a knitted polo shirt, and a fresh shave.

The boys dressed like their dads, and the masculine members of the Camp were almost universally a beautiful deep brown from the waist up, and the mid-thigh down. A surprising difference began to occur in their physical appearance, too. Many of them had been leading "soft" lives of overindulgence and insufficient exercise. Here they worked, hard, and out-of-doors. Paunches flattened out, flabbiness disappeared, and in its place was a ruddy, lithe look that took years off their ages. For many months people never ceased to comment on how this or that prominent business man had never looked so well. Then, gradually, the healthy lean look gave way to scrawniness, the glowing tan seemed weather-beaten, leathery; the clear, bright eyes came to have a tired stare, and wrinkles gathered from the unforgiving sun; the new youth vanished.

The tragedy was that the men had trained down involuntarily to the extent that when famine entered the picture, they had no reserves. They had already lost all their excess weight, and what they were losing now could not be spared. The cuts in rations were somehow more severe for them than for the women, who had as a rule been accustomed to eating rather little, and most of whom had gained weight during the first months on the almost exclusively starch diet. Whatever the final analysis of the causes may be, more men than women actually died of starvation and malnutrition.

At first the women wore their thin silk prints and cotton dresses, and at least the older ones wore their frayed girdles to the bitter end. So long as stockings would hold together, they were worn, then were reluctantly replaced with short socks or "peds" — topless socks that didn't show above the shoe. Younger women and girls wore their slacks all the time, until the ban on shorts was finally lifted, and then this most comfortable of all garments became the most popular. Before shorts were allowed (the Central Committee had ruled them out in the beginning because of the presence in the Camp of the Japanese guards), the younger generation chopped off slacks to a funny, awkward length once the fad in girls' colleges, leaving the bottoms unhemmed. They perfected their casual look by leaving their shirt-tails out, and wearing their hair in two tight pigtails; mothers sighed, but conceded it was probably a comfortable way to dress, if that was all their unnatural daughters wanted!

As shoes wore out, all but the very oldest ladies replaced them with the light, cool *bakia*, the pretty native shoe made with a wooden sole and one or two straps across the toe. As I described before, men's bakias had heavy, unshaped soles, crude leather straps, and were neither attractive nor comfortable, but women's were carved gracefully to follow the line of the foot, so that standing in them was comfortable and restful; they were never hot, and they required no socks. Some of them were elaborately carved and decorated, with high wedge heels. I had a twenty-peso pair of white ones, very high-heeled, and all the wood within the wedge carved away except graceful twisted columns; the white straps criss-crossed prettily to the ankle in Grecian style. They would have been sensational, I thought, at home. The wood used was usually balsa, so there was almost no weight to them.

Bakias require practice to wear safely, and the beginner turns her ankle, clacks loudly wherever she goes, and loses one every few minutes. But women and children both be-came so adept with them that they could run, dance, and flit up (not down—that had to be done carefully) the stairs al-most as easily and quickly as in shoes, and never make a sound, even on the concrete floors. The trick was to firmly grip with the large toe with each step. We learned to love them, and most of us acquired several pairs. But I must admit that they produced callouses on our big toes the like of which no lady ever attained before!

We kept our hair immaculately clean, and it seemed to some of us that the very primitiveness of our shampooing methods was a marvelous revitalizer. We washed in cold water, of course, with whatever soap we could get, or with-out soap, and dried it vigorously in the sun. And like the Filipino girls, we found our hair shining and lustrous. For comfort alone it was necessary to wash it often; and the ever-recurring scares over lice sent even the laziest scurrying to the old bathtub behind the building where shower heads had been installed for that purpose. It wasn't that uncom-mon for anyone to find lice in her hair, and the very slightest itch sent us at once to each other for CAREFUL INSPECTION.

Some of the women, especially those with very straight hair, let it grow and did it up in becoming coronet fashion, or in a braid. Tints and dyes soon faded, and at last re-vealed lovely gray or white or natural hues. This may have caused mental anguish to the owners, but most of them were charming that way; the real blondes were vindicated, and there were significantly fewer redheads.

On the whole, the standard of appearance among the women was as high as it could be. When the dry season limited the amount of water available, and first one system of rationing and then another was tried, all failed because the women would not curtail their frequent showers. And vanity was not dead: two women on our floor stayed up every night after hours to put up their hair in pin curls; electric irons were obtained from somewhere and were used so constantly that time schedules had to be worked out among the rooms to prevent breakdowns from overloading the system; clothing was renovated, made over, even turned inside out to create an illusion of newness.

Dorothy, the half-Spanish, half-Irish girl in my room, provided us with enough vicarious glamour for all. As delicate in appearance as a Dresden figurine, and as tough as a Texas pioneer, she combined in her one small person all the fire and beauty of both nationalities. Her hair was a gleaming copper, her eyes violet, her skin fair and lovely. Brought up in luxury, and married to an indulgent wealthy Assyrian who lavished upon her everything she desired, she didn't exactly descend to the level of prison life.

Her cot, even there in that harsh, ugly room, was covered with a rose satin down comforter. She arranged a small sit-down type dressing table in the bit of extra space near the door. And there she sat for half the daylight hours, every day, grooming herself exquisitely. Every glistening curl must lie in perfect position, and I saw her spend three-quarters of an hour on one; cream, powder, lipstick, and rouge she somehow managed to have, and applied them with artistry. Her fingernails and toenails were shaped and polished to crimson perfection; ears, throat and wrists touched with a drop of fragrance. When all of us were without even lipstick, we marveled at her supply.

I think Dorothy felt that she was a princess among peasants. When her beautifully tailored slacks and dainty dresses showed signs of sun and wear, they still fit her perfectly and were immaculately cleaned and guiltless of wrinkles. She never ventured out into the hot sun without a parasol, and never soiled her white hands for long with any of the drudging tasks that took their toll on ours. Her beauty sessions really left her little time for Camp duties, and although she tried several, none could hold her interest. With charm and grace, she either fulfilled her assigned tasks or left them undone, as she chose. For all her hothouse appearance, she was strong, and we knew it. She could do with less sleep than any of us, and her endurance could be startling.

One of her fascinating qualities was her linguistic ability. Quite as easily as we speak our own language, she could switch from Spanish (her preference) to English to French with never a pause for breath. She was Latin enough to make your head swim with her rush of words. Her English was perfect, a trifle stilted and accented; she held a real conviction that Americans were incapable of cultured speech.

Dorothy also had a talent for enslaving her friends, and one after another paused to admire, then remained to serve, and serve, for such luxuriousness in a prison camp was not easily maintained. The result was an effect of queen and court, in full assembly about the narrow door of the room, and a stunning flow of liquid Spanish conversation. With total unconcern and incredible selfishness, armed with both her father's American citizenship and her husband's British passport, backed all the way by those two doting gentlemen, she surrounded herself with admirers of both sexes and royally ignored rules, and achieved the impossible in a scarecrow world: She remained beautiful and glamorous.

Chapter 22:
ANY DAY - 1943

6:00 a.m.—Up long before daylight, as usual, and groping around for my *chenilas* and towel, I knocked off my tin plate again—you could hear it all over Camp, and I guess there were twenty women in there hating me. I can't remember what it was like to turn on a light or turn it off when I chose, or how it would seem to not be living in a suitcase. But I had a shower to myself, for a wonder—it was really early. While I was fixing my face a bit and combing my hair under the dim hall light, one of the other girls came out, and soon there were a half dozen, and then the rush was on.

8:00 a.m.—I decided to get into the breakfast line this morning for a change, since it was rumored there would be a banana. Now that they have it arranged so you can get your coffee at a different counter, I almost never get into the line. I cannot stand to eat the mush—I <u>know</u> it's still full of worms, and it's hot. I corrected my shorthand papers while I was drinking my coffee (stood in line for nothing—the bananas were only a rumor). Some things never change, I guess—one of my students, a married woman who would like to be a secretary, spells "urge" with a "d"—and five of the high school girls spelled "strictly" as "strickly" in their transcriptions. I must include a back-up spelling course along with the shorthand.

9:30 a.m.—But I love the teaching. I doubt if anyone ever had such a chance as this, where all the students are voluntary, and have so many obstacles to overcome—poor lights, no quiet place to study, a dearth of materials and no textbooks, and no planned future to work toward; yet they are so motivated to learn. One of my shorthand classes is composed mostly of Spanish girls. They learn incredibly fast—their language, like shorthand, is phonetic; and they themselves speak so much faster than we do. They are beautiful girls and fun to teach.

11:30 a.m.—In the typing class, I have all adults, who were able, one by one, to somehow smuggle or legally bring in portable typewriters. I have no textbook, so they are learning by the voice method, and they're doing fine. They are so enthusiastic. Sometimes it's quite a challenge. The reason that my classes are electives is that business classes are not required by the school system, which moved almost bodily into Camp. The regular school children, in grades one through twelve, are required to attend their classes, and I think they are happy to, actually.

12:30 p.m.—Since I do more than the required number of work hours, I am entitled to the beans at noon, but I can't take them every day; my poor stomach just won't stand for it. So I fixed some fruit and some toasted *poto*, and started re-reading a very patched copy of *Show Boat* while I was eating.

1:00 p.m.—Later, during quiet hour, the Spanish contingent held a convention in the room, and no matter how much we shushed them, they couldn't get their voices down, so Florence and I finally gave up and took our knitting out into the corridor, after we had showered and cleaned up. No visiting firemen today, so we accomplished a lot—ripped up an old sweater (college, class of '98—that's 1898!) for an elderly man who wants a dozen pairs of wool socks!

3:30 p.m.—It's fun to people-watch, of course. There's the little lady who passes us on her way to the shower, with her little bath apron, with a pocket for each toilet article; neat, efficient and sweetly funny. [In the very early days, to our deep dismay, we found a bathroom monitor at the door of the ladies' bathroom. She would issue two small sheets of bathroom tissue to each person entering—and that was all! This was almost the ultimate deprivation, and certainly an insult to the female personna.]

There's the German girl who wraps herself up in a peach satin and ecru lace negligee—what the well-dressed prisoner always wears on the way to the shower. I hope it survives the "rigors." And speaking of the shower, I got into trouble with the Sultana and her daughter the princess to-day—the regal Moro ladies (I have no idea why they were interned; perhaps they felt safer in here than if they were outside). It happens to everyone at least once: I snatched the wrong towel, and it belonged to the Sultana, of all people! I had not touched my body with it yet, but she ignored my apologies, and disdainfully ordered her daughter to get her another one from her room. To make it worse, while I was babbling that hers was just like mine, I caught a glimpse of mine hanging there, and it was not even the same color.

4:00 p.m.—It took us an hour and twenty minutes to get through the chow line for supper, and then it was bean sprouts and stew and rice, but we made ourselves a cup of coffee and allowed ourselves a cookie afterwards.

5:30 p.m.—Then down to the line again; they had a few hundred bars of laundry soap on sale at the canteen, and there were at least two thousand of us in the line (counting the children, who come in so very handy when it's "one to a person"). We took our chairs and knitting and went down early, so we managed to get our soap. We're praying that some day they will get hand soap into the camps.

7:00 p.m.—Then out to the plaza. There was wonderful music this evening, and a magnificent rose and gold sunset followed by an early moonrise. I miss my husband Norman especially during these beautiful hours. You can't help wondering—what is it like where he is? Is he all right? He's a good survivor, but he's strong and independent, and I can't imagine him in prison!

Florence and I had a great chuckle when one of the single women belonging to a certain mission group came out of the building to join her friends and greeted them with "Hi, fellers!" Our temperamental choir director was sandpapering another cigar box; he must be getting ready for next Christmas. We had to move our chairs twice to get away from the rasp of it. The featured music of the evening was the monthly rendition of the entire *Scheherazadhe* suite. It's gorgeous, but too noisy for in here; makes me nervous.

8:30 p.m.—We didn't wait for Don Bell's evening news-cast of menus and misdemeanors (he was a local American newscaster to whom we always listened in the evening on the outside, and it was an odd little comfort to have him giving us the "news"—even though the content was pretty drab). We quietly folded up our chairs and stole away to beat the mob to the showers. Later, we were comfortably seated in our housecoats near the blackout light by the time the thundering herd arrived. There's no other sound like it, when all those thousands of people, all talking at once, start pouring into the building.

9:15 p.m.—The Spanish girls were late to evening roll call —again—so we had to wait, and by the time we arrived back at the hall, there were no good seats. It was announced that they are starting medical shots again tomorrow, for dysentery, cholera, and parathyroid. It doesn't seem as though it could be six months ago that my arm felt like that. I hate shots. Someone told me that Bill, a strapping six-footer just off a college football team, fainted last time—before they even touched the needle to his arm. Oh, and the Comman-dant reminds us, the notices tonight said, that it is strictly forbidden to send notes out in the laundry (wish I had some-one to send my laundry to!) and we are warned for the last time that if there are any further abuses of this great privi-lege, he can "close the gate" at any time he wishes. More talk of the repatriation ship; no one knows yet who is to go or anything much about it, but there is much guessing.

The undercover news tonight was exciting. There were stories about our progress in the South Pacific, and with few exceptions, we have had to admit humbly that we never heard of most of those places, including the Solomon Islands, until war began to teach us something about our small world. The transcripts also have us doing big things in Sicily. That still seems so far away from the front lines of the war in Germany, but I guess it won't take much longer. We're be-ginning to think now that the Pacific War will be over before the European one, the way we are "cleaning up" down there

in the South. It would be nice to be home for Christmas—
and who knows?

11:00 p.m.—We put our knitting away at eleven, when
all the lights went out, but Florence and I curled up on our
chairs by the window, tucking our housecoats under our
feet to protect them from the mosquitoes, and talked there
until one o'clock, or whispered, rather. We do this almost
every night. It really is amazing with how little sleep one
can do, and we can always find so much to talk about. The
corridors look weird late at night, with the bats swooshing
down almost into our faces, and only the small blackout
lights burning. There are two older women, with faces revealing hardships, who make tea in the bathroom about
midnight, and seem to belong in the picture.

1:15 a.m.—Into bed at last—the room is always hot and
close. But this night I didn't have ants in my bed. Last night
I went to bed only to discover a whole swarm of ants, and I
was bitten. The experts say the ants were after the bedbugs.
Well, so am I, every day, and the ants might as well learn
right now that it's a losing battle. If I can't eliminate the filthy
creatures with boiling water and straight creolin, what chance
has a tiny red ant?

When the rain stops, it is quiet and peaceful. I like to
lean 'way out the window, and smell the air, so fresh and
sweet, like home . . . . .

Chapter 23:
LEGENDS FROM THE WEST
CORRIDOR

Nothing so enlivened and invigorated our conversation as the recounting of new and old exploits of our local heroes. The tales came by word of mouth, and grew as such stories will. Embellished or not, we loved them. These are some of the little epics, which traveled far and wide via the bamboo telegraph, and filtered through walls and fences to our eager ears, and this is the way we heard them. This is not the history of guerrilla activity in the Islands, for there will be records where that will be told accurately and completely for the great story it is.

I am sure that a certain Filipino *medico* never dreamed how much he was admired by several thousand prisoners. The little doctor had apparently been engaged in some subversive activities, as so many thousands were. Someone, tempted by the cash rewards the Japanese were offering for information concerning anyone working against them, must have betrayed him, and one day three Japanese officers climbed the stairs to his small, unpretentious office. They told him that he was known to have a gun in his possession, a death penalty crime, and ordered him to surrender. Sadly, trembling, with a great show of knowing when he was defeated, the doctor admitted that the accusation was true, and said, "It is here, in my desk drawer." Impatiently, then, and incautiously, they motioned for him to give it to them, so he pulled the drawer open, reached in and fumbled about among the rumpled papers, and drew out a hand gun— pulled the trigger three times, and escaped, leaving the bodies of the officers on the floor where they fell! We knew that at least some of this was true, for the Japanese paper printed his picture daily for weeks in a "Wanted" advertisement, with a reward for his capture, dead or alive.

Far up in the Northern Provinces, a Filipina won immortal fame and a place in our hearts almost as dramatically. Along a dusty, burning road a dozen American soldiers were working, barefooted, emaciated, ragged. Nearby in the sultry shade of a limp papaya tree lolled a Japanese soldier of some rank, occasionally bestirring himself to shout at the prisoners. The Filipino girl, head held high and shoulders straight under her large earthen jug of water, walked slowly down the road. Approaching the American boys, without a moment's hesitancy, she set the jar on the ground, knelt beside it and poured into a cup she carried water for each of them. When the guard noticed her, he watched for awhile without expression, then apparently losing his struggle with temptation, came over to the girl and demanded a drink for himself.

She rose with that superb dignity and grace of the women of her race, holding the jug, and even as he reached for water, in one quick motion the girl dashed the cup to splinters against a rock, turned her back, and walked back the way she had come. Perhaps the soldiers paid for her temerity, perhaps not —but how they must have silently cheered.

There was a colonel of the guerrillas whose daring and persistence became unbearable to the Japanese. Repeatedly, his ambushes of patrols and raids on outposts surprised and defeated them, while the price on his head doubled and quadrupled. At last, with the aid of the dysentery, malaria and malnutrition which forever struck so viciously at the men in the hills, the colonel was captured and killed, or more probably, killed, then captured. In the Japanese paper was a picture of the tall American, standing among Japanese soldiers. A long story under black headlines told about his being glad that he was caught, how tired and frightened he had been; urging all other resisters to give up and surrender themselves; assuring them they would be treated justly and respectfully by the Japanese. That picture—how it first startled, then haunted us—the gaunt body, in ragged clothing, hat settled stiffly over the <u>dead</u>, deep-lined face of a hero. It was the old wartime trick of standing up corpses, recording words that never could have passed those lips.

It would have been easy to turn against many captured Americans and Filipinos, either fighting men, correspondents, radio announces or fugitive civilians, if we had believed even part of the hundreds of direct "quotations" from them, printed regularly in the enemy paper.

One of our Santo Tomas prison camp heads once queried the Commandant along this line, asking "You people don't honestly expect us to believe the stuff you print in that paper, do you?" The Commandant replied, quite coolly, "Oh, no. That is for the Filipinos."

But a friend of mine told us, after he had been out on a special "day's pass" into the city, another side of that story. He had stopped in a little coffee shop for refreshment, and a Filipino slid into the chair beside him, opened up a copy of this same *Tribune* and pretended to read the paper, upside down. The American finally asked softly, "Why do you have your paper upside down?"

The Filipino replied, "Sir, that is the way we Filipinos are reading this paper."

The most spectacular and romantic legend of all grew up around the Cushing brothers, all three outstanding guerrilla leaders, but most particularly around the one named Walter. We had known Walter around the mining camps, an effervescent, wiry, unstoppable, tough, and likable miner. He was a natural for the part he played. An American, but half Mexican by blood, he was small, dark, incredibly strong and resilient. Years of prospecting for gold in the mountains of the Philippines had given him a knowledge of the country and the people equalled by few men. It was said of him before the war that even his Igorot *cargadors* (the mountain natives who hired out to carry supplies and equipment for the prospectors, and who themselves were swift and strong) could not keep up with him on his prospecting trips. His quick, tireless trot carried him far ahead of the carriers, even when he was breaking his own trail with a *machete*, as he did so often. He had penetrated far into the uncharted wilds, and was known to even the most primitive headhunters and tree-dwelling *negritos*.

At the beginning of the war, he gathered about him a group of natives, and they quickly grew famous as they daily outwitted the invaders who had half an army searching for him. Great rocks fell on troop trucks; patrols disappeared, now here, now there. He was like quick-silver, never still; and the natives worshiped him, so it seemed no betrayer could be found. Once we heard that Walter came alone to the house of a Spanish friend in the little sugar town of San Miguel, north of Manila. The friend cried in real agitation, "This is the worst place you could come. Every day the Japanese officers from the garrison come to my home to drink beer, and this is the time they come!"

Walter said, "Well, I'll hide some place, and they'll never know the difference," and was so nonchalant as to choose to lie under the bed, only a few feet from where the officers sat when they had their drinks. True to the tradition, wherever he went the word spread fast among the people, and while the Japanese still sprawled and belched in the stiff Spanish chairs, a horde of worshiping urchins assembled under the window of the house and burst into a shrill, sincere "God Bless America" for Walter!

Another time, an internee out in Manila buying for the Camp swore he had met Walter on the street, dressed as a Filipino cigarette vendor, white teeth flashing in his glorious smile, dirt and borrowed clothes his only disguise as he strolled openly through the streets, indifferently offering his wares to the men he came to see, and to the Japanese as well.

We were not sure we believed, but loved to tell it anyway—the one about his donning the robe of a Filipino priest and entering Santo Tomas prison camp for a visit. From sheer irrepressible bravado, he might have done it, at that. We know that our Central Committee and others had contacts with the guerrillas.

Then we began to hear that he had been captured, but no one could agree which of the many versions of the rumor was correct. All were romantic, dashing, unverified, and finally denied. And the legend continued to grow.

When the inevitable happened, and one Judas was found to earn the bloody pieces of silver, Walter is said to have "gone out in glory." The last story, believed by most to be authentic, said he was ambushed and trapped by an overpowering force, but shot it out to his last bullet, then sent that one through his own heart, true to his vow that he would never be captured alive. The Filipinos love a hero, and they will love Walter Cushing to the end of time and sing songs at their fiestas about the warrior he was.

The Baguio people in Santo Tomas loved to tell the tales about Dangwa, an Igorot. Few of these mountain pagans had been much educated, except through the scattered mission schools, and they were simple, unspoiled and sometimes dangerous. But Dangwa had an education and had traveled. He returned to Baguio, becoming the owner of a principal freight truck line, making him easily the wealthiest native in the Mountain Province. He turned his trucks over to the American Army when the call came, and from then on, discarded his American clothes, returned to the loin cloth (called a g-string there) and spear, and contributed more to our cause than any other one of his people could have. He was also badly wanted by the Japanese, and they sent frequent scouting parties to look for him, hiring Igorots to act as guides and interpreters. One of the things that pleased us so much about the whole story was that Dangwa himself, indistinguishable through dirt and tattooing from his brothers, served as interpreter or guide for many of these expeditions, leading the soldiers far into the mountains in the search for himself.

One night in the plaza a vivid, gray-haired woman with a charming voice held us breathless while she told us that the Panamanian Consul, a citizen of the United States repatriated with other consular and diplomatic officials, had actually returned secretly to the Islands on a submarine to contact, instruct, and supply the guerrillas. There were several recent American magazines right in the Camp to prove it.

About this same time, we heard the famous tale of Tomas Confesor and the big red apple he sent to Vargas as evidence of the nearness of the Americans (there are no apples grown in the Islands). Copies of his letter circulated through the Camp discreetly. These things were all-important to us, though such a small part of the whole.

Chapter 24:
SO HIGH A PRICE

Dealing with the hopeful, almost piteously eager people in a concentration camp must always have been a trying, emotional task. People tried so hard not to expect too much, but they wanted, ever so humbly but deeply, just some little message or privilege or word or promise. The answer was nearly always "No," or "I don't see how it can be done" to everything, and saying it must have been often difficult and saddening to the Camp leaders, who often did all they could and more than they should have.

In the spirit of true democrats, almost the first thing we had done in the Camp (and in every Camp) was to elect a Central Committee, made up of outstanding people from all over the Islands, from every profession. They ran the Camp, literally, from the beginning. They also served as a buffer, a liaison, between the prisoners and the Japanese, and they did this with wisdom, sensitivity, selflessness, and great courage. They were accessible to every internee, and listened. The Japanese respected them, were sometimes furious at them, but dealt with them as a legitimate representation of the prisoners.

Carroll Grinnell and A.F. Duggleby actually gave their lives in this cause. Mr. Grinnell, fine-looking, poised, and charming, worked at his job of Committee Chairman through almost three years, smoothly carrying on as liaison officer between the Japanese and the Camp population in the face of the bitterest criticism from both. And all the while, often unbeknownst to even his closest associates, and completely unsuspected by his intolerant critics, he was deeply involved in the most hazardous game of all—the underground activities which supplied military and civilian prisoners in all the prison camps, and active guerrillas on the outside, with money, medical supplies, food, clothing and information. He, with a very few others in the Santo Tomas prison camp, including Mr. Duggleby, actually borrowed and distributed where they were urgently needed, great sums of money from sympathizers or profiteers in Manila, with damning discovery always just around the corner.

They were doomed to disaster, and a few days before Christmas 1944, only short weeks before the final curtain would have saved and made public heroes of them, Mr. Grinnell, Mr. Duggleby, and two others were taken away by the Japanese. (The story has been told and retold, but it deserves a thousand tellings.) One of the other two men was a young salesman, who was in no way involved but had the same name as the older man whom the Japanese really meant to take.

As days went by and nothing was heard of or from the four men, the acting Central Committee Chairman, Earl Carroll, and other Committee members haunted the Japanese office for information, but drew blank silence. The Camp was in the charge of the military. Any sympathy that might have been found in a civilian commandant was frozen in the universal fear of their gestapo.

After the Americans came and conquered, it was through the chance testimony of a Filipino that the crime of another brutal execution was uncovered and the grave located, so positive identification could be made.

Little was known about the underground, or those who served it. A girl named Fay, whose husband was a prisoner at Cabanatuan, told me about one of the nameless hundreds who lived so dangerously for the love of their country and ours. She had been allowed for a few months to live in Manila with a neutral friend because of ill health, and after many very guarded inquiries, finally made a contact with one of the underground messengers—a Filipino boy. Fay told us that the boy would come to the house at night bringing a note from her husband and would wait for her to write an answer. Each time when he was ready to leave, he'd grin as though it were really funny, and say "Well, ma'am, I will say goodbye now but I will be back again, God willing." The risks were appalling, and everyone in the game knew it.

We heard that daughters of aristocratic Filipino families, who had never even combed their own hair during their extravagantly pampered pre-war lives, were dressing as *taos*—peasants—and with heavy baskets of tropical fruits on their heads, were appearing at the military prison camps, bribing and beguiling the guards into letting them inside to see the prisoners and sell their wares. Once inside, they snatched precariously at any unguarded opportunity to deliver messages and money to the Americans. They even endured publicly announced but privately-held investigations—a far cry from the cloistered, chaperoned, proud seclusion of their previous way of living.

Three Catholic priests, said to be Germans, were finally, after many successful months of mercy work, suspected and trapped with money and letters concealed in their garments. They were beaten and tortured at Fort Santiago; we never knew whether they survived. The Japanese as a rule dealt lightly with the Roman Church but had little success with their diplomacy.

Earl Carroll, twice Central Committee Chairman of Santo Tomas, and always a Camp leader, was also concerned in these matters, and knows probably more than anyone else alive the intricate details of the underground story. So much depended on the fearlessness and quick thinking of this handful of internee leaders, for they were the very focal point of the whole system in that section of the country, and the miracle is that they were able to carry on with it so long under the very presence of the Japanese Military Police.

AMERICAN RED CROSS
Washington, D. C.

Form 1616
Rev. Sept. 1942

International Red Cross Committee
Geneva, Switzerland

CIVILIAN MESSAGE FORM

Sender

Name Mrs. Ethel E. Allworth

Street Route 2

City Corvallis   State Oregon

Citizen of United States of America

Relationship to person sought Sister-in-law

Chapter Benton County Chapter, Corvallis Date 11-30-44

Message

(News of personal or family character; not more than 25 words)

Dear Evelyn:- We were all at Dot's at Thanksgiving except you
and Norman and Sonny and next year we're planning on you
three too. Everything is fine with all of us-Jacki-Son's
wife has been with us. Son is with the tulips and windmills
and we hear often. Jody is at the Good Samaritan Hospital
in Portland, a Cadet Nurse. Kent as tall as I am and Nancy
almost. Ed fine.
We've had a beautiful Fall. Gorgeous colors and lots of
fruit which is all canned or sold or stored. Harvesting and
seeding all done and now we're all getting ready for Santa.
Days are colder and its nearly time to go tree hunting.
Everybody is coming here and we'll be thinking of you.

Love

Ethel

Addressee

	Identifying Data
Name Mrs. Laura Evelyn Whitfield	
Address U.S. Civilian Internee	Birthplace Corvallis, Ore.
Santo Tomas, Manila	and date March 18, 1912
Country Philippine Islands	of birth U.S.A.
	Citizen of

Reply on the reverse side   Réponse au verso   Antwort umseitig

Chapter 25:
EVEN A WORD . . .

It was nearly a year before the Japanese finally allowed us to write a fifty-word censored message once a month to relatives and friends in other camps. With great relief, we resorted at once to this open communication. The secret method had always made Norman and me uneasy since the time one of our messages was intercepted, and the friend who had volunteered to get it out of Camp Holmes was beaten and warned of more serious punishment for a second offense. We hated to feel that we were letting others run such risks for us, and because of this, had sent very few letters to each other.

Some months the censored messages did not come through at all, reposing instead in the bottom of a wastebasket near the Japanese censor's desk. Occasionally a note would be so mutilated by his fault-finding that there would be nothing left to read. For the first few months, in line with the instructions that the notes were not to be affectionate, he diligently blotted out all "love" and "dear" and almost broke his pen on my husband's customary salutation of "My Sweet."

The notes we sent went through the hands of our own American censor first. His job was to check to see that nothing offensive or indiscreet reached the eyes of the Japanese. He was most helpful, too, endeavoring to put the more personal messages, such as those between husband and wife, or mother and child, on the top of the stack, in case the Japanese should weary of his task after the first few notes and discard the rest; this happened more than once.

He also tried to "snoop" a little for us sometimes, to see if our notes had been sent, or if any had come in that had not been delivered to us. He was on the outside a very able newspaper correspondent, and patient and cooperative in this job, and skilled. His reward was, more often than not, griping and intolerance from disgruntled and discouraged letter writers who, seeing no further than his title of Censor (in natural disrepute among Americans), considered him just another stumbling-block, a representative of official red tape to impede our freedom. He couldn't explain to everyone, either, or word of his helpful activities might reach the Japanese. His duty was not an enviable one, certainly, searching the hundreds of stilted little messages for that one incautious phrase that might cause trouble, or finding here and there a line of tragedy that would add to someone's burden. It could not have been a jolly occupation.

On an October day in 1942, one of our most fervent prayers was answered for some. The first bag of mail from home finally arrived. Internees hung around for hours awaiting the posting of the list of fortunate ones, each person sure his family had written and he'd have something. People waited on the big central staircase, hanging over the rail, waiting, hoping. Then the lists were up, and those who found their names were something near jubilant at the prospect of even a word from home. It had been like living in a vacuum. We couldn't imagine how things were there. No one knew whether he had near and dear young people in the war; whether his family was alive and well, nor what was happening. Parents with sons in the States were nearly beside themselves with worry. We weren't exactly "without a country," because we could and did talk about it constantly, even if we couldn't hear anything except propaganda.

Such a pitiful few there were, those precious letters in the first lot—something like sixty-five pieces of mail for four thousand people. And how I poured over even the outside of the familiar envelope of my letter, until my eyes were filled with tears and I collided clumsily with chairs and people as I hurried back to my room to read it. Always we had valued our letters from home during the years we had lived so far away; mail time had been the high spot of the day. But never has a single letter been so cherished and read and re-read as that one. I read it over and over to myself, and to my friends, and my sister became theirs as I read; even the small "family-talk" was some kind of news from home, and might have been written by anyone from those other families. There was a neat square cut out of the center where she had written something the censors objected to, and we spent time conjecturing what it might have been, for the beginning of the cut sentence was an innocuous reference to Spring's being late. She said she had written so many times, and I grieved for those lost letters, but felt like an heiress with my one.

Then I was in a fever to share it with Norman. I did not dare to take the chance of sending the letter itself by underground. So I typed a copy of it on plain paper, conspicuously placing the word COPY at top and bottom in business fashion, and took it down to the office. Mr. Grinnell promised to do what he could for me, but later returned it saying that the Japanese had refused permission to have it forwarded. For weeks, then, I watched my chance, and at last found a messenger to carry the copy out of our prison camp in Manila and contact someone who would deliver it to Norman at the internment center at Baguio.

There was nothing more, then, for several months. We smarted under the injustice of being denied our mail, knowing that under International Law (which we cited so frequently that it became almost too boring to mention at all), prisoners of war, whether civilians or military, were entitled to receive both letters and packages from home.

Once a Japanese diplomatic repatriate from the United States visited the Camp, and our Commandant called us out to hear a speech by the visitor on the mistreatment of Japanese internees in America. He told us about the brutal removal of all Japanese from the West Coast to the inland states; how their homes were confiscated by the government, and families were torn apart. We were quite disbelieving at that time, and not convinced that the conditions were as he said, although even then it was easily apparent that Japanese nationals in the States would be under suspicion. We had our own experience here, when those who had worked beside us through the years turned out to be military—we knew we had been infiltrated for years. In war, the innocent always do suffer; they lost their homes; we lost our homes; none of us had sought this wretched war.

Then the rotund little man, carried away by his own eloquence, made a most indiscreet suggestion—that the meeting be thrown open to questions from the internees. The Commandant looked very uncomfortable, but would have lost much face had he appeared to fear questioning, so of course had to comply. The first three or four questions were disarmingly casual and courteous, and allowed the speaker to become rather pompous, as though he were explaining the obvious to children. Then a man's voice boomed from the back row, "And do the Japanese prisoners receive any mail?" The Commandant began to shuffle his feet.

"Oh, yes, they have regular mail deliveries—censored, of course; most unreasonably, however," was the affable reply. And the Commandant rose and bowing profusely to his guest, apparently suggested that he had honored us sufficiently, and the meeting was closed, while chuckles and grins betrayed our little pleasure at having scored even a small point. We felt quite sure that the Commandant hadn't thought it necessary to prime the visitor on little deficiencies in the management of the camps, and was feeling a bit of chagrin now at the results.

The next mail appeared after the beginning of the second year, and it was all British and Canadian. There was a rumor in the Camp that the British camp in Hong Kong had received only American mail, but there was never a verification of that rumor! At any rate, we were glad to see our British friends have some of the good fortune, and the rest consoled themselves that if two mails had come through, a third one had a good chance of making it through the now-broken ice. I had never before realized the value of having Canadian as well as American relatives until I found that I again had a letter, from Canada, this time, and again just one of the many that had been written.

When the great vessel of bounty arrived at the end of 1943 with the Red Cross supplies, it also brought hundreds of letters for each Camp, and many individual packages sent from the "next of kin" through the Red Cross. It was three months, however, before distribution was made, and very few of the packages ever reached the prisoners. Those that did created a sensation. Carefully packed within prescribed weight and size limits, they contained as great a variety and quantity as anxious, loving, ingenious planning could attain. Into my one small package, my sister had squeezed a cotton slack suit and a dress, lingerie, socks, soap, toothbrush and powder, and a comb; soup cubes, dehydrated soups, cheese, powdered coffee, and vitamin and mineral capsules; and her understanding heart was revealed in the inclusion of a wonderful lipstick—I was queen of all I surveyed. How dear it was.

Nearly everyone had letters that time, and some received as many as twenty. Even a few snapshots somehow slipped past the censor and were shown to everyone who'd look. Then, for the rest of that last year, mail was received every two months or so, in small quantities, and under a new restriction of twenty-five words to a message. By a strange coincidence, it developed that nearly always the same people received most of the mail. One Texas girl never missed, and even in a very scant shipment would always have several. We missed only once out of all the times. On the other hand, there were a few who never received anything, yet knew well enough that their families were writing them. It was tragic to see their spirits sag with each new disappointment, and the whole Camp was eager to ask each time if they had not had some this time.

As dispiriting as receiving no mail was not being permitted to write, knowing as we did that our families and friends were longing to hear from us. I felt this particularly, for in the two letters I received before the end of 1943, there was no mention of Norman, an omission so obvious in our close-knit family that I knew at once that they had heard nothing from him, and did not know, even, that he was alive, but were carefully avoiding drawing attention to him in case he might be out somewhere.

I wanted terribly to get word to them about it, but we had no opportunity until August of 1943. Then we were told that we might each send one letter on the repatriation ship. So in December, two years after the beginning of the war, our family finally heard from us—a letter from me, and one from Norman. Before that, they had seen my name listed officially at Santo Tomas, and verified my presence there by a sympathetic early repatriate, who wrote them charmingly and intimately of what she had seen me doing there in the Camp. But there was nothing from Norman—no listing, no one had seen him. They left no stone unturned, wrote to every possible source of information, but the wall of secrecy was impenetrable, until after the arrival in the States of the *Gripsholm*, the repatriation ship.

The pile of letters I have recently seen that were received in answer to the family's inquiries is touching evidence of their aching concern. Their angst was as vivid to me while I was imprisoned eight thousand miles from them as though I had been talking with them daily. I could not bear to think of it, sometimes, and I even dreamed about it at night. My concern for my own well-being was small compared to this void.

Those little letters were so carefully and laboriously composed. We tried to reach a compromise between our conscience and heart; in other words, we didn't want to write anything that could possibly add to the worrying at home, but instead tried in every way to relieve it. Also, we would not put anything into the letters that would paint a falsely pretty picture of the conditions in the Camp for fear the Japanese would use it for propaganda. And this they immediately did, of course, whenever they found the opportunity. A few of the letters were even broadcast over Radio Tokyo, to their writers' intense chagrin.

After February of 1944, we were given the privilege of writing one twenty-five word message a month to our home, and several of those little yellow cards, beginning "I am interned at Japanese Army Internment Camp No.___. My

health is Excellent, Good, Fair, Poor (Underline one)" actually did reach the States, some of them long after the war
had ended and we were home. They told nothing, of course,
except that we were alive and thinking of them. Any that
were written in other than the stereotyped "Both feeling well,
working hard. Letters thankfully received. Tell everyone
hello. Love to all" pattern were dropped into the wastebasket by the censor. But it was an outlet for us, and there
was always the hope that they might get there.

One other type of message was occasionally received
after the middle of the second year: undated cables, sent
through Geneva to Tokyo, and thence to the Philippine
camps, sometimes so garbled through all the translations
that they were unintelligible. I had one with the enigmatic
phrase "Dne a hounded," and even my sister who sent it
has never been able to figure out what it should have said!

One of these cables gave us all something to remember.
A young British woman was called into the Japanese office
and told that she had a cable from her home in England, but
that it would cost her seven pesos before she could have it.
So she rushed back to her room and in a few minutes, with
the help of friends, accumulated the required sum, and too
excited and joyous to be annoyed at such a heckling demand
from the Japanese, hurried back to the Commandant's office and gave them the money. Then she was handed the
cable—informing her that her mother had passed away.

Other cables brought sad news, too, most frequently to
the English internees, who received many messages of deaths
by bombing or while serving in the armed forces of some
member or several members of the family. We discussed this
matter at great length in the Camp—whether it would or
would not have been better to wait until the end before telling
family bad news. It always came as a crushing blow,
particularly as the letters or cables were so excitedly
anticipated and so eagerly opened. On the other side, many
felt that it would be even more devastating to have the blow
waiting at the end of the weary road. There isn't any answer,

so it was never closed, but the cables themselves came to be received with dread.

One mother in the Santo Tomas prison camp later received word from her daughter in the States, telling her mother she had divorced her husband—who was in a POW camp. This mother took that news with such bitter disappointment that I wondered whether her daughter should have told her. Even though it was the honest thing to do— "Dear John" letters are always hard to take.

We knew there were some philatelists among the Japanese. Letters to prisoners of war could be sent without postage, so there were few stamped envelopes, but we knew which ones had been stamped, for the stamps were cut off. The Victory stamp, of course, was censored anyway, and we did not see it until after our release. In fact, our own censors returned one letter which Norman's sister had written us, informing her that the Japanese would not allow it to go through, so there was no use in sending it.

Sometimes we could laugh. The first package from the United States to reach Santo Tomas was sent by his family to a well-known business man for the Christmas before we were interned and delivered to him eight months later. He received the box, with the contents carefully listed on the outside, and the Merry Christmas seals still decorating the rumpled wrappings. It was so ridiculous—because of course there was not one crumb or article left inside. Like the woman who obtained permission to have her luggage brought into Camp, and received her seven trunks completely empty, he had the somewhat dubious consolation of knowing what had once been inside, anyway.

Material possessions came to have a special significance. If an object wasn't useful, or able to be made useful, it had no importance. Because of the lack of space, we were impatient with abundance. And a new attitude grew. We all knew the story of one dear lady, a friend of our family, who was allowed by the Japanese to remain in her home in Manila, because she was elderly. She could not bear to leave because it was furnished throughout with priceless Oriental and Spanish antiques which she and her husband had spent most of their lives collecting. Her husband and daughter were in Santo Tomas, always deeply worried about her. And when the bombing came, she lost her life there in the ruins of that beautiful home.

Most of us had left everything we owned when we were evacuated, and for most of us, we simply accepted that fact, and wasted little time and emotion on regrets. Since we were evacuated at the Christmas season, that first time, I sometimes thought wistfully of the lovely packages that we had received from home and never opened. But there were never any doubts in my mind that there would be other Christmases and other gifts, for the love that sent them was still there, waiting for us to come home.

PRISON GARDEN

THE ZIGZAG TRAIL

~ PART THREE ~
CAMP HOLMES

Chapter 26:
REUNION

It seemed a demeaning thing to ask concessions or favors of the Commandant, and we hadn't much respect for those who hounded him with their petty desires, leaving themselves open for humiliating snubs. Most of us wouldn't go near his office unless we were personally called there. We were content to allow the Committee to act for us, and the men on the Committee preferred it that way, too.

There was one matter, however, so important to me that I could swallow my pride, and did, for pride seemed a little meaningless compared to the strength of my longing to join Norman. When, on my birthday, I had my first message from him, I was surprised and relieved to learn that he was interned at Baguio. I had been almost certain that he was in the hills. The thought of getting transferred up to Baguio came to me at once, and I began feeling my way along.

First I made the rounds to consult anyone and everyone in Santo Tomas who might have some influence, or at least some sound advice. A kindly man named Jim Kibbee, the hardest working man on the floor, frowned worriedly at my idea, and protested that it wasn't safe for me to go, even if I could get permission. There was something in what he said, too, for the Japanese were still an unknown quantity to us, regarding their attitude toward women. Earl Carroll didn't give me much hope, but suggested that I write a formal letter of application, stating as many reasons as I could think of, to give to the Commandant.

Carl Mydans, the dynamic *Life* magazine photographer, was of wonderful assistance to me. His nimble imagination found many fine reasons for such a transfer, and with his help, I did compose a very lengthy written request and the Chairman delivered it for me.

In a few days, I followed up the letter (again at the suggestion of Mr. Carroll) by calling upon Commandant Tsurumi myself, literally dragging my reluctant feet into his office and past the disapproving white interpreters and Japanese staff members before I should weaken, or they should turn me back. Tsurumi informed me abruptly, with evident displeasure at my informal approach, that such requests were not yet in order, but conceded that he would refer it to higher authorities "at the proper time." And that was the end of that.

When Tsurumi was replaced, I repeated my request to the new incumbent, and the Chairman also brought it to his attention several times. We were told then that the whole Baguio Camp would be moved to Santo Tomas eventually, and that under no condition would anyone from the Manila Camp ever be transferred to the mountain camp. Although each subsequent request met the same answer, we were very skeptical, knowing that this Camp was already so overcrowded that another five hundred members would never be squeezed in, even if the Japanese Army could marshal enough rolling stock to move so many people. From the unimpressive and motley array of the army trucks they were using in the Islands at that time, we doubted if they could.

So now, I directed all my efforts toward having Norman brought to Manila, and he was working for it in Baguio, too. Neither of us seemed to be making any headway, in spite of the fact that both Camp Committees were trying sincerely to help us and the other families who were split between the two Camps.

About the sixth or seventh of July 1943, a sound of excitement spread through the Camp and touched our room where we lay drowsing in the sticky heat. We heard raised voices and quick footsteps in the corridor. Always sensitive to the slightest disturbance, we roused at once to inquire, receiving the breathless reply that trucks of people had just stopped in the plaza.

As we were hurriedly dressing to go down to see for ourselves, news bearers arrived saying "Baguio!" I didn't wait to hear any more, and raced for the stairs, then dashed down with my feet scarcely touching the steps. Surely, surely, I thought, Norman would be there; I just didn't have any doubts. I knew!

Bursting through the front door, I scanned those two small trucks eagerly, and found but one familiar face—not my husband's, but a former mining associate of his. The rest of the newcomers were strangers to me—mostly children and teenagers, who had been attending Brent, the private Episcopalian boarding school in Baguio. I was sick with disappointment, but still holding a small hope that there might be others on the way, I dogged the footsteps of the man I knew until he finally, in obvious exasperation, produced a letter from Norman, which helped, and told me that our request for his transfer had been deferred. He said Norman had been all ready to come, too; had even traded his one warm suit for some white shorts.

Along in April, the next year, already our third, trucks arrived from Baguio again, but this time I had been forewarned, and only loitered for a few moments on the fringe of the crowd about the new arrivals in the lingering hope that he might have made it, after all. Again, these were boys and girls from the boarding school who were caught there. Their parents were in Santo Tomas. Again revealing their special consideration where children were concerned, the Japanese had acceded to the parents' combined requests that all their children be allowed to join them. Even this had not been accomplished, of course, without delays and prolonged negotiations through the military.

Only a few minutes after the youngsters had registered and dispersed to their assigned rooms, one of them, a boy about thirteen, came to my room and asked for me. Never have I seen such dogged determination on a child's face, as he said stiffly, "Mrs. Whitfield, I have a message for you from your husband, because we weren't allowed to carry letters." Then he recited, obviously by rote, exactly what Norman had told him to tell me. I had a struggle with temptation to keep from interrupting him, just to see if he would have to go back and start all over at the beginning; but of course I didn't—it was such hard work for him, and his face was so red. And I was so glad for even a message. How dear this was.

In November, Carl Eschbach, the Chairman at Camp Holmes, the Baguio Camp, was permitted to come to Santo Tomas to take care of a large accumulation of inter-Camp business, and at that time, he made it a particular point to eloquently urge the Japanese to allow families divided between the two Camps to be brought together. By the time I saw him on the very evening of the day he arrived, he was able to greet me with, "Well, do you want to go to Baguio?" The Japanese had changed their minds again. After all the hesitation, we who had husbands or parents in Baguio were even given the choice of whether we wished to go to the other Camp or have them brought to Manila.

There was no hesitation on my part. Even though I had made such dear and close friends in Santo Tomas, Baguio had been our home. We loved the mountains and disliked the steaming lowlands, and I knew that both of us would be happier and healthier up there. Three of us chose to go, and at once began making our preparations. We were so thrilled, but almost afraid to believe. The "news" was so good that we felt we must hurry, or we'd never get to Baguio before the liberating forces arrived! Our anxiety and eagerness made the remaining month interminable, waiting for those slow, slow wheels of red tape routine to begin to turn. We gave up our Camp jobs, worked on our clothes, packed and re-packed and worked ourselves into a state of jitters.

On the morning of December 22, 1943, two years to the day since I had been unwillingly evacuated to Manila, we once more rode through the gates of Santo Tomas, and they closed behind us. But this time we watched the closing with cheers, thanking God.

In our party was a Catholic priest, Father Bob Sheridan, a ruddy and beautiful man who became a dear companion and friend to so many of us; a beautiful blonde teenager, daughter of a Baguio family; and we three wives. We had also with us one small child, who was the only one of us who viewed the whole affair with befitting solemnity. We were accompanied by the pretty girl's father, the Baguio dentist, who had been sent down as the representative of Camp Holmes to put an end to the Japanese procrastination, and to arrange for our trip. He was also charged with the important mission of being certain that the Baguio Camp received its share of the Red Cross shipment.

Our Japanese chaperon was the Commandant of the Baguio Camp, Tomibe, and a little interpreter named Tanabe accompanied him. Tanabe's English was vile, but he was of some service. Our driver was the handsome mestizo son of the renowned ex-Governor Hale of the Mountain Province. The truck was small, with bench seats along the sides in back, so that we sat facing each other, but we could all see out. We six transferees carried the small amount of luggage allowed, and our wonderful Red Cross kits, and several thousand pesos to deliver to individuals from friends in Camp Santo Tomas. When we were all arranged in the back of the truck, there was scarcely room to breathe, but we laughed and chattered excitedly, waving goodbye as long as we could see the crowd of friends who had waited with us since dawn for the truck to go, while Tomibe had a leisurely breakfast. We felt as though this were the crowning adventure of our lives.

It was incredible to be "out in the world" again. Manila was terribly, tragically changed. We saw nothing now to identify her as the "Pearl of the Orient," as she had been known for so long. In those normally thronged, colorful narrow alleys back of the *Escolta* and *Avenida de Rizal*, a lassitude lay as thick as the filth and dirty papers along the curbs. Many of the small shops were all boarded up, and in littered store windows the faded remnants of 1941's Christmas decorations still hung, limp and tarnished, among the strips of clustered flypaper.

Filipinos watched the truck idly as it passed, then a quick surprise wakened in their faces at the sight of the American passengers in the back. They waved at first rather tentatively, wondering what was going to happen to us, perhaps, but before they were out of sight, we would see the irrepressible grin break forth, and the awkward, wistful little gesture that looked as though they were trying to reach out to us. I had a feeling that they wanted to touch us, just for old time's sake. We waved gaily to them all, all the way, and only if there were guards around did we fail to receive warm response. I felt again the love I have always had for the people of this country, and my heart was so touched at the tragedy of their situation.

We strained to see all that we could of the passing world, entranced with a change of scenery, very conscious of being outside the walls. The Filipinos we saw out in the provinces seemed poor, and their wonderful native sunniness didn't seem to be there. Barrios were quiet and deserted looking. Even the dogs and pigs that had always made motoring down the highway an erratic game of dodge, were missing. Everything looked parched, the highway was pitted and littered, and we watched in vain for the straw-hatted, red-trousered road workers. The great "Far-Eastern Co-Prosperity Sphere" our hosts wanted so to establish seemed a long time coming. This was a war-weary countryside.

At the little town of San Miguel, Tomibe called for a rest stop, and after we had washed off some of the dust, he ordered a meal for us. We had food with us, and were not hungry, and we would never have chosen to eat at the little inn, which was run down and soiled. We wished only for a cold drink, just to quench our thirst. But we ate the sodden pancakes and drank the weak, peanut-shell coffee the Commandant had ordered, and realized that he really had been striving to please us when he selected the typically American food and drink, which he himself passed up. He sat wrapped in quiet dignity at the end of the table with us, conversing formally with some difficulty with Dr. Walker and with whatever help Tanabe could give. The rest of us ate in rather strained silence, occasionally making a commonplace remark, wishing we could get on our way.

When we came to the wide, shallow Abra River, we found that the long bridge had not been restored, and we had to cross on a crude coconut-log raft manned by natives who smiled sadly at us, but would not talk, as we were accompanied by Japanese and were obviously prisoners. The truck was unloaded by Dr. Walker, our drivers, and Father Sheridan, and run onto one raft, and we and our possessions crowded onto another, and they poled us across the broad, muddy river. With the unloading and re-loading of the truck, and the slowness of the drifting ferries, the crossing took several hours, while we baked and sweated and squinted in the heat and glare.

It was mid-afternoon before we started the familiar climb up the Zigzag into the mountains, but within a few minutes we could smell the pines and feel the delightful crispness in the air that always surprises with its sharp contrast to the languorous atmosphere of the lowlands. Near the top of the steep ascent, we again stopped to let the motor cool. We ate our sandwiches and drank our now tepid lemonade, and scrubbed some of the grime from our faces with the damp washcloths we had remembered to provide, making ourselves look as presentable as we could. We women took the kerchiefs off our heads and combed out the curls put up the night before for this great occasion, and applied lipstick and powder while Father Sheridan tsk-tsked at our vanity.

We drove through the outskirts of Baguio, and craned to see whether the picturesque town had changed as much as the lowland villages had. At four o'clock we were at Camp Holmes, and through the wide gates, and there were all our old friends, laughing and waving and calling our names, some crying in their sympathetic joy for us. But where was Norman? I jumped down from the truck into the arms of friends, then saw him running toward us across the parade ground. In seconds, my head rested at last on the shoulder I had ached for in the loneliness of the endless years.

We walked up and down the parade ground and talked and held each other far into the night, trying to bridge all at once the chasm of separation, feeling that nothing could ever be quite so bad again, now that we had each other.

Chapter 27:
HILLS OF HOME

My new prison had before the war been a Philippine Constabulary Camp. Its official title now was "Japanese Army Internment Camp Number Three," but it has always been known by us as "Camp Holmes" or just as the "Baguio Camp." It was located at La Trinidad, about five kilometers north of Baguio, in the richest agricultural region of the area. As a prison camp, it was as different from the Camp Number One, Santo Tomas, as the cities of Baguio and Manila were different. Manila is flat, hot, tropical, glamorous in reputation, cosmopolitan, a very large city. Baguio is the mile-high mountain resort city of the Philippines, its climate so nearly perfect that it was the city of choice for "R and R" for the military and for civilians all over the Far East.

No snow ever lies on the mountain peaks, but just often enough to be interesting a light frost whitens the tough blades of tall *cogon* grass in the early morning. Curling wisps of fog wreath the narrow passes and obscure the deep valleys below in the late afternoon. The days are jewel-bright and the cool air sweet, fresh, wholesome. Among the high-branched pines are exotic fern trees like elfin stage effects; begonias, orchids, and delicate ground ferns grow wild and thick in the shady depths of the forests. Dusty sun flowers and papaya trees edge the twisting, narrow roads; rice paddies, flooded for planting and reflecting brown and blue and white, or pale green with new life, terrace the hillsides from valley floor to the bold crests. Hibiscus, gardenias, bougainvillea, and poinsettias bloom in lush elegance in gardens and parks, side by side with roses, nasturtiums, pansies and petunias from home. This piquant mixture of tropic and temperate growth has a dazzling charm, and is part of the hold the Mountain Province has on all who have lived up there above the clouds.

In illimitable grandeur the mountain range, the *cordillera*, stretches off to the horizon, so that the heart fills with awe and peace in the sight, and man's affairs can become small-seeming and surmountable. We had the feeling that the prison camp became no prison when we could stand at a cliff's edge, looking past the wall, and drinking in that eternal panorama. We could let our eyes and minds "lift unto the hills" and the timeless beauty of that favorite psalm echoed in my memory reassuringly again as it ever had during the happy past.

In the lowland Santo Tomas Camp, heat and humidity helped drain away the last remnants of waning strength; here in the mountains at Baguio, we endured longer in the invigorating atmosphere. When transportation bogged down altogether and natives almost stopped trying to bring their reduced produce into the isolated, province-dependent, overcrowded city of Manila (more likely than not, when they did arrive with a cartload of vegetables, losing it to the Japanese soldiers at the first guard station), starvation closed its pitiless grip on the residents and prisoners there. Here at Camp Holmes, we still drew a meager life-preserving supply for many additional months from the natural abundance of Trinidad Valley. The Igorot mountain folk are sturdy, pagan people, and they were faithful to us, trying to help when they could, and never quite so dominated by the invaders as the lowlanders.

We could only guess at the number of cartloads of food the Igorots brought to our gate at Camp Holmes, only to be turned away by the guards. Occasionally one was allowed in. Dangwa once made a sincere offer to feed the entire Camp, before he became "wanted" by the Japanese, but the military would not permit that, either. Where there were thousands in the Santo Tomas prison camp in Manila, there were hundreds here in Camp Holmes. Of these things was our salvation composed. The difference at the end was not great.

None of what the Japanese called luxuries at first available to the Manila people had ever reached the little "forgotten camp" in the North. There was no great city to draw on for black market extras and hidden caches of clothing, tinned food, furniture, or medicines. Only one Red Cross shipment ever reached there. No shanties were built to relieve the congested housing, for materials were not procurable. Buildings were ramshackle, drafty firetraps, and up there in the mountains, sometimes cold. Movies, broadcasting systems, public markets, and "hired help" were out of reach entirely, and had no part in the primitive conditions under which the Baguio prisoners were forced to live.

On the other side of the picture, in those ugly wooden buildings there were no bedbugs nor scorpions. In the very limited extra buying that was sometimes permitted, the evil of profiteering was less evident until the last few months. Because the group was so much smaller, the weight of public opinion counted greatly more, and crime was almost nonexistent. The Camp Tribunal was seldom called upon to function. I never heard of any outright treachery, and do not believe that there was any.

Conditions were not ideal, by any means, and I couldn't testify that the atmosphere was one of pure loving-kindness. Feuds between individuals and factions grew out of all proportion from trivial beginnings. A kleptomaniac in our dormitory provided us with indignant excitement, while a paranoic brandished knives and raised a periodic pandemonium in another. Self-centered unadaptiveness reared an unrepentant head over space problems there as in any prison camp.

But these were mere *pecadillos* compared to the troubles in the larger prison Camp in Manila. Here, it was one thief, one psychotic, one brawler; and while the whole group was also relatively smaller, somehow the presence of these socially unadjusted never attained the same type of personally disruptive influence on the rest of us. When they became too rambunctious, they were literally brought down, quickly and effectively, by their neighbors.

The polyglot influx from other Far Eastern lands had only lightly touched Baguio. Most of the internees were American, with a strong nationalistic minority of British, one Chinese (a shy, delicate Anglican sister who remained voluntarily with her group), one citizen of Mexico, and a few American-Filipinos. We had two Russians, a man and a woman, both with American passports.

Jenny Zech, who was from Russia, will always be remembered by us for her passion for cleaning. Down on her knees we would find her daily "scrobbing" with a heavy brush and a big bucket of suds, venting constructively all her disturbance and impatience on the oily splintery floor. We had such affection for her, and admiration for her sturdy patriotism to her country-by-marriage. She never asked for sympathy, although her husband was believed to have been captured and imprisoned in a slave camp in Mukden, and she had received no word from him.

At the outset there had been a number of German refugees and Dutch missionaries in the Camp, and hundreds of Chinese who were segregated into a separate barracks. They menaced the health of the whole group in their miserable, cramped, totally unsanitary state. But all of these had been released within the first few months, leaving the Camp almost homogeneous, and consequently easier to govern.

There was a social division, however. The Camp population hovered around four hundred and seventy on an average, and was divided into two nearly equal groups—the mining community of Baguio, and the missionaries. (We loosely included among the mining group the business and professional people of Baguio who had made their living from the mining camp trade before the war.) Many of the missionaries were Baguio residents, too; teachers at Brent School, ministers of the city churches, medical and field workers from surrounding provinces. The greatest number of them, however, were students at the Chinese Language School, which had been moved from China to Baguio when Americans were evacuated from the Asian continent; or "old hands" from Japan and China. Every imaginable orthodox sect was represented, twenty-three of them listed on the Camp Holmes roster. The Lutherans, Seventh Day Adventists, Southern Baptists, and Anglicans had probably the largest representations, although others also had strong, active groups there.

The little building used for church services was seldom idle, with five or six denominational services to be held there during each week: the Anglicans daily, Lutherans on Friday and Sunday, Adventists on Saturday, and of course the Sunday schedule ranged from early masses to vesper service, with Sunday School somewhere between. Bible classes and roundtable discussions, choir practices, and catechism drill met where and when they might. On pleasant Sundays, the joint morning service of all except Catholic, Lutheran, Anglican and Seventh Day Adventists was held in the Sunken Garden. That was where Easter and Thanksgiving observances were held, and Christmas pageants presented against the background of mountains and pines, with a fitting pastoral touch lent by goats grazing nearby.

For the last year there was only one Catholic priest, Father Sheridan, who transferred from the Santo Tomas prison camp when I did. He held all his masses without assistance, served on the Camp Committee, and played baseball with equal *joie de vivre,* applying regularly to the Japanese for a companion to be transferred from another prison Camp, but never receiving even the courtesy of an answer from them. We loved this man, and his fine spirit was a boon to our Camp.

The mining game is an adventurous one, and miners in general are anything but effete; their work develops in them a pragmatic viewpoint that very often reaches the stage known as tough. They live in far away, rugged places, have no chance to put down roots and settle into a routine, for they are wanderers in the world—they work hard and play hard. It was only natural that some of the Baguio mining community, then, was immediately, innately, inclined to view the missionary group with something almost akin to suspicion, especially when they discovered that the missionaries slightly outnumbered them in the Camp. It took months of living together in a prison to buff down the sharp edges of bristling independence, to prove that the religious groups were less concerned with proselytizing then than with subsisting, just as the miners themselves.

A group of missionaries was taken to Military Police headquarters in Baguio City under suspicion of espionage (I heard it said that the Japanese military never could believe that these people were just there to help and educate the people, voluntarily giving up comfortable lives at home for spiritual rewards). There they were tortured and abused to the point that one of their number died in agony, leaving his young widow and tiny son in the prison camp. Both respect and sympathetic understanding increased perceptibly between the mining and missionary groups.

Many of the missionaries from the very first demonstrated inspired leadership qualities, and by the final year, not only the Chairman, but four other members of the General Committee were mission people. Many of the doctors and nurses who served at the hospital and clinic and at least two-thirds of the teachers were missionaries. Their services to the prison camp were certainly invaluable, and eventually, all but a few die-hards mellowed their initial antipathies and learned to make their friends where they found them. It was not too difficult to see that all of us were people together, and that we were all suffering from the same discomforts and weariness, whatever our occupations.

It was a good lesson in tolerance, and the final integration constituted spiritual triumph. There were two intermarriages within Camp Holmes between the missionaries and the miners. Several materialized later from prison camp romances. Norman and I found dear and lasting friendships among the mission people. This is an heroic occupation.

THE ROAD TO BAGUIO

Chapter 28:
NORMAN'S FIRST CAMP —
JOHN HAY

There were so many differences in the stories Norman and I had to tell each other. When the Japanese had picked up my Baguio friends and me at the Peralta Apartments in Manila in January 1942, we were taken directly to the Santo Tomas internment camp, and there we had remained until this transfer. The people who had stayed behind in Baguio, including Norman, by choice or from lack of opportunity, were either captured or gathered together voluntarily, and eventually found themselves interned, first at Camp John Hay, then finally at Camp Holmes.

Only the Balatoc and Benguet Mining Companies had succeeded in evacuating most of their employees to Manila to be interned at Santo Tomas. I had been at the Balatoc Gold Mining Camp with our friends Marge and Larry. Many of the townspeople and miners from the other gold mining camps were involved in a number of moves, but all within the immediate area of Baguio. One group hiked over the mountains to an isolated sawmill camp called Lusod, where Norman and I had lived for a year or two, high on a mountain, twenty-five kilometers from Baguio. This group was there at the same time that part of our standing army in the Islands evacuated through there. A few women were sent far up the Mountain Trail to the mission at Segada, north of Baguio—again, very isolated.

They all returned, however, to the protection of numbers offered by the gatherings at Brent School, the Pines Hotel, and some of the larger homes. A number took to the hills and remained at liberty for a year or two, but eventually hunger, weariness, fever, or the obvious futility of attempting evasion drove most of them into the relative protection of the internment Camp.

When our troops withdrew from Baguio, before the arrival of the Japanese, the civilians were thrown on their own resources, and immediately a committee was formed among them to meet the onrush of disaster. This committee, amplified by popular election at Brent, dealt with the Japanese as they came. A good many of the people had gone to the Brent School as early as Christmas Day 1941, rather than remain in their homes. Others awaited instructions from the Committee or the Japanese and stayed on at the mining camps, and were there picked up through the following days.

Norman, and other men and a few women, were at the Antamok Goldfields Mine, and there on December 29, the Japanese descended upon them, just a few days after the American forces had passed through the camp on their way to the lowlands, dumping supplies and gear all along the way.

The Japanese were naturally made very suspicious by this evidence so carelessly left about, and one soldier, pouncing on an army pack that had been tossed under the mess house, decided that the khaki shirt in it was the mate to the one on Norman's back. Neither could speak the other's language, and the bayonet was much too close to Norman's stomach as the soldier sought to frighten him into an admission of ownership, and it looked to Norman for a few minutes as though he were in very deep water, with no help in sight.

The invaders first herded all the white people into the halls of Brent, then two days later transferred the whole group to Camp John Hay, an American Army convalescent and recreation post, forcing them to walk all the way as the first of a thousand indignities they were to suffer. This was a full week before even the first four hundred in Manila were gathered up and put into Villamor Hall. So this was the first American prison camp, and my husband, whom I for so long pictured at liberty, was for my sake even ten days longer in prison than I.

During the months that they were kept at John Hay, and immediately following their removal to Camp Holmes, the treatment accorded them was senseless, inexcusable, and vile. They were given nothing and what they had was often taken from them. They could obtain their supplies only by resorting to the most surreptitious and dangerous methods, becoming accomplished "looters" in the process. They pooled their little resources to supply their own food and medicines, and under the guise of wood carrying, managed to thoroughly ransack a number of the barracks and officers' quarters at John Hay for the kitchen utensils, cleaning equipment and other necessities. Some of the missionaries who accompanied these foraging expeditions became known admiringly as the "looting parsons" in recognition of their successes.

An illegal shakedown by Japanese civilians stripped many of the internees of cash; even traveler's checks, insurance policies, passports, deeds and bank books were taken. As usual, attempts were made to hide money and jewelry to prevent confiscation. One man hid his currency in an overhead toilet tank, then spent a harried hour worrying that someone might pull that particular chain! Another stuffed his hoard of more than a thousand dollars in American currency between two wooden walls, and the rats chewed it to complete destruction. Jewelry was cached away where it seemed to the feminine owners that no man would think to look—the bottom of a cold cream jar was the favorite place for rings. (A woman in Manila told me that when she was picked up in her provincial home by particularly rough soldiers, they did make a search of her house, and the first place they looked for jewelry was in the bottom of all her cream jars and powder boxes!)

Two women, forewarned of the inspection, and unbeknownst to each other, hid their rings under adjacent stones in the flower border, and still unaware of each other's actions, got them mixed up when they retrieved them later, so that there was much ado until friends took a hand and straightened them out.

No water was provided for either washing or drinking during the first few days at John Hay, and the internees came near to a state of dehydration. In this weakened condition, they were easy prey for the first serious epidemic of dysentery that developed from the unsanitary condition of the Camp. They had not been allowed to bring in their collected stores of food, either, and for several days existed on weak soup and dry sandwiches.

Just after internment, when an expectant mother reached her time, permission was sought to transfer her to an outside hospital, but the military said, "She must wait until morning." Isabel delivered her son that night on the floor of a tiny room also occupied by others, with only the assistance that a woman doctor and nurse without equipment of any kind could give. The wee boy was named Richard Hawkins Scott, but known always, even by his parents, as John Hay.

A drunken general one night at a banquet ordered the mass execution of all the Baguio prisoners, and only diplomatic procrastination to a soberer reflection of a few underlings prevented the awful carrying-out of the order. All of the missionaries were suddenly released to live in Baguio, and then as inexplicably, without warning, almost immediately rounded up and unceremoniously dumped back into the Camp again.

Twice, our missionaries were taken to the Military Police Headquarters, confined in the noisome jail for many days, and questioned regarding guerrillas or matters of espionage. One of them told me later that it was the same thing—to the Japanese it was incredible that private citizens, working in a foreign land, would not be part of the intelligence system of their country, a suspicion that must surely have reflected exactly their custom. One of the Japanese who captured Norman and stripped him of his custom-made boots had the rank of major, and he had been a carpenter in the mining camp.

One of the most unendurable early restrictions in the Baguio Camp was the complete segregation of men and women, male and female, really, as it extended to the boys and girls, too. It was called the rule against co-mingling, as they termed it. High fences were even built between the areas occupied by the opposite sexes, and the fences were guarded. Across the no-man's land between, husband and wife were allowed thirty minutes' conversation once a week. My dear little friend Mary Kneebone told me that it was quite a sensation to try to discuss the selection of a name for your expected baby across a space of eight feet, with nearly five hundred listeners around you—even though most of them were sympathetic.

It was with extreme difficulty that even the doctors obtained permission to cross that barrier, to treat women patients, and the two women doctors (one of them pregnant) were drastically overworked. Picked men carried the food from the kitchen to the women's quarters. Consent was hard-won to allow boys and girls to attend classes together, and the girls were carefully chaperoned to and from school. A high school boy was beaten about the head almost to per-

manent deafness for rashly attempting to break the taboo and walk with a pretty classmate.

Among minor sins frowned upon by the Japanese was that of littering the compound. They carried this fetish for neatness (for the prisoners) so far that all persons were required to carry small tins tied to their persons while they were smoking, and many were slapped, both men and women, who were so forgetful or misfortunate as to disobey this ruling. This punishment was so deeply humiliating that no one ever forgot the experience.

One man was severely beaten within the Camp, and it is felt that he probably would have been killed had it not been for the absolutely fearless physical intervention of the incumbent chairman, Dr. Dana Nance. The victim that time was a benighted lawbreaker, caught once too often smuggling liquor into Camp to sell to the unwise few who hadn't become teetotalers for the duration.

This first wretched period was ruled by the Baguio military, but nominally in charge of the Camp was a man named Nakamura, immediately recognized through the masquerade of military *accoutrement* as a former boss carpenter at Antamok Goldfields (the very one who confiscated Norman's boots, which he was still wearing). Even if he hadn't been known, there would have been something faintly reminiscent about him, for in his English speech and affectation of mannerism, he was an Oriental mimic of his onetime American boss, a black-haired, high-tempered, long-legged lovable grandson of Ireland named Mike. Mike had "talked with his hands," and interspersed his most casual conversation with classic unaccented profanity; belying his sunny smile and slow drawl, he could and did "blow wide open" without notice. So Nakamura mimicked, apparently from a deep admiration, and the result was funny even to those who hadn't known Mike.

The husky, short Japanese, throwing his hands about unlike any of his race we had known, interpolating "Goddam" into every sentence, and ordering his erstwhile employers about in a genially bellicose manner, was fantastic. Even the Japanese couldn't believe in him, apparently, for he was soon removed and another local man, Hayakawa, son of a Baguio druggist, carried on as Acting Commandant until the arrival of Tomibe.

Hayakawa was a neat little nonentity, bribable but not trustworthy, whose laxness soon allowed many former grievances to correct themselves. For a long period, he had with him only a handful of guards, who spent most of their time lounging about on the porch of their quarters, so the smokers' cups, anti-commingling fences, and other injustices and inconveniences quickly disappeared. Guards did still occasionally tromp through the barracks at odd hours, with their long guns, bayonets affixed, either held dangerously in front of them as they walked, or on their shoulders. One slouched down the women's barracks steps to the accompaniment of shouts of laughter one day with a pink brassiere which he had picked neatly and unknowingly from an inside clothesline, dangling from the end of his bayonet.

A dearth of all vital necessities, tools and materials actuated a development in Camp Holmes of tremendous ingenuity. Substitutes were cleverly utilized with astounding results. Dr. Walker (the Baguio dentist), for instance, was not allowed to bring in his own fine dental equipment, which had been confiscated by a Japanese dentist. Yet a basic minimum dental attention was a must for the maintenance of any kind of normal health in the Camp.

Mustering every resource, and often through sheer force of personality and his quick intelligence, he collected enough tools and materials to do extractions and fillings; his drill was a Rube Goldberg contraption with a phonograph motor; he shaved soft Mexican dollars for silver for fillings; with the aid of the shop foreman, he even cast from aluminum a workable, perfectly fitting set of "lowers," prized by their owner as the masterpiece of inventive genius. An innocent comment on them would bring an immediate offer from him to let you take a better look, and you might find them being handed to you. They were admittedly a bit sensitive to extreme heat, and had a startling gleam when revealed in a smile or yawn, but were neither unsightly nor freakish, and the whole Camp was proud of them.

The cooks and dieticians faced the same dismaying lack of staple necessities, and their culinary arts were quite admirable sometimes. Doctors and mothers were not alone in their worry over the milk supply, for the entire Camp was much concerned that the children's needs be met. Among the substitutes worked out and produced while supplies were available were mongo bean milk (mongo beans are sometimes called cow beans, and are similar to soy beans; the natives sprout them, and we learned to do that, too, using the bean sprouts as a quick-cooking vegetable. You can find them in Chinese food, and in the market).

We also used, of course, coconut milk, which was also high in nutrition, although some of the children found it hard to handle. One or two cows were kept by the Camp, and did contribute some of the time, but native cows actually give very little milk, and whenever these were allowed to graze on the hill for a little while, they became very wild and it took a regular Wild West roundup to catch them again. This was a delight to the small boys but a strain on the volunteer cowboys!

A goat herd was acquired and tended by the Mennonite missionary group, and much of their milk donated, but they also gave but a scant bit each day. When the Red Cross food arrived, many tins of the powdered milk were turned over to the children's diet kitchen and hospital. Tinned milk was bought at whatever price and at every opportunity, but of course became unobtainable eventually.

There was never enough to go around, even at the beginning, and doctors were pessimistic about the later results in bone and teeth strength, but a valiant effort had been made. Children born in the Camp were nursed as long as possible by their mothers, some provident law of compensation giving the women the ability to do it in a country where the white mother seldom has milk for her baby. Mary, who was as slight as a flower stem, and who commemorated her baby's birthplace by naming him Terence Holmes, provided her son with milk for almost two years, until sternly stopped by her physician, who saw her own strength diminishing.

Spices and flavorings were provided through persistence in trying out whatever came to hand. Celery leaves, native cinnamon stick, hot little wild peppers, were all dried and powdered or ground, and helped to cover the distasteful, or to add a little interest to the plain, broken, poor quality rice. Native cacao beans were roasted and ground and used for a chocolate substitute, or even for flour, but I thought it tasted like medicine.

There was a period in the Camp's history when even salt was not available, and then the food was almost inedible. But most of the time we were fairly well supplied with rock salt, dirty and coarse. We roasted raw peanuts, when we could get them, and ground them into rich peanut butter. The little grain known as *bucacao*, a variety of kaffir corn, when properly processed, could be made into a malt powder or syrup, which was found to be what the sufferers from starch allergies needed to help them digest their rice, corn, and sweet potatoes. The latter, particularly, caused so much indigestion that they became almost detested. We called them by their native name, *camote*; they were small, stringy, but available.

Coffee was always used three times: a weak fresh brew one morning; a few extra pounds thrown in with the used grounds for a re-boiling the next day; and what remaining color and flavor there might be extracted by a good hard cooking for the third morning. The second day's brew was called "submarine coffee," the third day, "second sub," and that was coffee only by the grace of imagination, but by Americans, still preferred over the tea we could get from the Japanese.

As individuals, we bought native coffee beans when we could. Norman carefully roasted the green beans and ground them very fine, and after we had accustomed ourselves to the difference in flavor, it was good. We also submarined our own. By the time the coffee grounds were thrown out in that Camp, there was little besides appearance to identify them!

The smoking habit was almost as difficult to maintain as the habit of eating enough. Even the native cigarettes were off the market finally. For a period, the Japanese sold a limited number of their cigarettes in the Camp, but they were disliked. Many of the smokers simply gave up the habit. Others traded, scrounged, and substituted, learning to roll their own, and never realizing that quitting would in the long run make life easier.

The non-smokers who hoarded the cigarettes that came into their possession sometimes found them mildewed when they attempted to trade them off later for food.

We know we are all created equal in the eyes of our Creator, but even in the Camps this was sometimes hard to prove. One would assume that in such a place and under such conditions, every man would fare like his brother, but this wasn't exactly true. There were a few who always had more than anyone else, and there were some who suffered severest want from the first day to the last. The majority had times of comparative plenty, as such things are assessed in a prison, and times of dire poverty, even to starvation. Some would always share what they had when they had it; others sought only to store up for the future.

RICE PADDIES ON THE ISLAND OF LUZON

JAPANESE ARMY INTERNMENT CAMP NO. 3
Office of the Internment Camp Committee

Baguio, Philippines
May 10, 1944

Office of the Commandant
Internment Camp No. 3
Baguio, Philippines

Re: Change in Visiting Hours for
Dormitory No. 2

Dear Sirs:

The residents of Barracks No. 2, not involved
in the Family Unit Plan, have requested that the visiting
hours for men be changed to allow visiting from 7 A.M.
to 9:15 P.M.

Yours very truly,

Carl B. Eschbach
Chairman
Internment Camp Committee

CBE:d

Chapter 29:
NINE WHO LED

They attained their positions because they were so out-standing. They had to be that, to be chosen in secret balloting by a critical, familiar electorate. They were selected for particular duties, but it was more often than not impossible to separate the work of the individual from the work of the Committee as a whole.

The General Committee had nine members, the Chairman and two Vice-Chairmen serving as the Executive Committee. The nine met regularly once a week, and occasionally at special sessions between. They were served by a Committee secretary, who kept formal minutes which were posted for the Camp to read. I became secretary to the group that third year, an experience I treasure.

At the Committee meetings, all matters of policy, all internal problems, and ways and means for improving the living conditions, diet, and treatment of the internees, were discussed and voted on. Their most important function, perhaps, was the one of liaison agent between the Japanese and the prisoners. This Committee was the buffer, the protective wall that stood between the helpless group and its capricious boss. Life, liberty of thought and action, and general well-being were guarded to the greatest possible extent by the General Committee.

For example, in February 1945, the Japanese instituted a new rationing. We were allotted three hundred grams of cereal food (rice, camotes, or corn meal, or even casava root at times) for each adult. They then placed the ration for each child under ten at one hundred and fifty grams. Because we were self-governing, it was possible for us to divide the food equally, instead of so limiting the children to a diet which would not even be maintenance level. Had we been directly under the personal supervision of the Japanese, this justifiable subterfuge would not have been successful, and the children would have suffered.

When the Japanese propounded a new ruling, it was transmitted and interpreted for us through the Committee, and supposedly enforced by that Committee. Thus, instead of literal, right to the letter obedience to something that might have been ridiculous or harmful, we could make a show, in the right places, of abiding by the mandate of the Japanese, but as directed by our Committee. If there were no flagrant violations, almost never did the Japanese appear to think about checking on the enforcement themselves, or perhaps they were content with the appearances.

The Committee had a deep game to play, and everything to lose if there were any slips or miscues. Like the individual internee, the preoccupation of the Committee was always to get more food, to provide against famine in the future, while trying to meet today's needs too.

Bit by bit, they squeezed a little each month when the Japanese doled out the rice ration, until they had cached about the Camp with certain trusted members (who would have had a bad time if the Japanese had ever discovered the hidden sacks) nearly nine hundred pounds of rice for us, in case our rations ever failed totally. Extra Red Cross kits were hidden away, also, and when the need became dire, produced and divided among the internees as equally as could be.

They made it a point to see that the children and invalids received the eggs and milk produced within the Camp. They fought the Commandant almost daily, with only the weapons of their wits, for every extra buying privilege they could think of, bribed the Japanese staff, drivers and guards, borrowed money and bought on credit in their own names for the Camp, all this in the name of trying to safeguard those whom they were serving.

Because I think they did such wonderful work, and tendered such important service, I want to tell about the members of the last Committee, as typical of the quality of leadership the Camp had. This Committee was headed by Carl

Eschbach, with Philip Markert and Nellie McKim for his Vice-Chairpersons; Ward T. Graham, Louis B. Robinson, Vincent Gowan, Robert Sheridan, Marshall F. Welles, and A. E. Skerl made up the rest of that last incredibly courageous, ingenious, and very diversified Committee.

Vincent Gowan—Father Gowan to the Camp—was a scholarly Anglican teacher-missionary, who had set and maintained standards of schooling for the youngsters high enough, in spite of lacks and rebuffs, that they should be able to take their rightful places in schools at home after liberation. He guided the educational system and church affairs through stormy seas, and was highly respected for his erudition and integrity, and loved for his caring way.

Ward Graham was the finance man who also arranged many of the "deals" whereby we obtained more food than the Japanese knew or desired us to have. In his hands the important feat of arriving at and abiding by a balanced budget rested. He prepared intricate and all-important statistics for later reference. Louis Robinson, quiet-spoken and imperturbable, was in charge of the over-worked, beset utilities department. Both were top mining men from the Baguio District, accustomed to authority and practical business methods. They provided a good balance wheel for the whole group. Both Ward and Louis had families in the Camp—young children and beautiful daughters; both had impeccable reputations and were strong, intelligent leaders.

Dr. Welles was a young missionary physician in charge of the health, medicine and diet, and he brought the full strength of his abundant energy unsparingly against staggering odds. His was a 24-hour-a-day job, and each decision he made could be crucial. Marshall and his wife were attractive, dedicated missionaries who would devote their whole lives to their cause, to God and their fellowman, in far points of the globe.

Dr. Skerl, usually called Gus, was the only Britisher on the Committee. He was a reserved, brilliant geologist, with a line of initials following his name to attest to his scholastic record. He managed the work details, and his dextrous charting and graphing befuddled and impressed the Japanese, and his austerity and imposing appearance, and cryptic comments, kept in line those internees who would rather not work. Dr. Skerl was our chaperon on that first evacuation trip down from Batong Buhay. He was tall, black-bearded, deeply tanned, and very, very British.

Bob Sheridan, the only Catholic priest in the Camp, was our Internal Affairs Manager, which meant that on his shoulders rested the never-settled problem of space. He was also a spiritual leader, a dear friend, a jolly companion, and a stalwart Committee member.

I seek gentle words to describe the beloved woman who made it possible for us to deal with the Japanese open-eyed. Nellie McKim—"McKim San" to the Japanese—was also a missionary born and raised. She had spent most of her life in Japan, and her fluent, perfect command of the written and spoken Japanese language proved an unparalleled weapon for us. She served as our interpreter and the service she gave to us in that capacity was so invaluable that everyone wondered what we would have done without her. Through her, we were informed. Without her, we would have been lost in the maze of deliberate misinterpretations and evasions of dealing with those who held us captive. She was serene, attractive, with gay eyes and a quick, sweet smile. When the Japanese spoke to McKim San, it was in respectful tones, for she knew their language and their customs, and when she bowed in charming courtesy, there was no servility in her bearing. They even feared her, and finally at times excluded her from the joint meetings so that she could not relay the actual words the Japanese didn't wish to be known.

Second on the Committee was Phil Markert, one of the key men in International General Electric's Far-Eastern staff. He had a mind like a rapier, little patience, and enormous fortitude. Phil was not a tall man, but carried such an air of assurance and mastery that the Japanese stood almost in awe of him, and his delight was to push back the very limits of discretion in "telling them off," in a universal language; and his bearing was so manifestly superior that he got away with it. He could be smoothly diplomatic when he wished, however, and was the author and instigator of many a *coup d'etat* for our benefit. Norman and I knew him as intensely loyal, and at a later time I was deeply grateful for that.

Carl Eschbach was a minister of the United Brethren Church in Baguio. He had been re-elected, almost unopposed, to that last Committee, for the internees realized that he was the outstanding citizen of the Camp, and was regarded as our best hope during the final months. Tall, slender, blonde, with courage and humor to match his intelligence, he seemed to know no fear, and time and again he literally snatched a burning branch from the fire of Japanese wrath to avoid disaster to the Camp. He was just, honorable, and sweet, slow to anger but firm in his convictions, with the saving grace of a marvelous sense of the ridiculous. His sense of humor certainly was the sanity preserver of all who had to deal directly with our hosts.

With the two others of his Executive Council, he deftly defied the Commandant who replaced Tomibe, to stave off the hatred this Oura felt for all Americans. Oura was forced to respect these three leaders, and his harsh policies were many times thwarted by their quick wit. They would sit there in meetings with him, and while he ranted and raved, they would hold their tempers, exuding patience. When Oura was finished, or paused for breath, Miss McKim would turn and interpret the whole, succinctly, with "lecture."

These were the nine, then, who guided us through the final term. They were infinitely loyal, unstinting in their efforts; they did not always agree, but were so well integrated as a Committee, they could present a solidly united front of optimum strength and efficiency.

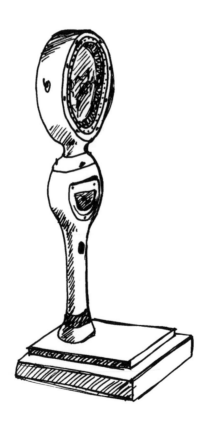

Chapter 30:
FREE AT A PRICE

Soon after I arrived at the Camp Holmes prison camp in late December 1943, a new system for calling the roll, similar to that at the Santo Tomas prison camp, was inaugurated. Dormitories were divided into sections, and a monitor was appointed to be responsible for each section. Each night the monitor checked to see that all his charges were in their places, then turned in his report to the chief monitor, who tallied the totals, and submitted the itemized account of internees' whereabouts to the Japanese. It was an easy, undemanding routine, and under it both internees and monitors almost at once became lax. But it was through no fault of the monitor of one of the men's groups that it also created the opportunity for a dramatic escape from the Camp by two young men in April 1944.

Our most treasured privilege was access to the hill just above the compound. We were allowed to get a pass from the office and roam around over this hill, within certain wide limits, and we climbed the steep trail as frequently as possible, sometimes for the day, taking a picnic lunch (those wonderful perishables from the Red Cross) and drinking water. There on the crest beneath the pines, we could rest, luxuriating in a sense of liberty that did much toward steadying our nerves (like the shanties in the prison camp at Santo Tomas), and keeping us well and strong. Picnickers scattered as widely as possible, and the nearest approach to privacy that we ever attained in concentration was ours on that hill. So it was that on one April day, Richard Green and Herbert Swick, young, husky, unattached, impatient of the shackles and longing to be a part of the real battle to come, strolled casually and quite legally out of the Baguio prison Camp, onto the hill, ostensibly for a little relaxation—and never returned. Since there was no roll call until nine at night, they had the whole day to make good their escape. Both were miners, and knew the country; their plans were well laid, and their contacts secure.

When the distracted monitor of their group could delay no longer in reporting their absence that night, a thorough search of the prison Camp was made, then reluctantly, as late as possible, the information that two members had failed to check in was turned over to the Japanese.

Almost instantly, the word went out and the whole Camp was aware that Herbie and Richie had gone over the wall. Reaction varied. Most of us were thrilled, and everyone crossed his fingers for the boys. But apprehension laid a cold finger across our hearts, too; everyone in our prison Camp would indubitably pay, how dearly we could only surmise. At one time, the penalty had been set at ten lives for every escapee. In the prison camp at Santo Tomas, three Australian seamen had been executed and the entire Camp punished by severe deprivations. It was daring, certainly dangerous—was it worth it? Could they do enough good on the outside to warrant risking the lives and welfare of hundreds of prisoners? We were sure they believed so, but our own very sober reflection gave an uncertain answer.

We prayed fervently, all of us, that they would never be captured. Their fate would have been far more horrifying than mere death. Herbie, particularly, had burned his every bridge, for he already had a record with the military police, having once been a part of guerrilla activity.

There actually wasn't much Camp censure for the boys. Our prisoner philosophy granted that they had the right to try, anyway.

Events moved rapidly to a climax the following day. In the morning, first the men, then the women, were called into mass meetings with the Japanese Commandant, who asked for any information anyone could give. No one knew anything, naturally. Commandant Tomibe thoroughly scolded us all, and presented a very grim prophecy of the consequences, which he confessed were entirely out of his control. He seemed genuinely upset, and we had a feeling that he, personally, was more sorry than angry, although he must have understood at once that the incident would be a bad blot on his own career as Commandant.

A plane circled over the hills all through the day, and search parties of Japanese military beat through the tall *cogon* grass and brush. The roads were guarded, and patrols fine-combed neighboring barrios. The Military Police made their abhorred appearance in the Camp early. It was obvious that there was much more involved than the mere recapturing of two escapees.

This was, to the Japanese, complete vindication of their suspicions that the guerrillas were in close contact with the internees; they had no doubt that the boys had gone to join the men in the hills. They questioned our General Committee thoroughly, but were told only that the plans for the escape must have been made in total secrecy, for no one knew that they had any such intentions. Then the military seized the men who had slept near, or had been closely associated with Swick and Green.

One of these, an older man, was returned to our prison Camp the same day without being questioned, but Gene Kneebone, Swick's buddy, was retained by the Japanese. Later, Bill Moule was taken to the Commandant's headquarters, and finally, Jim Halsema. All three were young. Bill Moule had been a recent victim of infantile paralysis, and was still crippled from that. Our worst fears were confirmed almost at once. The three men were tortured—starved, beaten, given no water, incredibly hurt.

Finally, when the prison Camp was nearly broken with bitter sorrow and sympathy for the victims and their families, Tomibe himself could stand it no longer, and somehow managed to persuade the Military Police that they would gain nothing by continuing their inquisition. He must have quoted the Japanese equivalent of our old saying about getting no blood from a turnip. Perhaps the fact that they had killed a young missionary in that way during the first year had an effect. At any rate, Tomibe did obtain their release, and he brought the men back to our Camp the next day, Sunday.

The very sight of them was enough evidence of their nightmare experience. They were isolated at once in the hospital, and found to have dysentery from the filthy prison water they did have, and their bruised and lacerated bodies needed healing care. Months later, Jimmy Halsema still lingered in the very shadow of death as a result of his beatings.

Frustrated and vindictive, the Japanese captors retaliated by rescinding the privilege of leaving the Camp at all except under heavy guard and on authorized business; they required morning and evening roll call taken by the Japanese staff; extra guards were posted; they "closed the gate" once and for all to any outside buying; and built another fence around the compound.

None of this was so severe as we had expected, although we regretted losing our high hill, detested the formal roll calls, and felt the pinch of decreased food supply. But we felt sick whenever we thought of the three men who had really paid. The only redeeming feature was that Swick and Green were not captured. This we were sure of, for had they been, the Japanese would have been quick to make of them the sternest example. Certainly no one would now take the responsibility of torture or death for neighbors and friends, for now we knew what would happen—before it had been just a guess.

The most far-reaching result of the escape episode for our prison Camp was a change in Commandants. Tomibe was a gentleman. He had been more cooperative and sympathetic, and far more courteous, than either of his predecessors, and certainly than his successors. But he had lost all face now, and was broken to a low clerical position in Manila, replaced by Lieutenant Oura as Commandant, and Lieutenant Sakashita as Officer-in-Charge of the greatly strengthened garrison.

Both Oura and Sakashita immediately established their policy, based soundly on a dislike of all Americans, and it was with reluctance that they permitted any privileges.

Sakashita was a well-trained military career officer, and he eventually softened his attitude and was more just; Oura was a peasant farmer who had worked his way up through the ranks as far as lieutenant, then was placed in charge of our prison Camp by, we were all sure, exasperated superiors who couldn't abide him either. There were many times when he was not rational, and even his aides cautioned us that this was the case.

He was certainly poisonously prejudiced against us, and in 1944 the very name of President Roosevelt was anathema to him. He would concede nothing. Approached on the subject of increasing our food rations, he would bellow: "If you need food, get it from your President Roosevelt who started this war." Carl sometimes answered frankly that we would be delighted to get it from our President, and he would be only too happy to send it to us. All that the Japanese had to do, he would say, was to let the ships come through and enough food and money for all would be sent gladly and at once from the United States.

But Oura would grunt sourly, "No ships. Besides, the United States has no food either. The people there are starving. They have nothing but horse flesh to eat."

When accurate, comprehensive charts, showing the sharp decline in body weight of every prisoner, were presented to him, he refused to believe the figures, shouting that the American doctors were all "damn fools." Then, to show us that he thought we were not telling the truth, he had his staff take the weekly weights, and when their findings showed an even more formidable downward trend, he dropped the whole matter and declined to talk about it. [Our weight losses were only too valid from week to week, but just to be sure that the impression was right, we did not eat breakfast before the weighing. We wore as few clothes as possible, and some said they even exhaled as they stepped up on the scales!]

Commandant Oura launched almost daily on a scathing diatribe against the iniquities of American habits. He said we were too soft, too fond of luxuries (other Commandants had accused us of that one, particularly), and greedy. He claimed that all Japanese had been living for years on less food than we were at that time receiving. Carl would simply reply that we were Americans, not Japanese, and would surely starve if more food were not given us.

Then Oura fastened on the idea of a prison Camp garden, inspired by suggestions from General Kuo, the Number One of all the Camps in the Philippines, who was thought to be responsible for much of the suffering and all of the lack in that last year. Oura decided that now we must raise all our own food, for soon no more at all would be provided by the Japanese, who needed it for their army.

We had tried in vain to convince previous regimes that we would like to have a Camp garden. Individuals had managed to raise a few vegetables for themselves in choice bits of land about the prison Camp, getting their starts from the cut-off roots in the vegetable-preparation room. Almost everyone had a few string beans and a little lettuce growing on some tiny plot of ground. But the officials had, up to this time, been so uninterested that they would not provide tools, fertilizers and seeds. They had also refused permission to use the areas suitable for gardening, since they lay just outside the fence or down in Trinidad Valley. One abortive attempt under Tomibe to get one started in the valley had been nipped in the bud by the military's refusal to let the volunteer workers go out.

Oura banned all private efforts, however small, so we planted marigolds in front of our four lettuce plants. The Japanese Commandant now demanded that every man, woman, and capable child in the prison Camp spend most of his time in a community garden, for which he designated a rocky hillside above our Camp, and a clay gully below. He threatened us with all sorts of penalties if we didn't comply, so for the sake of keeping what little we had, we organized ourselves into daily gardening details.

A mean-looking carabao (buffalo) and a native plow were brought into the prison Camp, and used for several days by a few men who weren't afraid of the beast (it is a widely-

held belief that the carabao has no use for a white man, and
it was felt to be a dangerous job to handle one) to plow up
part of the specified site below. Then the rest of us tackled
the poor, heavy soil with hoes, shovels, and picks, women
chiefly de-grassing while the men turned over and tried to
cultivate the soil. Children were supervised for an hour or
so daily on a little section of their own in the Sunken Garden. The starting of Fall term in the high school was delayed for a month so the teenagers could help. Onions, lettuce, camotes, and beans were planted, and a few other native vegetables.

It was backbreaking, disheartening work, and it was
forced labor. Not many of the internees were by this time
strong enough to put out any amount of physical effort, and
heads would swim and hearts pound suffocatingly at the
exertion, there at this five-thousand-feet-high altitude. Neither did we ever expect to harvest the crops we were being
forced, with armed guards stationed about, to plant. One
by one, exemptions were achieved—first for the elderly and
unwell; next for those who already were doing heavy or full-
time jobs; finally, for all but those who had no other work to
do, or had volunteered to make a show of keeping it going.

Dr. Skerl was required to make a daily, weekly, and
monthly accounting to the Japanese of the number of work
hours put in by the internees. Oura maintained that we
gave far too much of our time to the hospital and kitchen as
a group, and to private cooking. We knew, but found it use-
less to argue with him, that these were the two most vital
functions in the prison Camp now that the general health
condition was so poor.

So we handed the responsibility of the whole matter to
Dr. Skerl, and never did an embezzler more assiduously pad
his accounts than the bearded geologist did those work reports. Everyone was given credit for working, even the few
who had never lifted a finger for the prison Camp. It became a standing joke that if you passed the garden, he
counted it as a work hour there. Many people made their
appearance, armed with a shovel or rake, to sit for an hour

in the sun, out of sight of the guards, and ever on the look-out for a chance inspection.

Half the hospital staff was cut off the official list and ac-credited to vegetable-raising, although they actually went right on with their regular duties. Mothers with small chil-dren, who had been exempt from most Camp details, were put down for hours of bathroom duty. It seemed a clever ruse, and it worked, but the risk of discovery lay ever at the door, and a single mishap might have precipitated an ava-lanche of trouble.

Commandant Oura was enraged that we didn't show proper respect to our Japanese captors by bowing, and he demanded it constantly. In the first few weeks he was there, before Tomibe left, it was obvious to him that our relation-ship with Tomibe was one of respectful amiability, and feel-ing that this did not extend to him, he attempted to coerce respect. He it was who finally barred Miss McKim from the meetings. His own interpreter mirrored his desires.

Where Tomibe had been handsome and immaculate, Oura was physically uncouth. He kept his head shaved, but not his chin. He wore wrinkled shorts and wooden clogs. In his uni-form, donned for special occasions, when VIP's were due, he still seemed somehow uncomely and poorly groomed.

Yamato, his interpreter, was a wonderful character. When he came into the prison Camp, he first of all talked to Miss McKim, who bubbled afterwards that he was a "Sunday School boy, all full of sweetness and light."

Laughter blew refreshingly through our day as we read the first of his "vital memorandums" to the internees of the prison Camp, that for our own peace of mind, Mr. Yamato felt we should not concern ourselves with the social affairs of the outside world—so we would have no newspaper af-ter this. Besides, he added, there was a paper shortage! It was no great loss to us insofar as reading matter was con-cerned, for it contained nothing of real information.

He was a very small man, with a copybook command of English, and immediately became a figure of fun to the pris-oners, although he was actually in a position to do us harm if he chose. He issued weighty "vital memorandums" concerning our conduct and interfered with our prison Camp government and our little customs. He was often perplexed. A school teacher, he was actually well-read and was even familiar with English-language classics. He was ponderously pedantic in his manner and loved to converse eruditely with the Americans and British. Yamato always wore a full uniform, and sometimes tripped over his sword, which was very long.

Roll call was a solemn occasion to Yamato, and he made the most of it. He devised a ceremony and presented Carl with a written schedule to memorize. First, the internees would assemble in a horseshoe formation, the sections standing a little apart from each other, on the parade grounds. Then the Chairman or Vice-Chairman would accompany the official roll-caller, one of the Japanese staff (usually himself, for he hated to miss it), to the center of the horseshoe. The Chairman would then call the internees to military attention, inform us that "We will now have roll call," turn and bow formally to the staff member, who would thereupon come forward, greet the internees with a "good morning" or "good evening" salutation, repeat the announcement of roll call in Japanese, bow and be bowed at by all. Then he and the Chairman would make the rounds, stopping at each group and receiving the section report from the monitor, observing while the group counted off in confirmation. At the end of the ceremony, the Chairman and staff member would return to the center of the parade ground, and formally dismiss, after another round of bowing.

What he hadn't counted on was the characteristic inability of the American to resist clowning in the presence of pomposity. From the first attempt, there was something wrong, and Yamato sensed it but couldn't define it. In complete gravity, Carl informed us frankly that we were lined up there for roll call. Then Carl would execute a snappy military about-face, his lean height dwarfing his companion, and bowed graciously to Yamato. How it could seem funny to us I don't know, but there was a puckish glee in watching Yamato struggle through his little ceremony. He would be immediately greeted in each group with the monitor announcing the number present: "One on duty, one in hospital, one in jail," and the counting off would begin. Then he must transfer his whole attention to that. Groups with the small children were especially worrisome. At first, he ordered that the children, even tots, be taught to say their numbers, but this resulted in chaos. Helpless laughter engulfed us at the sanctimonious-appearing, tall, dark young missionary who boomed his own number, "twelve"; then in falsetto added "thirteen" and "fourteen" for his tiny girls.

Yamato never lost hope, and to the end was still trying to invest his beloved roll call with the proper dignity. It was even worse when it rained, and the rite had to take place within the separate barracks. Mr. Yamato would arrive to find women scrambling down out of their suspended beds, dressed in odd wrappers or coats over pajamas. When they lined up along the aisle between the bunks, there would be scarcely room for the soldiers to squeeze through, and I truly believe that neither our General Committee nor the internees detested the aggravating business any more than all of the Japanese, except Yamato.

Another one of Yamato's most cherished duties was censoring, particularly the monthly yellow-card messages. Virginia McCuish and I were working in the prison Camp office by this time, so we collected the little messages, printed on bits of scrap paper, then with Yamato sitting beside us, reading each one, and copying them onto the cards. He arbitrarily (and enigmatically) divided the cards into three stacks, and try as we would, Virginia and I could never determine what this sorting meant. We had a privately-held hunch that it was purely for effect.

This would have been an ordeal for us, but for two things: first, we were eager to promote any means of communication, of course; and second, Yamato never allowed us to be bored. The nicknames baffled him, and he asked us to explain "Bud," "Pop," and "Ducky," his studious brow heavy with concern over their absence from his ever-present pocket dictionary. After the day when we had seen our first American plane overhead, one message tried to subtly relay this great piece of news with the single exclamation "Eureka!"—an interjection Americans commonly use to exclaim triumph upon discovery. This was too much for Yamato, and my explanations were so necessarily vague that we floundered into very deep water for a quarter of an hour, when suddenly his eyes brightened, and he cried out the most unintelligible word I ever heard.

Repetitions didn't clear it up for me until suddenly my memory functioned, too—more creakily than his—and I realized he might have been trying to say "Archimedes," referring to the early Greek inventor who shouted "Eureka!" ("I have found it!) to announce a scientific discovery. This was the one and only time in three years I actually sat and laughed with a Japanese captor. We were both so relieved to have reached an understanding, and in our laughter he even forgot to object to the unorthodox message, or to ask to what it referred.

We had a small Camp newspaper issued daily by Jim Halsema, who was on his way to becoming an international journalist chronicling the "legitimate" news, such as baseball scores, supper menu, announcements, releases from and entrances into the hospital, number of dysentery cases, and special church services. This paper was of course submitted to Yamato for censoring to see that we were not concerning ourselves unduly with outside affairs before it could be posted on the bulletin board. In November of 1944, on Election Day at home, a straw ballot was held in Camp, and the next day Jimmy printed a headline in red letters across the top of the typewritten pages, announcing "ROOSEVELT WINS, 4 TO 1!"

Yamato sent for him at once, and brandishing the paper at Jimmy, queried excitedly, "You have had news from America?" Jim patiently explained about the straw vote within the prison Camp, and assured him that no, we had no word from America regarding the real election there.

Yamato was most relieved, but still worried about that headline, then triumphantly was inspired to write neatly, with his official red pencil, just below the headline: "This is a joke." And thus it was posted for our happy pondering. [Apropos this election, we tried to get some information about election returns in the States from the Japanese, but they wouldn't tell us anything, and only through their continuing to revile President Roosevelt did we realize that he had been re-elected. We had to wait for liberation to hear about Mr. Truman.]

Yamato was really making a career of his censorship toward the end. When the itemized lists of all the personally-owned books in the prison Camp were called in, he had each owner, in alphabetical order, bring his books to the office, where he laboriously skimmed through unfamiliar technical and religious volumes to ascertain their suitability for his charges. We thought he did this just for fun—he returned every book.

Other Japanese staff members with whom we were much in contact were young Hayakawa, who had served so long as Acting Commandant, and who was pleasant enough; Suda, very genial on the surface, but capable of cruelty; Tanabe, not given to brilliant performance, but innocuous; Kaito, known as "Joe College" for his high-style uniform and slick hair, very young and ill at ease with us; and Masaki, who was our friend.

Masaki was well bred by Western standards, and he spoke English more fluently than any of the other Japanese on the staff. Oura spoke no English at all, except for some quite fluent profanity, and Yamato's English always sounded like a translation. Masaki was transferred to Camp Holmes from Los Baños with a "bad record" of sympathetic treatment of the prisoners, and soon we found that he would always at least try to help us. He had no authority, and his hands were tied by Oura, but he was of some assistance to us.

We worried a little about him at first. He seemed so friendly, so genuinely concerned for our welfare; we felt he must either be playing a deep game with us, or was a traitor to his own country. But he was neither. Masaki had a Western education, and the unnecessary suffering was as abhorrent to him as it was to us. Further, he was accustomed to our ways, and found them congenial, and with his good language skill, there was little or no barrier to overcome. Eventually he was in trouble again for his continued friendliness, and for the last weeks was not allowed inside the prison Camp. But Masaki died fighting near Baguio for his country, which absolved him from any hint of disloyalty.

Kaito, too, is dead, and we know now that he was terribly afraid all the time that would be his fate. He never became either friendly or hostile toward us, and would have been quickly forgotten except for one incident.

On a morning in September in 1944, Kaito was delegated to take roll call. But that morning Porro was bombed and shelled (down on the Coast below us, miles from Baguio and Camp Holmes, but from our mountain gallery, we could see the smoke and hear the guns—the first, for us, in the retaking of the Islands). The result can be imagined. Internees crowded to the edge of the bank, gazing down toward the scene, hushed with our tense listening, pale with excitement. At eight o'clock we grudgingly tore ourselves away to line up while Kaito stood uneasily waiting, not knowing how to meet the situation, well aware of the distant booming.

Even in formation, the listening and straining went on, and he could not command our attention. At last, with a supremely disgusted gesture, the boyish conqueror said aloud, in English, "Oh, what's the use!" He turned and walked away, while we dispersed excitedly, but with a chuckle, to vantage points to see if we could see any of the action below.

Chapter 31:
PRIVATE COOKING

The prisoners in Camp Number Three, Camp Holmes, in this mountain village of Baguio, were housed in three long dormitories, and half a dozen small cottages that had been moved into the grounds from surrounding sites by the internees themselves, under guard. One of the large barracks was occupied by men, one by unattached women— that is, without small children; and in between, one by women and the younger children. In the center building, all but one end of the first floor was occupied by the main kitchen and the dining hall, which was also used between meals and during the evenings as a recreation center. Back of each dormitory was a shower room, and there was one small makeshift kitchen.

On the lower level of the prison Camp was the hospital, the "Sisters' Cottages," where two groups of Anglican nuns lived in semi-privacy, and the "Baby House," reserved for mothers of infants and well isolated from the rest of the living quarters. Later, a sheet-iron edifice was erected down there, and it became known as the Ark, because when it rained, the box-like building fairly floated in standing water.

This, though, is the tale of the kitchen, and the "private cooking" so disfavored by our captors, and so vital to us. As it came from the Central kitchen, the food was cooked, and that was about all that can be said. That is no reflection on the chef, the Russian former chef of the Pines Hotel in Baguio, noted before the war for his skill with gourmet cooking; nor on the kitchen crew, who labored long, hot hours. The ingredients were inferior, seasonings hard to get and at best, imitations; utensils were awkward and inadequate, and the quantities cooked too large for much attention to flavor. It seemed to me better than the chow line at the Santo Tomas prison camp, and when we were first transferred, we thought the food comparatively fine.

But it was drab, and because we had to depend on seasonal vegetables that were available, we had worse than monotonous runs on certain items. During cabbage season, there would be cabbage every day for weeks, and the best efforts of the cooks to vary the menu by serving it boiled, fried, or raw, couldn't disguise that it was still cabbage. Cucumbers had their turn; we had months on end of chayote, a particularly savorless, "ninety-percent" white native vegetable. One of our doctors coined that term and applied it to the bulky, watery vegetables which grow indigenously in the Islands. So we received our rations from the line, and then the women took over from there.

They hustled their pots of food into the little kitchens, and there seasoned, spiced, re-cooked, and renovated every meal to some semblance of appeal. While vegetables, fruit, meat, flour, eggs, and shortening could still be purchased in the extra buying, even in small quantities and of doubtful quality, elaborate cooking took hours of every woman's day.

Recipes using the ersatz items we were able to buy were invented and passed along, so that there was a great similarity in the meals of all the families. For example, fried rice was a standard dish. The plain rice from the line, often broken and of the poorest grade—what we called sweepings, worse than gleanings—was dumped into a frying pan with chopped onion, garlic, green pepper, tomato, and meat when available, or whole peanuts. Well-seasoned with the coarse rock salt and native pepper, and nourishing, this was the men's favorite.

Muffins were popular, too, especially when it was no longer possible to bake our raised bread (for which we made our leaven from bananas). The muffins were made with a mixture of casava (almost a pure starch) and rice flour or corn meal or *bucacao*. When eggs became a memory, bananas made a nice substitute; then they disappeared, and it was found that the muffins could still be made with just flour, leavening, liquid and shortening. When the shortening was gone, we substituted the unscented cold cream that came in the kits; soda was used for leavening (I paid eighteen pesos, nine dollars, for my last quarter pound, and used a quarter of a teaspoonful for each batch of muffins), and soda-mint digestive tablets filled in when there was no more baking soda. As flour stocks dwindled, the corn meal mush from the breakfast line, or soft rice (broken kernels cooked to a mush in an excessive amount of water), was substituted for half the flour quantity.

The final recipe was a memorable, haunting concoction we called *"gup cakes"*: half a cup of cold mush, sacrificed from the skimpy breakfast portion, half a cup of corn meal, soda dissolved in vinegar made from fermented fruit peelings, a pinch of salt, a few grains of sugar if you had it, a dash of native cinnamon to kill the taste of everything else, and sour coconut milk or water. We used the last of our cold cream to grease the tins. The batter was spread into pie tins to make a crust, or into butter cans to make muffins, or into tall tins if you wanted steamed bread—it didn't matter how it was cooked, the soggy result was still gup cakes. A variation was provided by adding some coconut residue, but even

coconuts became non-available eventually. We ate it, because it was filling; the memory still brings a tinge of nausea, and the sight of large jars of unscented cold cream in a drug store makes me feel green.

Men stood back in awe and wonder as they watched their wives perform the daily miracle of this anything but private cooking. For each stove there were sixty or more women. As a dish was finished, it was removed from the hottest areas, and shoved to the back, until by the time the meals were ready, kettles, coffee pots, and muffin tins were piled six deep at the back of the stove, while from ten to twenty women stirred, tasted, peeked at and tested their cookery around the front edges. It was humanly impossible that this mad scramble could be accomplished in divine harmony, and sometimes the words grew as hot as the scorched faces of the women in the favored positions, where all the other women wanted to be. There was an air of cheerfulness, even so, and most of the altercations provoked giggles and grins from the bystanders. Cooperation and even graciousness were manifested, too, more than impatience and selfishness.

The first day that I braved our little kitchen, with its huge flat-topped stove and cockroach-infested sink, I stood back appalled at the very thought of trying to invade that formidable phalanx of female determination about the stove. But if I wanted to cook, I knew I'd have to get in there somehow. So I watched my chances, until I finally saw a slight gap in the defense, and then, blessing my small size, I meekly edged my proudest possession, a new homemade frying pan, into the fray, accepting gratefully the condescending or friendly advice I received from all sides.

By the second day, I was bolder, and in my temerity committed a *faux pas* that earned me a bitter enemy at once. I moved a pan! Just a few inches I did push it, but while I was still committing this heinous crime, a thin, gray-haired woman bore down on me with an unnerving shriek crying: "I didn't think one woman would do such a thing to another woman. I never heard of anyone's being so cruel! Women don't do things like that to other women!"

I was so dismayed at this outburst that I could barely stammer an apology, while the audience gathered around, and encouraging comments were muttered into my burning ears. It finally came out that I had moved her bread, in the process of raising, onto a too-warm spot, and the lady couldn't believe that such abysmal ignorance concerning bread-making could be. She never quite forgave me for my unfortunate deed. I privately then thought that it was quite funny, and Norman howled when I told him about it. But I proceeded with more caution thereafter. And I soon learned from my own sad experience that it wasn't at all funny to find a bit of your scarce food burned or spoiled because someone had moved your pan from one place to another.

It was a mystery to the masculine observer, too, how we managed to identify our own pans of food. Most of the utensils had been manufactured right there in the prison Camp, and were made of tin cans; beaten-out galvanized iron was used for frying pans; muffin tins were small butter cans fastened together in racks of four, six, or eight; coffee pots were tall cereal tins with spout and handle soldered on. And as everything we were cooking depended on what we could get on the line, there would be ten frying pans of fried rice, a dozen peanut loaves; four or six steamed breads; and a multitude of muffins, which had to be browned directly under the coals at an open grate in the front of the stove. Occasionally someone would make a mistake, and it was sometimes firmly believed to be deliberate!

Our private cooking was a painful thorn in Oura's flesh. He first ordered us to cut it down to a minimum. Then when he developed his gardening phobia, he banned the cooking altogether so that we could spend our time in the garden. We compromised finally, when it began to look as though he really meant to carry out his threat to forbid the use of the stove, by assigning details of two women each for duty in the kitchen for an hour's run. We would prepare our muffins or fried rice beside our beds and take the pans of food, ready to cook, to the kitchen window, where it would be turned over to the monitors on duty. Thus, when the inspectors came by, it appeared that the amount of cooking going on had been greatly reduced—if they didn't scrutinize too closely the astounding activities of the two wild-eyed, damp-browed women bending over the stove. Keeping track of a dozen skillets of frying cornmeal mush, several coffee pots, pans of muffins, and toasting coconuts, while stoking the fire and boiling endless kettles of drinking water, with a weather eye out for the state of done-ness each dish had reached, shouting out the names of the owners of completed cooking—this required Herculean efforts and complete self-sacrifice.

The situation was a little relieved by the presence in the Camp of a number of electric hotplates, on which the owners and their friends did all of their cooking, using the kitchens only for baking. But Oura considered this just a dodge, and demanded that the hotplates be collected and stored in the office. They were, for awhile, until our General Committee convinced him that all the women were spending "much time" in the garden and no time at cooking. Dr. Skerl's fabulous work charts had much to do with that convincing.

The most anomalous habit of all internees and prisoners in every Camp was our insatiable collecting and exchanging of recipes of former days. Women were not alone in this—dozens of men compiled voluminous notebooks of other people's memories of favorite dishes. In the course of every conversation, food never failed to be mentioned. Often we deliberately cut off the subject, in tacit agreement, only to find ourselves reminiscing eagerly again, minutes later, of meals we had eaten, and culinary triumphs we had witnessed and remembered too vividly, or simply what we'd like to eat. [The French artist in my room at the Santo Tomas prison camp had been inspired to make up some attractive little French recipe books to sell at Christmas time, and she couldn't fill her orders.] Cooking was a contagious habit, and even some of the old men tried an occasional pan of fried rice.

My friend Mary Kneebone became famous in Camp Holmes for the muffins she made with soap powder given her for Christmas; she thought it was flour when she used it, but after one bite, hastily sought the person who gave it to her to find out what kind. Then she improved the opportunity by passing them around generously to anyone who came by.

The most nauseous dish I was ever required to taste was a dreamed-up pudding of cornmeal mush—flavored with garlic and browned to a turn; the creator was enthusiastic!

Chapter 32:
CUBICLES

Knowing that internees at Los Baños had been allowed for some months to live as family units, and that the same privilege had recently been granted Santo Tomas prisoners, a movement toward that goal was begun by some resident prisoners in Camp Holmes during March, 1944.

At the first presentation of the question to the Camp Holmes personnel, a startling phenomenon occurred. As though a stick of dynamite had been thrown into the midst of us, the whole prison Camp was split sharply into two bitterly warring factions, and the controversy that made some history at Camp Holmes was on.

Marshaling their forces, quite unaware of the impending explosion, the "pros" presented their confident, obvious and commonsense reasons for wishing each family group to have a separate living space. As though they had been stung, the "cons" leaped into action, publishing their obvious and commonsense reasons why the suggestion should be over-ruled at once and *in perpetuum*. The battle became a bit tough in spots, and personalities inevitably got tangled into it, with both sides firmly believing their own viewpoint was so right that only blind prejudice and self-seeking could be motivating the other faction.

The plea for family housing came from those of us who felt that having their family all together would ease the strain, and aid in bringing some happiness into a rapidly saddening situation. There was quiet reasoning along the lines of companionship, convenience, and the wisdom of fathers being with their children and wives in a time of approaching crises, the nature of which we could not predict. We didn't ask for new housing—just an adaptation of the present. We couldn't understand why all married couples were not just as eager as we were to live together in some semblance of home life, some effort toward being together in at least a modicum of privacy.

It seemed abnormal to us to continue the wretched separation of families when there was any possibility of correcting that old grievance. We stood aghast at the scathing denunciation we and our plan received, finding such a reaction from married people incomprehensible. Friendships were strained, and even our General Committee involved itself in the sharp division of opinion.

The opposition first questioned the wisdom of the move from a physical standpoint, which of course hadn't been mentioned by the advocates, and so far as I knew, had received little consideration from them until it was aired by the other side. Many sincerely believed that, after years of physical separation, living together again would result in a large number of pregnancies, which all agreed was certainly not desirable. The question could scarcely be argued, so the proponents simply denied such a thing would happen, and let it go.

The opposition also insisted that from the same standpoint, the whole idea was indecent—that no real privacy could ever be attained, and "married life" in public was primitive, animal, and worse! This angle was not generally advanced by the single, but by the married opponents; and the answer was a hot flinging back of the insinuation into the laps of the originators, with the old platitude that they must be judging others by themselves. This kind of bickering was not only futile and undignified, but we recognized it as harmful, hurtful, and wiser heads sought to cool it down. But bitter words were spoken, and some of the discussions had a decidedly earthy tinge. Of course, very few persons entered into this phase of the conflict, but those who did barred no holds.

A more impersonal reason against, and by far the most convincing, was the lack of space, and the necessity it would create for moving many who would not benefit by it. Plans were drawn up and presented involving the least number

of displacements, but there had to be an adjustment somewhere, so it was finally settled that the little building then
serving as school and church would be converted into additional living space. This brought righteous and telling protests from the educators and some of the religious leaders,
but about that time, a new schoolhouse and office-building
was completed, so that it proved no hardship to relinquish
the little old building.

Permission was then obtained without any apparent difficulty from the Japanese, whom we assumed to be unaware
of the raging battle among their prisoners. To put the plans
into effect, and over the objections of the still unconvinced
and irate few, the upper floor over the dining hall was partially converted into family quarters, and the husbands
moved in.

Allotted spaces were curtained off with anything that
could be found—sheets, blankets, matting, wallboard. It
required a little adjusting for everyone, but within a few
weeks it seemed a normal situation and the hue and cry
died away. So, the eight families who put up *sawali* partitions and moved into the ex-school, originally a goat-pen,
did so without much further argument. Fathers joined their
families in the "Baby House," and the "Ark" was rearranged
into living quarters for families. Even the store building,
when the store had outlived its usefulness, was converted,
and plans were under way to make additional "cubicles"
available to more families in other barracks, as more and
more succumbed to the idea, once it had been demonstrated
a success.

Children could hardly understand the new regime. One
little girl summed it all up the first morning she wakened to
find her father in the same room, just getting out of bed.
She stared wide-eyed at him, until he asked her why, and
the tiny child shook her head and replied, "Daddy, you look
so funny! You don't have your glasses on!"

It wasn't all painless, amusing, and fun. Quarters were
severely cramped, and there was a period when husband
and wife had to learn all over again how to live together.

The men had become accustomed to a bachelor's existence, with its lack of some of the graces and small attentions to formalities, and they frequently shocked their wives at the beginning. And the women had long been established in their spinsterish routines, and they found their lives a bit different—the continued presence of a man in the house could be challenging. But it was certainly exhilarating and nice, we acknowledged.

The peace and contentment we felt simply radiated through the prison camp. That cold, empty loneliness that always followed the goodnight kiss, when each returned to a separate dormitory, had been hard to bear. In the evenings, there had been no place for a man to sit with his wife in the rainy season except in the stuffy, crowded dining hall, under the garish unshaded lights, surrounded by bridge players and noisy youngsters, or on the chilly, windy porch of the barracks, which was frequently rain-swept and uninhabitable. If one or the other were ill, it was uncomfortable and inconvenient to visit each other, and nearly impossible to be of any help. Women were not welcome in the men's barracks at any time, and only very grudging consent was given to a man's appearance in any of the women's sleeping quarters.

The cubicle plan literally changed our lives. The dining hall was almost deserted, for the newly-settled couples were unwilling to forsake their precious privacy for even an evening, and it was easier and more fun to hold their bridge games or little "get-togethers" right at "home." I knew a genuine feeling of security, for the first time in thirty months, lying there beside my husband during the anxious nights. Even the hunger didn't seem quite so acute—we had funny little customs of our own that helped, like doling out ten peanuts apiece, to be eaten after we had gone to bed!

We could sit at our own table, with a real cloth and napkins and a little bowl of flowers, and serve the unpalatable food onto our crockery plates, and make private jokes about it all. Life seemed more gracious. Norman couldn't help laughing when my coordination failed me and I immersed my whole nose into the coconut milk I was trying to smell for freshness, so that what might have been frightening or exasperating to me became funny; I teased him about his growing tendency toward forgetfulness, so he could be amused by it, too, instead of fretting. We had exactly the same problems and trials, and now we could totally combine our attack. It was a different world for us. And we were just typical of the way the family-housing was affecting those who accepted and tried it.

We quickly learned to speak in low tones, and tried to keep our ears closed to sounds from the other side of the thin walls, unless there was something amusing to hear, when we shamelessly — blithely — eavesdropped, as did everyone else. We loved to listen to Walter Tong, who had been separated from his family until his recent transfer from the prison camp at Davao, brushing up on his fatherliness and drilling his ten-year-old son on geography and arithmetic. We entered quite freely into the conversations with that delightful family from our side of the *sawali* wall. We weren't the only neighbors who chuckled with pleasure to hear the serious young minister on another side of us describe the way he courted his pretty southern wife. We enjoyed our group in the old goat-pen — the Mennonites in the corner cubicle who had audible circle prayers at their evening parties and were always there, always ready, when anyone needed help; the pipe-smoking, witty wife-daughter-granddaughter of missionaries in the opposite corner whose terse comments on life in general brought shouts of laughter from the rest of us. We listened with sympathy and wonderment to the patient, unrewarding efforts of one of the Lutheran missionaries to teach by rote his earnest creed to the two toughest kids in the prison Camp, little British offspring of one of the Hong Kong evacuees. All of our cubicle mates were missionaries; all were splendid people — and we were all young.

Feeling like brides again, we wives hurried to make our cubicles homey and attractive. Curtains, furniture, and decorations were devised and arranged. Our "apartment" was eight by ten feet, with a window and a doorway. We suspended our bed from the rafters, to save space, and climbed up to it on a ladder. Norman found a crumpled, rusty set of springs on a prison Camp junk pile; and on these we laid our lumpy mattresses, and while the bed sagged threateningly, it was far more comfortable than the wooden and bamboo slats to which we were accustomed. Beneath the bed, Norman built me a dressing table and kitchen cupboard combination. Our dining table was beside the window from which we had a superb mountain view. He fashioned a settee from bamboo slats, and put up shelves on the level with the bed for storage (we had little to keep there, but it was nice for the mice!). Outside the window, he hung a bamboo window box for my nasturtiums. I curtained off the corner for our clothes, ironing board and broom; made curtains from the extra sheet we had after pooling our possessions, and a cover for the settee with my worn yellow bedspread, which we didn't need up near the ceiling.

The room had a center light, and we had a reading light over the bed, "borrowed" by my ingenious husband from the Japanese Commandant's office when the building was in the process of renovation and left open for an hour. Beyond this, we had two stools and my folding chair from Manila, besides the settee, to sit on; a fork and a spoon each, and one sharp knife made there in Camp; two pottery plates and cups, a frying pan, coffee pot and muffin tins; a dish pan. We felt wealthy. We had love and laughter and faith and a better understanding of the difference between "need" and "want."

[When a typhoon struck us that last year, we had to resort to some extreme measures to keep our little castle intact. I have such a vivid mental picture of Norman, Walter Tong, and two of the other men who lived in our goat-pen struggling to keep the roof on. They tied heavy ropes to the corners, and stood there in the wind and rain literally "keeping a roof over our heads!" It was a major effort, and they were storm-battered, but successful. I have no idea now how long they courageously stood their ground.

That was the same typhoon that gave Norman a bad moment on another day. I never had weighed a great deal, and the very slimming diet we were on had reduced me somewhat further. But I didn't think of that when I opened our door out into the storm. Instantly, a powerful gust simply picked me up and "blew me away." Landing in a sitting position in the mud, I sat and laughed insanely while Norman watched in stunned panic, his face white and his mouth open.]

The eight families adopted a kitten for mouse control, and named her "Cubie." Norman and I had her a good deal of the time; her prowess as a hunter became renowned, for her rations were as scant as ours, and there were days when to spare even a teaspoon of rice seemed hard. She dined well only on the days when we had *dilis*, native anchovies, dried and odorous, and served complete with heads and eyes!

Not all of the married couples in Camp took advantage of the chance to live together. A few joined our immoral ranks from time to time, but many were still unconvinced that it was a good thing. One of the arguments was forever refuted, however. Only three known pregnancies occurred during the last year, and one of these with a couple who had been very opposed to the Cubicle Plan. Two of the babies were not born until after repatriation; the other baby, of a missionary couple, was delivered a day or two after liberation.

From one other viewpoint, the cubicle controversy was interesting. It included everyone in the prison Camp, miner or missionary. The old men whose native families awaited them outside had much to say against the move; the bachelors and unmarried women were indifferent except where it touched their own living space—some were opposed and some thought it all right, as long as they themselves were not dispossessed in the shuffle; but the two rival factions were composed almost equally from both the mining and missionary groups, so that for once, the miners could not blame the trouble on the missionaries, nor the missionaries on the miners!

Just after we had moved into the cubicle, large details of men were taken out to several of the surrounding mining camps to demolish buildings for the lumber, and whenever one of these crews returned to the prison Camp, our possessions were augmented. The men returned loaded with whatever useful materials they could find still loose in the abandoned, already-looted camps. Norman proudly presented me with the broken head of a pick-axe; we always felt that it might be useful someday, although we did not quite know for what. And I remember so vividly Father Sheridan climbing the rocky steps up to our level, waving two curtain rods delightedly in my direction, calling out, "Look what I found, Evelyn. Do you want them?" Indeed I did, and accepted them in the spirit in which they were offered — sincere, if amused, gratitude for added treasures, mirrored in the ruddy, happy face of the kind priest who looted them so I could hang my curtains properly.

Chapter 33:
WAITING

Perhaps if we hadn't kept ourselves so keyed up by think-ing that the end was always just around the corner, the endless waiting we endured would have been easier. But in everything we did, that discouraging time-killing was in-volved. We waited in lines, we waited for decisions, we waited for our turn to cook, to wash, or go to the bathroom, or buy a pound of peanuts—we waited for deliverance, and the exhausting patience it all required was nearly superhuman.

Even at the Camp Holmes internment camp, the "chow lines" began forming hours before the meal was scheduled for serving. The old-timers, who slept much of the day and roamed through their barracks at night, and had little if any prison camp work to do, were planted solidly on a long bench near the entrance to the dining hall long before daylight, and resumed their posts early in the afternoon to doze or spin yarns, or complain about almost everything, until time for the supper line to move.

Even the children were trained to take their playthings and get a good position an hour or two early, so that their busy parents could go on about their occupations until sup-per was nearly ready. It became so bad that in order to get one's portion, the internee had to plan on an hour and a half at the very least in the line.

Norman didn't get back to our prison Camp until nearly four o'clock in the afternoon. He was a member of the "wood crew" which supplied us with our fuel. They were out of the prison Camp, under heavy guard, all day while they did their cutting near Trinidad Valley. When he did return, he had to have a little time to shave and shower, so I fell into the habit of taking a book or my knitting over to the line about three-fifteen, to hold a place for him until he came to relieve me a little before four-thirty, the serving time. Then it would take him another half hour or more to get through the slow-moving queue, so together we consumed nearly two hours a day just collecting our supper.

This built up into an unbearable aggravation after so long a time, and sometimes during the last months he brought in the rice and watery stew, or *camotes* and cabbage, with a glum face and irritated comments foreign to his resilient, cheerful nature. But if we did rebel, and wait to go in at the end of the line, the food was cold, and sometimes there was not enough to go around.

Occasionally something would happen, as we stood there, trying to check our nervous impatience, to break the deadly monotony and give us a needed laugh or bit of diversion. Such was the day when that delightful toddler, Terry Kneebone, playing with his wooden toy truck beside an open drain, dropped a wheel and watched in comic dismay as it rolled into the ditch, and then with an absolutely radiant amusement at such a great joke on himself, turned and announced to the entire chow line, "Dee whizz, I dopped it in the dutter!" and beamed with satisfaction at the shout of joy from his audience.

The worst fate was to find oneself standing next to one of those perpetually gregarious souls who would seem to thrive on crowds and repetitious small talk. Then you were deprived even of the retreat into reverie or reading, and while you strove for the courtesy to answer pleasantly the trite observations and rehashed rumors, you involuntarily held a brief discussion with yourself about assault and battery or even mayhem!

One woman, in particular, was our nemesis. She was a self-contained, eccentric spinster with an incomparable proclivity for finding the weak spots in one's armor, unerringly managing to take the opposite view of anyone else's opinion, whether you had expressed it or not, and she talked incessantly, with imperturbable friendliness. She "really thought last night's supper was awfully good." We gagged at the recollection of the dried fish and coarse rice mixture.

She "loved the rain" while we shivered miserably, soaked to the skin through our inadequate clothing. She "couldn't stand the children,"and our hearts were gripped with anguish because of hungry babies. Worst of all, she thought the Japanese "had their rights." Maybe they did, but we were in no mood to hear about them.

At night, we waited for the others to quiet down so we could go to bed and sleep, or they waited for us, depending on who was having the bridge game or prayer meeting. Norman waited for me and I for him, for our work hours didn't coincide. During my work at the Commandant's office, we all waited for the Japanese to make up their minds and say "yes" or "no" to the day's items of business.

And so the precious time was killed, the wasted dragging hours became an obsession; but we learned, painfully, to do it without losing our sanity, and the submissive patience of the prisoners was almost a pathetic thing to watch, after their release, when they finally could have been free to revolt.

The most undisturbed person in the prison Camp was one who long since had ceased to consider time; an angular, sibylline creature so indefinite in her appearance that only the birth date recorded in the office gave any clue to her age. She was an old-time school teacher, who had lived for all the years anyone could remember in barren rented rooms or native hotels in Baguio. Emaciated, scraggly, with her wiry gray hair clipped short, and wearing shapeless garments pinned precariously about her bones, she spent her days by the kitchen door, nibbling off infinitesimal bites from her crackers and cheese, or drying and cracking prune pits or stirring with a dirty, skeletal finger the dubious contents of her tin can cup. Sometimes she lurked about the stove, darting into the mob or around it to snatch a kernel of corn or grain of rice or even a crystallized drop of syrup from the hot surface with her bare fingers.

Her mannerisms and attitude were that of a poor little church mouse, yet hidden about her person she was known to have thousands of dollars in good currency, enough to buy and sell most of us, perhaps. This they discovered when she was taken to the hospital and forcibly undressed during an illness. She was a vegetarian, and dabbled in the occult. She loved to foretell and prophesy. She would corner one of us and say, in her slow, weak voice, "Missus, you are now in your sixth incarnation. In your seventh, you will be more fortunate."

One day she seemed to be dreaming off into space as I flitted by at my usual breakneck pace, but she called to me and said, as from a far place, "Mrs. Whitfield, do you see that lovely pink cloud? I've just been out there, floating on it, out through the blue, blue sky on a beautiful pink cloud." I swallowed hard, seeing the woman before me, sitting there at the stained table, clutching in her grimy hands the thinnest slice of cheese, and a wee crust of bread she had picked up somewhere—a different vision. She had her contentment within her. Did I? For that moment, I wanted to fly with her on that pink cloud, through that blue, blue sky!

I waited for her, too, for months—at every roll call time, when I was monitor of our section, and on many nights finally had to go out and hunt for her. I would usually find her standing behind the kitchen gazing at the stars, or by the sink, washing her teeth in one of our community water dippers! But she did not worry about time a'wasting, and maybe her vagaries were easier to live with than my surging impatience.

While we waited, we dreamed. The men talked among themselves and to their wives about spectacular new business opportunities in a post-war world of universal reconstruction. The women drew house-plans and discussed in minute detail where they would like to live and why, and what a post-war future might hold for them, too. And the pretty, forlorn girls, to me almost the most deprived group in the prison Camp, must have reached out to a time of dreamed-of gaiety and glamor, with boy friends, dates, pretty clothes, college and dances—the things they were missing in their growing up. Like the rest of us, they had no privacy; like the adults, they did their prison Camp duties. They went to school, gathered in their little groups, always under observation, of course. If their shorts were too short, there were multiple "tsk-tsks." If they were a little loud, people turned and looked. There were no secrets. Many were separated from their parents. They must have learned, like the rest of us, much about patience, self-reliance, and faith, but they also must have wondered about those vanishing years of girlhood.

Chapter 34:
I SAW THE STAR!

Not many Japanese planes were ever to be seen at once in our vicinity, and usually any that we saw were alone, gliding along lazily, not high, too familiar a sight to give us any pause. The wheezy "daily mail to Tokyo" flew over every afternoon; now and then a few fighters came our way; but they all bore the old familiar emblem—the "fried egg"— and we had no interest in them.

But one day—the sudden glint of silver wings in the sun—so high that it seemed at first we had been deluded, disappearing into the clouds, then flashing again against the blue vault of the sky, going so swiftly that even at that great distance we knew this was speed beyond anything we had ever seen—jerked our senses awake and like a light spreading through a darkened doom, our instincts "alerted" and proclaimed that this was no Japanese plane! No! It was too unlike, in action and color and sound. Of course, we could not positively recognize it as belonging to any other nation, either. We hoped, and we believed, it was American, and were thrilled to our toes at the thought. By our grapevine, we had heard how close our forces were to the Philippine Islands, but we were at last tiring of these bits of news so often found to be only rumors.

The whole prison Camp was simmering, and then in a few days, two planes were seen, not quite so remote, but streaking across the heavens at a speed uncomprehended by us. Strangely, one looked black and one silver, and they were an entirely new shape. Still we could not make out the insignia. The cry of "Look, look!" brought us tumbling out of the barracks to catch a glimpse that left us trembling. That very night, a thunderous noise awakened us—the reverberating throb of a low-flying plane, rushing like a meteor over the rooftops. We were sure! We had never heard plane motors that sounded like that one.

And then—another story, for a shining airplane skimmed over the prison Camp, circled and dipped a wing before it zoomed away, the trail streaming behind it spectacularly, and the people sang a great refrain: "I saw the star!"

It <u>was</u> American, and now we knew for sure that the others were, too. Someone in another part of the prison Camp reported that Japanese guards had scuttled into their newly-dug foxholes and tried to fire at it with their rifles. Furious at our cheering and waving, Commandant Oura immediately issued orders that hereafter, no matter what happened, we were not to make any such "undue demonstrations," and added that he had given orders to the guards to shoot into the crowd if we did—only the way he put it was that the guards might become excited and shoot; his meaning was clear.

Moments of exultation or sorrow, danger or rushing relief, never elicited a wholly unanimous reaction or response. The sad little woman whose impatience with the children had disturbed us scoffed at our jubilation, declaring that the Japanese were fooling us. But she stood alone and apart, for the beautiful star on the wing was enough, and the rest of us were treading the very clouds in our mounting excitement.

And now, we saw other planes. We couldn't identify the types, for they were new since the war, but we knew they were our own. One day, we counted nearly a hundred. Norman came dashing into the cubicle shouting—"Planes, honey, hundreds of them, all ours!" They were hurtling over us so close now, and everything stopped while we watched in absorbed delight. The silver, double-fuselaged pursuit ship excited us the most, for it gleamed ethereally in the brilliance of the tropical sun. It flew high and fast, and the innovation of its graceful lines called forth all our superlatives. We likened it to a kite; sometimes it seemed almost transparent, and then we affectionately nicknamed it the "jelly fish." We had not been formally introduced to our henceforth sentimental favorite, the P-38.

Then we heard a great rumor! The Island of Leyte had been invaded! And two weeks later that rumor was positively confirmed, and we organized ourselves in readiness. Norman and I, and probably most of the other families, plotted a secret rendezvous in case something happened that caused us to disperse. The Safety Committee prepared a plan for taking care of the helpless ones in the event of emergency. All ablebodied men were deputized for special responsibilities.

The Japanese imposed black-out regulations, and inadvertently dropped pieces of exciting news by denying them. They were busily occupied these days in digging their foxholes, and Assistant Commandant Suda, particularly, spent a chagrined hour at the hated labor while small, curious Americans crowded to the edge of his pit and pelted him with questions about it. They also built another barrier around us, and barred us from the workshop. The order went out that all cutting knives were to be turned in at once. [Every man carried one, some double-edged stilettos, some made in the Camp, all razor-sharp. Many of the men had practiced throwing knives until they had become dead-eye experts.] At odd hours, the Japanese searched the barracks and cubicles —we weren't quite sure what they were looking for. They were nervous and grumpy, and even the staff was armed. We saw barrios being burned in the valley below us, and troop movements up and down the Mountain Trail.

The future was eerily unpredictable. We thought of everything—paratroops landing right in the prison Camp (not so far from possible, either, for it was in just that way that the dramatic liberation of Los Baños did occur); guerrillas striking and rescuing us at the crucial moment; pitched battles between the opposing armed forces on our doorstep (as it happened in Manila). We considered some grimmer things, too, but left them unspoken. However, liberation conflict was coming; we knew it was near, and life or death for us hung in tenuous balance. The actual outcome was the farthest from our thoughts.

And, in the meantime, another Christmas (1944) was upon us. We had been so sure that this time we'd be at least on our way home, but it bore down inexorably, and had to be observed. Food was appallingly scarce, but a little something extra was somehow scraped up for a Christmas dinner. We ate with the Tongs and Carl that night, at a long table outside under the stars, a "last supper" sort of an affair, ending with the singing of carols, and quiet talk.

We were tense and weary, with our breathless waiting. Hunger and dread and hope all mixed together had already touched us with a feeling of haziness. We could see ourselves daily becoming less coordinated, more likely to be clumsy, both physically and mentally. Our memories were bad—weeks ago we had given up our bridge games almost entirely, not even capable of following through a club convention, and the effort of concentration on trumps and tricks robbed the game of any pleasure. We were distracted, bemused, sometimes irrational. Carl would remind me to remind him of something at the Commandant's office, and then neither of us could remember what it was. One telling a story would become inextricably tangled in a maze of forgotten names and elusive events, and give it all up.

At night, we constantly dreamed of food—smelling and seeing great juicy steaks, iced orange juice, hot bread. In our dreams, our mouths would water over huge dill pickles; but not even in our dreams did we have the satisfaction of actually eating these envisioned wonders. We were finding it necessary to rest during the day. Tempers were at trigger point. Yet with all this, we were in tremendous spirits, and felt ready for the *denouement*, wishing only it would quickly materialize.

Two nights later, it did. We were sitting at the table; supper dishes were cleared away, but Norman and I were having our submarined coffee, when we heard the mellow Southern accents of the couple in an adjoining cubicle explode in excited undertones. When we could stand it no longer, we called out to ask what it was all about. The young minister came close to the *sawali* wall and softly, breathlessly, replied that he had overheard one of our General Committee members saying to another that they were all wanted at the office—the Japanese had told the Executive Committee that we were to be moved, at once!

While we were debating the possibility of such a turn of events, Carl was there at the door, asking me to come to the Commandant's office to take minutes for a special meeting.

The Japanese Commandant had indeed called our Executive Committee to his office, and informed the three bluntly that the entire prison Camp was to be transferred to another place within the next forty-eight hours, half at a time. There was no chance to ask for explanations, for he was inscrutably formal. He demanded that the internees be advised of the impending change immediately, and said that Yamato would furnish further details.

Carl summoned the rest of the General Committee, and the members of the Safety Committee, and requested Mr. Yamato to honor us with his presence at the office.

While we waited for the interpreter, Carl sketched the bare outline of his own slight knowledge of the matter to give the rest of those present a background. Then, playing his role for all it was worth, Yamato made his entrance, entering the building as pompously as a parade, then standing stiffly in the midst of the big Americans. He said, in his stilted phrases, that before the twenty-ninth, all the personnel of this internment Camp were to be evacuated to another place—ah, no, he couldn't say where, but yes, probably Manila; he was not at liberty to tell us why. He reiterated that we were to be transferred in two equal groups, the first to go the morning of the twenty-eighth (that would be tomorrow), the balance the morning of the twenty-ninth, December 1944.

Trucks would be provided—ah, no, he couldn't say how many. Each prisoner should take only a bedroll and his clothing—Yamato designated some irrelevant measurement allowable. He agreed that special provisions would have to be made for the hospital patients (including the elderly man who lay at death's door from a heart attack, a paralytic, two starvation cases, and others so critically ill that they could scarcely be kept alive—we shuddered at the thought of the toll the excitement and strain of the long, rough truck trip could take).

The General Committee at once asked what would happen to the forty-five Americans on the outside, some in hospitals and convents for special care, some in their homes. We were assured then and later that they would be brought down to us, although we know now that there was never any such intention nor concern for those elderly or ill people, and their tragic fate was sealed in advance.

Then Yamato departed, leaving the main issue as cloudy as ever—the motive behind the move, and the destination. It was like jumping blindfolded through a mysterious door. There were a good many reasons we could express why we didn't want to go, but no such arguments could be given time for hearing now. We felt that something big had to be happening somewhere near for them to take so radical a step, and in our reactions there was certainly agitation, something of both exhilaration and dismay, and an overwhelming sense of climax.

After a quick discussion with the General Committee, Carl dictated the announcement, and I typed several copies, my wayward fingers tripping on the keys in my distracted state. Then Phil took the notices over to be read and posted in the dormitories. Blackout was lifted for the evening, until midnight, and the prison Camp blazed with light. We could hear the swelling hubbub from the living quarters clear over at our office building, where members of the two Committees and several emergency assistants pored over plans. They chose the group to depart the first day, deciding what to take and what to leave, and what should be done with the internment Camp and personal property that couldn't be carried—futile consideration. My pencil flew over page after page of shorthand notes of announcements of schedules, lists and instructions. Yamato was called in again a time or two to settle ambiguities that kept revealing themselves in his first explanation, but he was of little assistance.

In the central kitchen, vats of coffee were recklessly brewed, and the breakfast mush served to any who wanted it. Norman reduced me to wry, resigned laughter by bringing me a great bowl of the stuff, which I loathed—but I ate it and felt refreshed and quieter for having a full stomach. Men and women both hastened to use every cooking facility, private and community, to cook up their meager, hoarded supplies, reasoning that if we couldn't take our utensils and equipment with us, it seemed very unlikely that we were going to have an opportunity for any more cooking of any kind. We were determined to leave no food behind, no matter what Oura said. With a prescient distrust of their promises that food would be available, we unanimously sacrificed clothing and possessions to make room for food.

The laundry sinks and buckets were all in use, too, all through the night, as women worked to prepare for any exigency. To complete the confusion and wildness of that scene, a short circuit caused a small fire to break out in the women's dormitory. For the first and only time, the great new fire bell clanged a strident alarm!

Men captured and butchered our small herd of livestock and flock of chickens, and the meat was cooked for distribution to the internees to take with them. Everyone was working, sorting through his trove of queer treasures peculiar to his never-too-understandable prison philosophy, discarding with a shrug or a sigh, packing at last, and always eating!

The first section's luggage was out on the parade grounds for inspection before lights out at midnight, and most of us, completely worn out from the unusual exertion, were ready to call it a day—and night—but all during the rest of the night we could hear people tossing about, and low murmurs of disquieted talk. Long before daylight, we were up and about again.

A double portion breakfast was served to those who were to leave, and they were given cooked rice and meat to take with them for lunch *en route* (the rice soured and the meat spoiled in the humid heat of the lowlands before it could be eaten—it seemed that everyone forgot you can't keep food in closed containers in that humid, hot atmosphere). A little after seven in the morning, trucks arrived. People were packed in atop their possessions, and quickly gone, leaving a litter of last-minute castoffs on the parade grounds—sweater, a stick-horse, camp stools, buckets, and one treasured baby-carriage. No attempt was ever made to leave the prison Camp in a presentable condition. Great piles of garbage and trash cluttered the roads and barracks.

All that day I worked in the General Committee office, packing records and equipment to take with us, destroying carefully anything rejected, typing announcements and running errands. Norman made a late foray into the prison Camp garden to dig *camotes*—our only worthwhile harvest from that sterile hillside. The rice *bodega* storehouse was left open, and we helped ourselves, filling paper market bags and stowing the forbidden supplies in our bedrolls.

Just before Christmas, one of our special deals had worked, and for fifteen hundred pesos, we had been able to smuggle into the prison Camp from our Chinese grocer a few pounds of peanuts and several balls of the crude, dirty brown sugar that was all that remained of the output of the Philippine Islands' great sugar industry. Norman carefully roasted all the nuts, and ground some of them into butter; we always boiled the sugar to make it usable, but thought it would be much easier to carry in the sticky balls, already wrapped in banana leaves, so postponed the process—a grave error. Our craving for sweets was so overwhelming that we kept nibbling at the filthy stuff, and the price we paid was high.

By nightfall, we were ready to go, and in one final splurge, with Carl Eschbach and the Tongs, we had a party, with splintery ice cream made principally from water with the last tin of Red Cross preserved butter whipped into it, and sweetened with the brown syrup. The little cubicles, so trim and immaculate two days before, were shambles. Our method of getting rid of what we could not take had been to throw the discards out the door and down the steep bank below—and thus went the folding chair that had meant so much to me, and my handmade dishpan, and the bamboo tubes Norman had carved so prettily to hold our spoons and small knickknacks; there went the settee, and the table, and the ironing board, also hand-carved; all thrown overboard in one last gesture of renunciation of what had been. We all sat around on our bedrolls and suitcases, and ate from coconut shells, and laughed at our latest dilemma.

So, on the morning of the twenty-ninth, the rest of us were loaded onto luggage-piled trucks, and rolled out of the messy, bare prison Camp, reluctantly leaving Carl, Phil, and another member of the Safety Committee behind to take care of unfinished business, and our kitten meowing forlornly in the new dawn.

As we descended to the lowlands, the long convoy of light trucks wending its way sluggishly down the narrow Zigzag Trail, most of us had a premonition of finality. I had lived seven of my ten years in the Philippine Islands in the Mountain Province, and my heart told me now that this was a last goodbye. Nothing was left to us but the memories of the delightful years of living; our home, possessions, income and savings were gone, along with the lovely Far Eastern things we had enjoyed accumulating. Now, we had only each other, and the hope of coming through alive so that a fresh start could be made somewhere else in the world. That was all, but it was enough. We were far past the stage of regretting lost material possessions; all we asked was to get out of the mess we were in—to see peace in the world—the end of war and enmity and the harshness of anger; to have all men free; to go home.

A gruesome moment on the mountain road shook us out of our pensive mood, when we passed one of the trucks that had been ahead of us. It had accidentally wedged itself under an overhanging cliff, and we realized with a shock that there had been a glimpse of a headless man still standing under the rock, decapitated when the truck jammed against the massive, sheer wall.

We were sitting in the back of the truck, bouncing about between suitcases and trying to dodge uncomfortable protuberances from those suspiciously bulging bedrolls. The lowland heat slowly wrapped itself about us as we neared the bottom of the trail, and we began shedding sweaters. No rest stops were allowed, and with alarm most of us began to detect a familiar discomfort in our interiors, and knew our first regrets for the unboiled sugar and yesterday's unaccustomed extra eating. Panic gripped us, as diarrhea threatened and the drivers refused to stop.

The town of Binalonan was our first stop, at long last, and here the trucks were unloaded, with Yamato explaining that a new convoy would carry on from here. We were dumped into a large dusty plaza, and after some persuasion the guards gave the women and children permission to go, a few at a time, across a field to a crumbling old Spanish church, apparently abandoned to the bats and weeds. It offered no privacy at all from the curious eyes of an entire Japanese garrison quartered nearby in a schoolhouse. By now our suspicions were confirmed, and we knew that nearly all of us were due for a siege with this dreaded and obnoxious physical problem, and we were frantic.

All the rest of the day we lounged in the baking plaza, fighting off the hordes of red ants and scratching their stinging bites, until in the late afternoon the Japanese Commandant arrived by car. After some palavering with him, Miss McKim dejectedly translated his command that we each were to at once make a bundle of a few necessities and start walking, as the relief trucks would not arrive until the next day. We were, he had coldly stated, to walk the rest of the way to Tarlac, some sixty kilometers—a feat he and we knew to be impossible. But we took our water bottles, mosquito nets and tins of food, and started with the guards trudging down the road— children, elderly ones and all.

This was an impasse undreamed of. Some of us were wearing *bakias*, and turned our ankles cruelly on the stony, rough road. No one had the strength to walk six kilometers, let alone sixty. The heat rose in suffocating waves, and our sweat-soaked clothes clung annoyingly to backs and legs. The sun was merciless. There were among us the frail; there was a solemn hush as we moved achingly toward an improbable goal. Oura dashed past us, back and forth, in his car, and we wondered if he were gloating.

We should never have been so gullible, after all our training, but we were too weary to think clearly. We knew our captors changed their course of action frequently, and they did it this time—unless, as some bitterly thought, the whole affair had been a silly hoax. We had plodded for only a short way when the guards were ordered to stop us, and we were directed into a grassy yard shaded by giant bamboos, where we flung down our loads and sank down to try to relax, to wait for the next vagary of our hosts. Half an hour later, the tropical rain that had threatened through the sultry afternoon came pouring down, driving us to the shelter of the old brick residence, vintage of Spanish times, now being used as a warehouse and at the moment filled with idle soldiers.

They were making tea over great open charcoal fires in the terrace (paved with once-exquisite, now broken and filthy, tiles still surviving from that luxurious olden time). So we motioned to them that we would like some of the boiling water to make coffee. Just as we were accomplishing this, Miss McKim arrived from another talk with the Commandant, and almost grimly announced that all the men were ordered to go at once back to the plaza to load the abandoned luggage onto the trucks which had just arrived. This was a frightening blow—it was not pleasant to be left without our men in the midst of the soldiers, but there was no help for it, so all save one young man who was just able to walk went off through the rain with Miss McKim. The soldiers paid little attention to us. We waited through the dragging minutes uncomfortably, praying for our safety and the protection of our men.

Finally the trucks rolled down the road and stopped in front of the old building, without the men! Oura drove up and motioned and screamed unintelligible commands to us, but we had no interpreter, and he was in a frothing rage before we understood that he meant us to load our bundles onto the trucks and climb on. With much difficulty we obeyed, for the trucks were high, and already stacked with luggage. We were deliberately slow, too, in a nervous dread that they might drive off with us, leaving our men behind. The men had apparently been rushed with their loading, for the conglomeration of suitcases, bedrolls, and market bags looked as though it had been thrown in helter-skelter, and we could do nothing to make it better. There were fewer trucks than before, too.

One of the women took this moment to break. She threw a tantrum. I missed the beginning of it, but hearing the commotion, I looked around and beheld a completely ludicrous, bizarre sight—the overwrought, petulant woman, too heavily laden with possessions she hadn't been able to bring herself to relinquish at the plaza, stumbling toward the truck, and Oura following her, black with anger, spanking her derriere with the flat of his sword! Her own blaze of temper dissolved into hysteria, and fear, and the rest of us were near that state ourselves as we watched incredulously and helplessly.

The men came toiling down the road and clambered onto the trucks, hungry, wet, and out of sorts. And there we sat, until darkness closed down, before a truck moved.

We were far more uncomfortable now than before. The luggage shifted badly, bruising and squeezing us as we perched precariously on top. The moon came up nearly full, and we could see as though it were day as we drove slowly southward, the convoy halting every few miles of the way, with the guards shouting to each other, relaying the orders from truck to truck. We weren't allowed to get off the trucks during these stops, and our demands and pleas for rest stops were disregarded, although even the guards could see that many were actively ill. Once we halted beside a high wall, and I made a desperate attempt. Taking a small girl who was near to tears in her trouble, I stepped from the truck to the wall, and headed for some tall shrubbery, but that moment Oura came by and saw me. He shrieked angrily, probably thinking we were trying to escape.

For hours we had been meeting Japanese troops moving north by the thousands, all on foot, pulling their equipment themselves on bull carts or *carromatas*, bicycles, and wheelbarrows. It was a silent, sinister flow, and strengthened our conviction that our move was a direct result of something important that was either happening now or about to happen. We could see them clearly, and they appeared to us as poor. Here and there, ineptly camouflaged beneath an empty native hut, there would be two or three small tanks, or stacks of ammunition and supplies. Occasionally planes flew over, and we held our breath wondering if they could be our own, spotting a nice fat convoy beneath for a bombing target.

In one place, in ghostly moonlight, two Japanese soldiers labored in a macabre struggle to get a bony horse on its feet, but the horse was dead. As we passed the airfields, we could see hundreds of wrecks pushed off to the edges, evidence of old and new bombing.

A new thrill was introduced near Manila when the truck drivers began succumbing to exhaustion and falling asleep at the wheel. Alarmed cries could be heard all along the line as one after another of the trucks careened crazily off to the edge of the road, but the drivers always managed to pull back just in time. The guards, too, seemed deathly weary, and slumped at their posts in the corners of the trucks, sleeping nearly all the way.

Since leaving the mountains, we had seen no Filipinos, and it seemed a queer, empty world, with all the roadside barrios silent and deserted or dark, there in the white light, the warm life of the native scene stilled. There were great holes in the paving of the highway, and the continual swerving to avoid them gave us a dizzy sensation, like *mal-de-mer*. Through a gritty haze of aching fatigue and pain, we kept a tense grip on the spirit of high adventure we wanted to feel, but the ravages of that long night were too severe.

The normally four-hour trip took us twenty-two hours of arduous, fretful travel, and we drove into Manila just as day was breaking. Still we wondered dully where we were being taken, though the bets were strongest on the Santo Tomas prison camp.

Instead, we by-passed the ancient university, but by just a few blocks—and stopped at last at the iron-bound gates in the gray walls of Bilibid Prison.

~ PART FOUR ~
BILIBID

Chapter 35:
THE GRIM, GRAY WALLS

And now, in distressing reality, we were in prison. Of all those in the Philippines, only old Fort Santiago itself could compare with the bleak grimness of Bilibid. Built in Spanish times, complete with dungeons and inner cells, it had been used until just before the war, when the New Bilibid Prison, a few kilometers outside Manila, had been completed. The order had been given by President Quezon to raze Old Bilibid, and the demolition had been started, to be halted again on that December day which the Japanese celebrated each year with shouts of "Banzai!" and bows toward their native land.

Of the main concrete building, the third story had been removed, leaving only the floor; all the plumbing was removed, and the bars and glass taken out of the windows, so that great gaping holes remained, with temporary covers of rusted, bent corrugated sheet iron. Where the third story had been, pieces of wooden support beams still stood, broken cross beams with jagged ends hanging loosely from them by a nail or two, and swinging in the breeze. Against a darkening sky, Bilibid was theatrically reminiscent of the setting for a horror movie.

The whole prison was surrounded by a high, thick concrete wall, with sentry boxes at the corners, and divided into a number of enclosed compounds. The courtyards were bare, hard dirt. A few beautiful old mango trees had survived neglect and the elements to bring a tiny hint of grace and cherished shade into the dreary aspect.

Bilibid had been filled with military prisoners of war since the Fall of Bataan in 1942. As we later learned, of the thousands of American G.I.'s who had been captured by the Japanese, all but 850 had died. Many who had survived, in spite of the cruelty of captivity and wretched conditions, had been shipped off to Japan, and many of those were lost at sea. Now one of the compounds, and the concrete former prison hospital, had been vacated for us, and into this stone-bound area we were unloaded on the morning of December 30, 1944.

The friends who had come down the day before met us with open arms and hot coffee at the very entrance, and hospital nurses stood ready as one woman after another descended from her cramped perch to collapse in tears or even unconsciousness as she attempted to stand. Almost oblivious to my surroundings, I found myself folded into the safe, loving haven of Mary Kneebone's thin arms, and she guided me up the front steps and into the building, then placed in my hands that wonderful cup of hot coffee. Then, with courage to look about, we took in the situation, while we compared notes with the first arrivals. We had been told not to bring our mattresses nor cots, that beds and mattresses would be provided. And there they were—the wooden frames and torn straw mats, indescribably filthy and disgustingly alive with vermin. There was no kitchen, no cooking utensils, no food.

A roof in the rear of the compound sheltered several open brick hearths, and there the internees were building bits of fires to boil water for coffee and tea. Two latrines had been dug and half enclosed in ragged *sawali* walls out in the courtyard. A spindly yard faucet or two brought brackish water for washing, and after prolonged boiling, drinking.

The back courtyard was a cemetery, filled with the graves of the former military prisoners who had died of starvation and disease, or had been executed—lines of bullet marks against the building's wall bore mute testimony to the history of murder there. The inside walls of the building were covered with penciled names of those who tried to leave some information behind for whoever might find it.

The place was filled with heartbreak.

As always, our first thought was to clean up, and as soon as our aching legs, spent bodies, and cramping stomachs would allow, we set about trying to do that. Our small, priceless bottles of creolin were unpacked, and we scrubbed clean spots on the concrete floor to lay our bedding, wherever we could find an unoccupied space, avoiding like death itself the crusted pads littering the foyer. Then men with handkerchiefs tied over their noses and mouths carried the offensive objects away. The Japanese captors refused permission for us to burn them, for they were the property of His Imperial Majesty, the Emperor of Japan. All we could do was dump them into the farthest corner of the compound.

Our General Committee met as soon as Phil arrived (Carl was delayed for several days while we fretted in our anxiety for him), to organize the "housing," sanitation, food supply and other vital matters. The Japanese failed consistently to cooperate, and we overcame our obstacles with enormous difficulty. By persistence that amounted to nagging, we got some cleaning materials, a cereal ration, latrines, and extra faucets installed for laundry. The covers over the windows were raised and propped open to let in the air and light, and we put whatever effort we could muster into "house-cleaning" for days.

All the families remained together; the only attempt at segregation was the assigning of unattached men to a small wooden building outside, and the single women to the central hall upstairs. Elsewhere men, women, and children were quartered together in the wing sections of the two floors of the building. The hospital was set up in a group of open cell blocks in the rear, and the remainder of those barred cages were appropriated by some of the prisoners for sleeping quarters.

Norman and I had pooled our small resources with the five Tongs (Walter, Peg, Eloise, Curt and Annarae) and Carl Eschbach, and we became then a permanent unit of eight, securing, preparing, and eating our food together, and sharing the work and our woes and triumphs like a family. It was relatively wonderful for the two of us—these dear people had become precious friends to us. We arranged our Spartan beds—two thin blankets and a sheet on the concrete, with the net tied a little above—in an area near what was obviously once a bathroom, but was now an open, roofless balcony. It gave us an outdoor living room, with a view of part of Santo Tomas, Quezon Boulevard, and the Tondo slum area. That was where we "lived."

The first night had been a revelation to me concerning bedbugs, which I thought I knew only too well from my education in Santo Tomas. We had foolishly made our bed on a wooden platform, thinking it would be less hard than the concrete. Even in the moonlight, I could see the little black specks moving around on the inside of the net, across my pillow and even over Norman's sleeping face. An hour of it was enough for me, and raw with scratching their bites, I retreated to the front steps for the rest of the night, while Norman slept soundly on, with never a bite on his body the next morning to verify my story, although the sheet was pocked with small blood spots.

Our men went right to work to devise furniture for us from the wire, pipe and boards found in junk piles left from the demolition, and charcoal stoves from large tins. We found charcoal in the cinder paths, and set up housekeeping anew, but without any of the little niceties we had been able to contrive at the Camp Holmes internment camp in Baguio.

This was life in the raw. Whatever our difficulties had been formerly, they were multiplied a hundred times now. Food rations from the Japanese guards had been halved again, and only the rice, sugar, *camotes* and peanut butter we had brought along against orders, and our few remaining tins of Red Cross food, kept us going. One of the Japanese was bribed or coaxed into engineering a truck of tiny "monkey" coconuts, which we could buy at fifty pesos each. So one day we would have rice with a grated coconut, and the next, rice with a four-ounce can of meat—for the eight of us.

From the food line, we received a hundred and fifty grams of cornmeal a day, alternating with rice every sixth meal. The only vegetable was steamy, gritty *camote* greens. Sourish soybean residue came to our mess from the guardhouse leftovers, and a nasty Japanese food called *mitsu*, from which gravy was made for the mush. Sometimes they sent cassava root instead of cornmeal or poor, fibrous purple *camotes*, and both of these raised havoc with our digestion, which was already touchy. Frequently, the servings of greens were almost too small to see. There was never any fruit.

If we had thought that we had no privacy before, now we learned what that really meant. It was impossible to dress and undress under the old standards of modesty, so we forgot them. Our first attempts at getting into our clothes under the precariously-hung mosquito nets disgusted us with their awkwardness, and after all, a mosquito net is hardly a screen. We emerged from those attempts steaming, disheveled, and cross, so that was abandoned. We simply assumed no one was looking, and I think that was true. The classic remark in our recollections was made by a weary Irishman to a complaining maiden lady who was sure he was "peeking" when he said, "Lady, even if you had a ham sandwich in your hand, I wouldn't be interested!"

At night, we lay within arm's reach of other people's beds on each side. We learned not to care—much. Sometimes, though, that closeness to sweaty, restless, uncomfortable humanity was the epitome of prison itself. There was no escape, no place to go, no fresh air, no space. The elderly man right next to our pad used a coffee can several times in the night to relieve himself. People snored or whispered or groaned. No one could really sleep much; it was as though the world were coming to an end. It was so dirty, so dingy and ugly and bleak. The nights were long, and filled with the longing to be free.

Latrines and shower rooms were both only casually screened with the coarse *sawali* wall, and completely open to the skies, so that the Japanese guards, or anyone on the second floor or roof of the building had an unobstructed view. Later, we partially remedied that when the men unearthed some huge pieces of filthy green mosquito bar to drape across the tops. The Japanese most indignantly protested that such use of His Imperial Highness's property was not dignified, and were only kept from confiscating the nets at once by being warned that dysentery, which they seemed to fear above all things, would surely run rampant if the latrines remained unscreened and open to the flies!

We washed ourselves the best we could, but the water was dirty, and we were dirty. I distinctly remember rolling the black dirt off my arms; feeling unclean, shabby, under-fed—exactly like the pictures of the impoverished people in the slums of the world. Now I knew how it felt. Now I knew.

Eight-year-old Curt Tong was given an extra portion of food one day by one of the guards, and hungry as he was, what he did was so poignant to me that I wept. He brought the morsel, intact, to our eight-member "family"—to share.

From the South Balcony, we could occasionally catch a glimpse of the military prisoners in the next compound, but efforts at communication—by printed signs and pantomime —were harshly squelched by guards on both sides of the wall. The distance was a little too great to permit positive recognition of the altered forms and faces except with the use of the one contraband pair of field glasses in our compound, which were used cautiously but almost constantly, especially after a young war widow among us discovered her father in the ragged, tragic group across the wall!

We simply could not ignore the sordid details of this phase of our prison life, the degradation of our physical existence, and the danger signals. How tenuous was our hold at this time on the present, much less the future. This was a dark portrait, without any outward sign of grace—but the grace of spirit was still there, and laughter and courage and optimism were not noticeably diminished. And the contrast, the reason, was that we actually began to feel at this time and in this place an unbounded elation that lifted our lives above the hardships from the day we were trucked back to Manila, into this stark prison. Pain is more memorable than pleasure, and our time at Bilibid is a harsh recollection—yet the thrill of what happened there lives on, too. The grim, gray walls are only a backdrop for a kaleidoscope of excitement, breathless expectation, and hope!

Chapter 36:
CRESCENDO

While we were still scrubbing our knuckles raw to remove the crust of contaminated filth from the tough concrete, before we had eaten our first meal at Bilibid, we had the answer to our despair. For the air above us became filled with vibrant sound, and we crowded to the gaping windows to see great silver-winged bombers and their lethal escort of fighters piercing through the overcast, headed north with the grace and speed of swallows—<u>our</u> planes, bent on destroying the forces that held us captive and blighted the lovely land, intimidated and corrupted our Philippine friends, spoiled China, brought to ruin Java and all the other helpless little countries inundated in their terrible siege.

Every day those planes came, in greater and greater numbers, often pausing over the city to drop their bombs unerringly on ammo dumps, airfields, arsenals, and ships in the Bay. Then the Navy dive-bombers went to work, and day after day they pounded at Grace Park, where Japanese planes crumpled to wreckage on the field as the deadly little ships flew over, then peeled off with rhythmic regularity one by one into a breathtaking dive, almost to the ground. Then each plane would fling itself back to the sky like a bird, circle to its place in the formation, and dive again! We hung out the window, forgotten plates of rice clutched in sweating hands, gasping in terror as it seemed that nothing could ever pull out again from that precipitate downward rush—then letting out our breaths in a long sigh of relief as each one did come up, every time. The crashing of their bombs and spitting bark of strafing guns kept us spellbound.

Antiaircraft fire spotted the sky about the formation of planes at first from all directions, and rained sharp bits of metal and stone into the courtyard and onto the roof, then with robot precision, one after another of the nests was silenced by our bombing. Once, in all the times we were observing, so closely that no detail could be missed, one of our planes was hit, and exploded there in the air. With wet eyes, we saw the pieces float lightly to the ground, and three parachutes open and drift slowly downward. We prayed from our hearts that the boys could be rescued, and tried to console the children who cried bitterly over the beautiful plane that they felt they themselves had lost.

Parts of Manila began to burn again. Great explosions shook the earth when oil dumps, gasoline storage tanks and stores of ammunition fell to those plunging, deadly-accurate missiles. Every night we stood on the balcony and watched great bubbles of flame rise and explode from gas fires. Tondo burned, and we could see the flames sweep through that crowded slum, envelop and consume the railroad yards, smolder and leap again. Flashes of light and the distant rumbling of big guns came to us from the East, where sporadic fighting began to develop into importance between impatient guerilla forces and the enemy.

After dark, a lone, rackety-sounding Japanese plane "hedge-hopped" across the rooftops of the city, its red tail light blinking like a drugged firefly—and no other aircraft of theirs did we see or hear for weeks.

Down the street a radio blared a news broadcast nightly, and we gathered in dead silence, even contriving an ear-trumpet from an old tin light shade for a greater concentration of the elusive words, catching now and then: "landing"—"raid"—"Cavite." We wrung our hands in our desperate desire to piece together those snatches of sentences, to know what was happening! What we were witnessing we knew must be but a piece of the whole. Where were we landing? Commando raids, or bombing raids? What kind were they? <u>What</u> about Cavite, just a few miles from us? Was that where the counter offensive was beginning? The tantalizing fragments could not be fitted into a pattern, and we were beside ourselves with our desire for news.

Two nights we lay rigid, listening to what must have been the wholesale evacuation of all the Japanese forces from Manila, going North. Did that mean we were using their own tactics and landing at Batangas, Antimonan, Legaspi? Then, a few days later, the trucks were heard rumbling back again, and the tanks, and the sharp rhythm of marching feet. Now what? Oh, the suspense of those moments! What did it matter that we staggered when we stood up too suddenly; that knees, ankles and wrists were swelling until the skin about them was taut; or that dengue fever was already epidemic? We were so caught up in the suspense and bewilderment and mad conjecturing that we simply ignored those inconveniences.

The General Committee office work was more demanding than ever before. We cleared a space near the entrance to the foyer, and there, amid the turmoil of coming and going, children playing about us, far too accessible to the people to know uninterrupted moments, our Committee carried on the anxious work of internment Camp management, and hurried to write the finishing chapters to the official history they had been compiling for months. Meetings, for the sake of privacy and concentration, were held on our balcony. Occasionally there, too, Carl Eschbach and others had important conferences with a friendly member of the Japanese staff who came with us from Camp Holmes, Masaki. But one day, word was received from him that the friendly little enemy had been denied entrance, and we knew he was in serious trouble for our sakes.

We missed Masaki, for he it was who brought us the first news of the formidable American landing at Lingayen (a few hours north of us) only a week after it happened, and during the next few days kept us posted as well as he could on what was happening up there. Now we looked always to the North, and blessed the balcony for its direction.

Commandant Oura, incensed at us as usual for everything we did, objected now to our watching the planes, and ordered the window flaps closed and all holes overlooking the street below to be boarded up, then ruled we must stay away from any window or doorway during raids. So we crouched below the sills, or stood back out of the sight of the sentries, but watched however and whenever we could.

A new commander was assigned to us, superior to the blundering lieutenant, with the rank of major. His name, Ebiko, meant, oddly enough, "Son of a Lobster," and was translated by some of the internees with a slight substitution for "lobster." We saw little of him, and Oura still stomped through the compound in fractious cognizance of the non-bowing. One day, his temper flew completely out of control, and with his sword he slashed down all the clotheslines, just to show us, I guess. He then came raging into the office and told Carl that from then on, anyone who didn't bow would be beaten. He forbade any cooking, and we in the office kept a sharp eye on the gate so that when he or Yamato appeared, we could send out the warning for all hot plates to be out of sight.

The Baguio garrison had been replaced largely by husky Taiwanese, and there were a third at least as many of them as of us. Under the cool surveillance of Japanese officers, they stalked their beats in deadpan remoteness. But when they were unobserved, they manifested a clumsy friendliness that was a welcome relief, even sharing tidbits with the children. Sometimes it was fine white sugar, or a can of milk, or a piece of fruit; much oftener it was a plate of exotic Oriental stew that made us shudder with distaste, but we tried everything, and if it weren't tainted, let the children have it as their constant uncomplaining hunger was a quivering pain to us. They, like the adults, were looking fine-drawn, and were almost too docile, too quiet.

Then, on a day near the end of January, 1945, I was typing in the office nook when a shattering roar brought me to my feet with a dizzying jerk. Everyone rushed heedlessly to the doorways and windows, and we had an instant's glimpse of two small planes, gorgeously marked with that beautiful star, hurtling across the prison, scattering the pebbles from the roof, so close were they—and gone almost before we knew they were there, so fast were they flying.

These were the first low-flying planes of ours that we had seen, and this was almost too exciting to bear. I rushed back to my typewriter, inserted a fresh sheet of paper, and in a few minutes had a new notice for the bulletin board, to remain there just long enough to be read, for it was not for Japanese eyes: "NOTICE: It is officially confirmed—they were our planes!" Always the thought came to us—maybe this is the beginning of our rescue.

Carl told me that the Japanese had requested a list of ten of the outstanding men in the internment Camp—outstanding, that is, not only for their position within the Camp, but for what they had been, or achieved, and their position in their communities prior to the war. His name, and Phil's, were to head the list. A few words of description or explanation were to be given concerning each of the men. He had no idea what it was all about, but with grave reluctance we complied, listing a retired American Army colonel (quite elderly), the superintendents of two of the Baguio gold mines, a former governor of the Mountain Province, the dentist, a doctor, and two others. We submitted the list, and thought it strange that we heard nothing more about it—then.

The General Committee was feeling more deeply than ever its responsibility for the safety of the people, and held frequent lengthy meetings on the balcony, guarded by Peg Tong from the encroachment of idly curious internees or the surprise of unscheduled Japanese inspections. They discussed in keen seriousness what safety rulings they could make and enforce. The subject of possible street fighting, which the Japanese in off-the-record conversations said would never happen, or a revengeful attack by the guards, or even shelling and bombing of the prison wall, were scrutinized in every imaginable aspect, and plans were laid for coordinating our actions with Santo Tomas and the military prisoners in the next compound.

The internees were quietly informed, a section at a time, of what action would or might be taken in several eventualities. Tension mounted. More men were added to the emergency group, and instructions and precautions were detailed for everyone to read. What else could we do? Beyond these steps, it seemed there was literally nothing <u>any</u> of us could do, except hold to the faith that had kept us safe this far. We watched, and listened, and prayed, and talked quietly among ourselves.

Yamato appeared, like the guards, with a net over his newly-acquired helmet, and an absurd camouflage of *camote* vines trailing from it down his back and shoulders. This was funny enough to make us forget a little our nervous preoccupation, especially when impudent children followed him plucking the leaves from the stems.

A woman's scream sent our hearts into our throats and we ran to the courtyard to find only that one of the girls had caught and killed, to her own intense and horrified amazement, an enormous rat. Screams, tears, temperament—they couldn't be tolerated at this moment.

Soy beans were substituted in our diet for part of the cereal ration, and we almost enjoyed the change until their unfamiliar fat content sent us racing to the latrines.

It was nip and tuck now whether a new baby or the American rescue would get there first, and the mother lay sweating in misery in the hospital, a victim of dysentery. None of the chronic invalids had succumbed from the move, but some were day by day sinking, and doctors were beset with anxiety. One young woman had become a living skeleton, and weighed only fifty-seven pounds. Men were gaunt, hollow-cheeked. A blonde English girl with a hyphenated name and blasé manner stood behind a chair, gripping the back firmly, and without a sedative or a tear had a troublesome tooth pulled. The little American flag so laboriously sewn by all the women of the internment Camp—wrongly once, and the error had been spotted by a Scotswoman—lay in readiness, for we thought we'd be needing it soon.

And it was, suddenly, the third day of February, 1945.

Kaito was in full uniform these days, swanking about with his long sword and big revolver, burnished belt and shoes and helmet, but his young face was haggard the night of the third, and he sank informally onto the edge of Miss McKim's pad, in the lower hall, as though it were a relief to talk a little there with her. They discussed a few matters rather absently, then she queried casually, "Tell me, Kaito San, where are the Americans today?" He rubbed his hand distractedly over his face before replying, but said without reserve, "They are at Tarlac. Two, three days, perhaps, and they will be here."

We were eating our supper on the balcony when we saw our observation planes, half a dozen or so of them, flying low and slow over the streets, leisurely—or was it sinisterly? As though by the magic of a conjurer, a crowd of Filipinos appeared in the street beyond the prison, and moved *en masse* like sleep walkers in the direction from which the planes had come. Forks clattered to the table, and we rose, bemused, eating forgotten. Milling restlessly about from window to window with the crowd, I found myself at the other balcony, and leaned through the window space. Then a cry tore from my throat—for rolling down Quezon Boulevard, a few blocks away, were enormous tanks—and they were firing at the buildings along the way, and being fired at. Excitement

snatched me from the window and sent me racing, weakness
forgotten, through the building to find Norman, shouting like
a mad thing, "American tanks! American tanks! Out there—
the biggest things I ever saw!"

Everyone heard, and thronged to look. And Kaito heard,
as he was worriedly muttering his "two, three days"—and
blanched to ivory pallor. He jumped to his feet, crying in
his own tongue, "<u>How</u> can they be here?" and ran from the
building.

Up to the forbidden roof surged the men, then back down
again, beads of sweat gleaming on their foreheads, laughing wildly as they told us "We heard a voice, yelling, 'Hey,
Harvey, I thought you knew this Goddam town. Where in
hell are we?' and another guy answer, 'Well, hell, I do know.
We just took the wrong turn back there.' Those were American voices, and that was good ol' American cussing! This is
it, gals!"

Then, as anyone would tell you, everything broke loose
in Manila. Machine guns, grenades, bazookas, mortars, rifles,
big tank guns—they all blurted their deadly fire into the
streets. Across the alley from us, an ammunition dump in an
old frame house was set afire and filled the night with explosions and a lurid glare. Shouts, running feet, and rumbling
wheels swelled the din.

Bullets ricocheted against the building and whanged off
the window flaps, and the men rushed us down to the first
floor ordering us to "get down and stay down!" The Taiwanese guards, looking ferocious and inhuman, came
through the foyer, their boots ringing hard on the concrete,
and the passage way was quickly cleared ahead of them.
We saw in horror that they carried "Molotov cocktails"—
beer bottles filled with gasoline. They tramped up the stairs
to the roof. Our men, making a quick survey of outside
conditions, reported that a drum of gasoline had been rolled
in front of the gate. Our position seemed to become every
second more dangerous. But we were past caring.

We couldn't keep ourselves down. Only when a burst of
firing sounded as though it were on our very doorstep did

we duck behind the low concrete partitions that divided the sides of the foyer into sections. As the endless, horrendous night wore on, lagging second by second, children drooped in spite of themselves, and hasty forays were made by volunteers to the second floor to get nets and pillows, and the sleepy, weary babes were bedded down to sleep in the ceaseless noise of the battle. Occasionally, when even the tremendous stimulation couldn't stiffen sagging knees and tired backs, an adult would slip under the net with the little sleepers for a few minutes' rest, but we couldn't sleep or lie still, and out we'd crawl again, to watch the leaping flames and the white burst of shells.

The excitement roused our appetites to the pitch of torture, and during a breathless lull, two of us scuttled to our "larder," producing the last can of salmon and a tin of hash, which we opened and ate by the spoonful—manna from heaven. One of the men even slipped out to the kitchen and crouching involuntarily from the sound of whizzing bullets outside the wall, and the rain of shrapnel on the iron roof of the kitchen, made coffee. For a little while, we stood around the old piano, with a dim candle shaded almost completely, and ate and drank—it was wonderful.

The nurses and doctors, and volunteer assistants, carried on the work of the hospital, remaining with the nervous sick people, aiding them in total darkness when they called, standing by intrepidly.

All through the night, alternating crews of men fanned a fire in a charcoal stove there in the midst of us to keep heat under a hospital sterilizer filled with all the soy beans we had left—tomorrow we'd eat, if we were alive!

It was a scene from Dante, there in the foyer: long shadows dissecting the bodies of gaunt, half-clad people sprawled on the bare concrete floor, or standing in clusters about the stark pillars; flushed children sleeping in their parents' arms or under crookedly-tied nets; the squatting men, their small flame hot on their perspiring faces, stoking and fanning like gnomes about a witches' fire; white-faced nurse's aides, coming in for an hour's relief. A dull, crimson glow, murky with smoke, highlighted faces and gesturing hands—now there was no other light. Outside, it was all livid flashing and the thundering bedlam of war.

Kaito came in, near midnight, and with an awkward "bygones-be-bygones" air, offered his hand to a few of the General Committee, saying goodbye, then was gone. Yamato followed, and bowed ceremoniously in his farewells to many—but he was to be seen once more, in the final act.

When the whiteness of dawn finally broke through, we dared to venture forth to the latrines, each adult with a child by the hand, whether his own or just one that happened to be near, and to consider breakfast, which the cooks somehow prepared, sketchily but undauntedly. We took advantage of every lull to go up to the second floor, ostensibly to get something we needed, but actually to <u>see</u>.

A mortar shell burst within the courtyard, singeing someone's washing still hanging forgotten on the clothesline, and leaving one woman gasping because where it burst, she had been standing only a moment before. Fragments littered the yard, illustrating vividly enough the danger of lingering out of doors. A small boy picked up some harmless-looking object and brought it into the building, and for the next fifteen minutes the Safety Committee grimly fought small phosphorous fires and the child and his playmates were smeared with soothing ointments and their spreading burns bandaged.

Still we were wondering what was next, and not until ten o'clock did we receive a clue. This was Sunday morning, February 4th. We couldn't begin to picture what this day would bring. But at ten, Carl Eschbach was sent for by the Commandant, Major Ebiko—Oura had been among the ships that passed in the night, apparently. There at the outside office, Carl met for the first time the Commanding Officer of the military prisoners, a cadaverous colonel who, as highest ranking officer among the prisoners, was their leader and spokesman.

To these two men, Ebiko made a terse speech, and delivered the final literary effort of Mr. Yamato—the "Liberation Paper" with a crossed-off date of January 7 above the current one of February 4.

At eleven, Carl returned to our compound, and sent word to have all internees gather at once in the foyer. We waited in an unbreathing hush while the guards marched, two by two, through the midst of us, their rifles lowered and faces blank, out the front door forever, as quietly as that. Then Carl stood up on the desk, and in his clear, mellow voice, read to us what was on that paper:

MESSAGE

1. The Japanese Army is now going to release all the prisoners of war and internees here on its own accord.

2. We are assigned to another duty and shall be here no more.

3. You are at liberty to act and live as free persons, but you must be aware of probable dangers if you go out.

4. We shall leave here foodstuffs, medicines and other necessities of which you may avail yourselves for the time being.

5. We have arranged to put up sign-board at the front gate, bearing the following context—

Lawfully released Prisoners of War and Internees are quartered here. Please do not molest them unless they make positive registance [sic].

When he had finished, there were cheers and tears, and a husky attempt at singing "God Bless America" and "Star-Spangled Banner." Our glorious home-made flag was at last produced, and run up on the flagpole. The chapter of our imprisonment was officially closed. In prison we certainly still were, unguarded and in danger; the future was no more

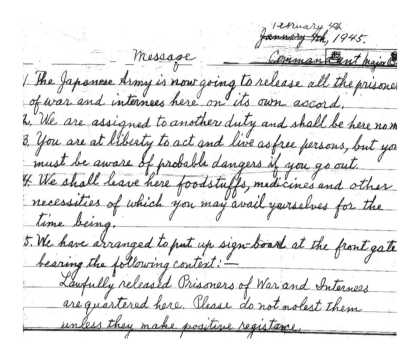

February 4th
~~January 7th~~, 1945.

_____ _Message_ _____ Commandant Major

1. The Japanese Army is now going to release all the prisoners of war and internees here on its own accord.

2. We are assigned to another duty and shall be here no m

3. You are at liberty to act and live as free persons, but you must be aware of probable dangers if you go out.

4. We shall leave here foodstuffs, medicines and other necessities of which you may avail yourselves for the time being.

5. We have arranged to put up sign-board at the front gate bearing the following content: —

   Lawfully released Prisoners of War and Internees are quartered here. Please do not molest them unless they make positive resistance.

certain than it had been ten minutes before. But we were our own again, not captives—free of bondage. Free. What a word. What a thought. Thirty-seven months for me— longer for some, less for others. And we had survived, to be _free_ again. God bless America!

The rest of that incredible Sunday we waited. Carl called upon the colonel, and they discussed and rejected the immediate possibility of contact with Santo Tomas officials. It would be rash to attempt to leave the prison. Incidentally, the colonel asked that we lower the flag we had so proudly raised, as it was endangering us all—a target not to be resisted by the enemy all around us. The neighborhood was filled with the Japanese, and the sight of the Stars and Stripes was sure to draw fire into the prison. So we hung it in the center of the foyer, and beamed upon it each time we passed. The gates between the two compounds were opened, and in the first hour some of the men from both our civilian internment Camp and the military prison Camp passed through it, to mingle and get acquainted, but the military prisoners were under strict martial law by their commander, and indiscriminate visiting was not allowed.

We kept away from windows upstairs, but from a safe distance back, strained to see what we could. When action came too close, we were called below again. That day, February 4, 1945, has become to me now a hazy dream of emotion and suspense, complicated by a hangover from sleeplessness, utter weariness, and hunger. From the moment of liberation until nine that night, memory lends me only sketches. About dark, Carl Eschbach was again in the other compound, and we were waiting for him to return to see what news he could bring. He came back and set us tingling with his story:

"I was talking to the colonel and some other officers when there was a loud pounding on the front gate from outside, and a voice called out, 'Hey, howdya get in there?' A prisoner shouted back, 'What we want to know is howdya get out of here?' The voice outside asked 'Who are you, in there?' The prisoner answered 'Prisoners of War.'

"Then heartily, with laughter and excitement, but huskily, too, the one on the outside said, 'Oh, no, you're not. We're here now! Help me get this damned gate open, will you?' And then he came in—a young fellow—major, I think, so strong and confident, and he almost broke our hands shaking them. He said the First Cavalry had forcibly liberated Santo Tomas the night before, but didn't know where the military prisoners were—and he was dumbfounded when I told him about the civilians being here, too. His own outfit, the Ohio 37th, has surrounded the prison, and they are our liberators!"

Half an hour later, we had our own thrill, when our outside gate resounded to exuberant knocking. Internees rushed to remove the cross bar and swing back the creaking great doors, and two big soldiers walked in. We engulfed them, and listened raptly as they told us how they came to be there. They had hiked at double time all the way down from Tarlac in a race to get to us, and were sweat-soaked and dirty, but looked so huge and magnificent, even in their bone weariness, that we could barely refrain from clinging bodily to that vitality and assurance.

The following day at Camp Bilibid was filled with American GI's, and outside the walls five great tanks came to rest. We tore down the view-obstructing curtains and barriers ordered by the Japanese, and hung from every window and balcony to wave at and call to the troops in the streets below, and they returned the greetings enthusiastically. It was overwhelming; we were not sensible; filled with joy and gratitude and so tired we didn't know what we were doing.

Shots would ring out, and we ducked below the walls quickly, but just for a few moments. We proudly spotted a sniper in a church tower, and reported him. Cold terror clutched us once again as we sat watching the street when Peg's face turned white, and with a scream she threw herself flat, crying "There's a sniper in that window across the street—he pointed his gun right at me!" She had looked down that threatening rifle barrel for a startled instant before she realized that he was aiming directly at her. Soldiers rushed to the house, and uncovered a sniper's nest there. All the houses along the street were cleaned out and occupied, and our own GI's were blessedly covering every bit of the old stone wall—how great that protection seemed to us!

From quite early that morning, the downtown section had been another focus of interest. We were certain that all the big buildings must be filled with Japanese, for they were under heavy fire from our guns. But one by one, they seemed now to be bursting into sudden flame, and we understood that the Japanese themselves were firing them, probably first saturating them with gasoline. It became a terrible spectacle, as the ocean breeze fanned the fire into a roaring holocaust and flung it across the skyline. Brilliant embers were carried from one street to the next.

Soon we could think of nothing else, for it was only a short distance away, and we could feel the heat and see and hear the crackling timbers fall away. What could ever stop such a tremendous blaze in a dry, wooden city? What was there possibly able to prevent its devouring all of Manila?

The street-fighting, heavy gunfire, and burning towers made a spectacle unbelievable and horrifying. Beautiful Manila—Pearl of the Orient—city of flowers: orchids, hibiscus, gardenias—and broad avenues and flame trees—what would be left? And what would happen now?

By eight o'clock, through the darkness we could see all too plainly that the fire had moved perceptibly much closer to us; at eight-thirty, we received the word that we were to be evacuated—to pack only what we must have, for the men would have to walk part of the way to our destination and carry the suitcases. This was war, and there were few extra trucks to be commandeered from the troop movements. Some of us had already made preliminary preparations, expecting that something like this would be necessary.

Carl and Phil were both gone, inopportunely delayed at an initial conference at Santo Tomas, so I hastily packed our bag, then hurried to the office to collect what I thought was most vital to be saved from our internment Camp records, turned some of them over to General Committee members and carried the rest. I also remembered, for a wonder, to provide myself and Dr. Skerl with copies of the internment Camp roster—and it was not two hours before I was asked for that list by an American Army officer.

By nine o'clock our gate was opened, and a long procession of stretchers, manned by the 37th Division GI's who had liberated us, gave us our first startling glimpse of the rest of the boys on the other side of the wall. By nine-thirty, every person of the thirteen hundred and seventeen former Bilibid prisoners was outside, the military prisoners loaded onto trucks and gone. Our men, under heavy escort, started off on foot down the luridly lit street; and we women and children lined up in the alley at the south entrance, waiting for the trucks and jeeps that quickly assembled to remove us.

The fire was actually just across the street from the prison by this time. The soldiers were in a sweat of anxiety to get us out of there, away from the roaring, onrushing blaze, and the constant danger of sniping from dark windows and alleys. But they were inexpressibly tender and sweet, lifting us each one so gently, holding the small children close against them for a moment; smiling radiantly and answering our warm gratitude with "Oh, thank <u>you</u>, ma'am. This is the first pleasant thing that's happened to me in two years!"

Then through the streets we sped, and everywhere the crowds of Filipinos cheered and waved, and threw kisses at us, like a New York victory parade. The streets were filled with American military personnel posted to guard our progress, and <u>they</u> waved and smiled and shouted. Warmth and a kind of joyousness welled up in us—that wonderful sensation of being wanted and loved, after the years of hostility and coldness. Here we were the very center of affectionate, delighted friendliness, and we loved every one of those fighting boys who thought nothing was too much to do for us, and who fell all over themselves to offer the tiniest service. It made us feel humble, and proud. And all this time we were riding through that crazy scene of destruction and fear and danger, guarded on every side, but vulnerable as never before in our lives.

Then Ang Tibay! This was an abandoned shoe factory just outside of town, at that moment being used for United States Army Headquarters, our immediate destination. Willing hands and smiling faces of hundreds of GI's in battle clothes reached up to us as we stopped at the old frame building. In former years, we had passed this building so many times without a glimmer of premonition of its place in our destinies. The soldiers took us up to an open, rickety balcony, and we found gracious guides to warn us that the bathrooms did not work, and they were "mighty sorry but the latrines aren't finished yet, but they will be really soon;" that there would be coffee and tea in a few minutes; that there was more room farther on. They sought out the children and loaded them with candy and gum, and one husky Adonis flashed a white smile of pure love at me and asked me if <u>I</u> could use a Hershey bar!

The internee men arrived soon after we did, for our trucks had hurried right back for them, and they had walked only a few blocks. Norman came up the stairs grinning like the storybook Cheshire cat, our suitcase carried as lightly as a pound of butter on the broad shoulders of the uniformed lad with him. Norman told me that when the soldier had picked up the suitcase, he had protested that he'd carry it himself, and they had a laughing tug-of-war before the matter was settled by the big youngster simply taking it away from my husband and starting off with it. The Tongs and we found a spot to lay our sheets and to string our nets, had some hot coffee, and were wandering about in a gleeful haze, chattering with our friends, hearing only faintly the boom of the mammoth explosions to the south of us.

Norman and I sauntered over to the rail of the balcony, and leaned against it carelessly for a moment, then broke off our happy, weary talk abruptly. There below us, in the pallid glare of unshaded lights, was a scene that time can never erase from memory—the eight hundred and fifty Bilibid Prisoners of War, survivors of the infamous Bataan Death March—men twisted, maimed, starved; some delirious with fever, and some hopelessly mad. They had been strong, robust and young only three years ago, like the brown and ruddy soldiers hovering so solicitously over them. Now they were wrecks, ghosts, all that was left, rejected even by the enemy—and they merely sat on the edge of their cots with bent shoulders and empty eyes, or lay in pain-filled torpor, their bodies meatless skeletons or thick with the hideous swelling of chronic malnutrition.

A few of them wandered about, nibbling indifferently at the "emergency ration" chocolate given them, or fumbled awkwardly with stiff fingers to open a clean, new package of cigarettes. On one cot, two crippled young men with old, sad faces sat playing a game with thick oily cards, careless of their fate or the moment's importance. A psychotic broke away from his attendants and danced erratically out onto the floor before he was captured and subdued again by compassionate medics. A perfectly bald man directly under us sat erect on his cot and rubbed the naked stumps of his two legs.

When we could no longer bear to look, we turned away, keeping close together, and my husband said huskily to me,

"My God, honey, compared to them, we've just been on a three-year picnic!"

It was three in the morning before we settled down for rest. Wildest rumors had been floating through our people—the old Bilibid prison, as the Army had suspected, had been mined. When the fire reached it, had blown up. No, it hadn't blown up, but it had been looted. It was Santo Tomas that had blown up when the fire reached it. The Japanese were counterattacking. The Japanese were coming toward us from the North. And so it went, each story more sensational than the last.

A few hours earlier, at midnight, we had gone down to the front of the building to hear our first "Stateside"news broadcast, telling us about the invasion of Manila, ending with a throat-filling "Star-Spangled Banner." Shortly after that, Walter and Peg and their children and we opened two four-ounce tins of ham and eggs, the last of the kit, and ate them right down, not even considering tomorrow's and the next day's meals. Then, with two sleepless nights behind us, and another nearly gone, we lay down upon the wooden floor, and fitfully dozed, too exhausted to even rest, until daybreak.

In the morning, we women felt a new urge to look presentable, and painted our lips and cheeks with the stubs of lipstick we still had, and combed our hair into a semblance of order. Then, with little Annarae Tong, I went to seek Norman, who had not waited for my vanity to satisfy itself.

Outside the building was a sprawling, bustling United States Army camp, mushroomed overnight into being. Generals MacArthur and Kreuger were both said to be there, in an office or residence building appropriated for headquarters. Trucks, tanks, and "ducks"—which of all the new equipment astounded us most—lined the highway beyond and filled our side road. Soldiers were everywhere, with grins and cheery greetings, and affectionate pats for the lovely child with me.

I was thinking hard about a cup of coffee, and someone told me that it was around somewhere, so we started a little private hunt. Walking into a likely-looking machine shop, we found a smiling GI, who without asking, handed Annarae a canteen cup of milk—real milk. Her brown eyes sparkled, and she tipped the big container up, and literally absorbed that cupful. It was empty when she lowered it and handed it back, with a beatific expression and white mustache, to the touched soldier. He cleared his throat, then asked her, "Well, look, do you think you could use a refill?" Her little head bobbed emphatically—she could, and did.

Both of us smiled until our faces hurt over her contentment as we wandered a little farther along, and then saw Norman. The three of us stopped to talk to a group of soldiers beside a giant tank. They asked if there were anything they could do for us, and when we mentioned coffee, produced at once canteen cups filled to the brim with a scalding, delicious brew, which we sipped cautiously while we stood and visited eagerly with them. Then <u>we</u> asked what we could do for them, and one after another, they gave us their names and asked us to write "Mom," when we got home, just to tell where we saw them and that they were fine—and right then, they did look it. This was the start of a long list that every internee soon carried—our one sincere, if infinitesimal, gesture toward expressing our gratitude to our rescuers.

Breakfast was very late, but left us almost overcome by its bountifulness, and we couldn't begin to eat up our servings. Then there was lunch soon after, and our shrunken stomachs warned us about the dangers of overeating—when we disregarded the warnings, we were sick; then when that was over, we ate some more, and through the hot day, drank quarts of the reconstituted lemonade that is part of the army rations.

Late in the afternoon, Dr. Skerl made the official announcement to us that we would be returned to Bilibid in the evening, and brought us the news that one of last night's rumors had been all too well founded. The prison had been thoroughly checked, and no mines were found. The fire had abated, and was no longer dangerous to the prison. Santo Tomas was intact and had never been threatened. But Bilibid had been looted, and he warned us to expect the worst.

Carl arrived before we left, with a case of milk! He had been as anxious about us as we were concerning him, but he was filled with satisfaction over the arrangements they were making to feed us, and called a short informal meeting of our General Committee to divulge what he had learned. He spoke sadly of the internees at Santo Tomas, saying they seemed in bad condition, and told us about the loss of Carroll Grinnell and Mr. Duggleby and others, and described the thrilling capture of that internment Camp by our forces. Phil had gone on over to Bilibid to await us there.

The Army waited until nearly dark to return us to the city, and it was an uneasy trip. Snipers fired on the lead trucks, and they were forced to turn back so that the whole convoy was held up until the way was cleared again. We felt singularly exposed in the big open trucks, which weren't speeding as they had in the darkness of the night before, but eased along warily; but our elation still bubbled over and smothered the unease of that dangerous hour.

There were no lights in the prison, and strictest blackout was in force for our protection, but in the light of the full moon, we could get an impression of utter chaos. The smell of souring rice and of smoke made the building insufferably close, and everywhere we stepped we could feel paper, mattress stuffing, and slippery gooiness under our feet. With sticks and our feet, we gingerly pushed back the wreckage to clear a bed space, and tried for a little sleep on the bare concrete, knowing that the next day was going to call for all our strength and resources. I giggled sillily once in the night, thinking what "shipwrecked Kellys" we always seemed to be these days, and Norman chuckled wryly beside me at our foolishness. My hip bones were bruising themselves on the concrete, and it was truly impossible to rest in any position. But still, we were actually <u>all right!</u>

We did sleep a little, and when we awakened, bruised and stiff again from our stony bed, it was to a scene of complete shambles. The looters had done their work thoroughly and well. Not one object in the prison had escaped their wanton vandalism. Clothes, food, and anything else that was perceived to have any value was gone. Papers, books, diaries and pictures were torn up and strewn everywhere; mattresses and pads, what few there were, had been ripped open for hidden money, I suppose, and *kapok* was stuck to everything. The remnants of Monday's unfinished supper glued the whole mass together. In the office, the records we hadn't saved were ruthlessly torn and scattered; hundreds of aspirin and sulpha tablets had been dumped out of their containers onto the floor.

The first part of that day was spent going through the gummy trash for pictures, which had been ripped from their frames and discarded, and any small possessions rejected as worthless but still of some use or value to us. While we were deep in the mess, word came that General MacArthur and General Kreuger and their staff members had arrived to greet us, so we stretched wearily, wiped off our hands and our sweaty brows, and trudged off to see the great men.

MacArthur's strong face was glowing with satisfaction and his real emotion, as he cried *"Mabuhay."* We applauded and waved—they were our rescuers—but at that moment, we may not have responded with our later-felt enthusiasm even to the hero of the Pacific, so disgusted were we with the wreckage about us. They were so clean!

When they were gone, we pushed what was left into big piles, and the men carried it out in stretcher loads, to burn in the yard.

And now began a strange interlude in our lives that is hard to put into words. The battle of Manila raged all about us; in fact, we were in the dead center of the conflict, with our American heavy artillery to the north, firing on the Japanese positions across the Pasig River to the south of us, and the enemy fire responding across our very heads. At first we winced and ducked at the white blinding flashes, followed by a tremendous roar, and the great shells passing swiftly overhead, like the sound of freight trains, we said. Then we learned to take that in our stride, and ceased even the involuntary upward glance that strove to see the shivery rustle of those projectiles.

Sometimes the shells fell short, and burst so near that we crouched without thinking. A mortar battery within the same block with us pounded incessantly at targets beyond. We could see the shells for an instant as they rose from the tube. From the south balcony, our view of the battle-scene across the river was unobstructed, and the heart-rending destruction of the beautiful city was being accomplished while we watched dazed, numb.

Early one morning, a lone Japanese plane sneaked in and dropped one bomb, squarely on the tanks outside our wall, bulging the thick concrete and startling us almost out of our senses. It gave us plenty of thinking to do, too, about the consequences had that aim been not quite so good, for a hit five feet to the left would have been tragic for many internees. Even as it was, gratitude for the narrow escape was marred by our grief when we learned that four tank crew boys had been killed. Thereafter, the unearthly "Black Widow" radar planes patrolled the skies all night, and we had nightmares and restless half-waking dreams that the droning motors we heard were Japanese again. [Even yet, the sound of a single small plane has for me a vaguely upsetting effect.]

It seemed strange not to have the Japanese around within the prison, and we caught ourselves watching for them. There were many stories about what had happened to our particular group, but we couldn't verify any information about them then.

Camp Bilibid was now filled with American soldiers from early morning until late at night, every boy in "our outfit" who had a few hours' relief seeking the company of these civilians, especially from a home state. Norman and I even had a guerrilla captain call on us, and prevailed upon him to stay and share our lunch, while he told us his unusual story. He was the one man who ever made good an escape from Bilibid prison and got safely to the hills, and for the last eighteen months he had led a band of these mountain fighters. We guessed him to be a Creole, and while his talk was rusty and a little rough, he was gentle and friendly, and we admired his bold life. An added interest for us was that he had been through Batong Buhay, and had seen the houses, and found them empty; many of them, in fact, he said had been damaged by a tremendous slide on that steep mountain slope.

The Bilibid water mains had been broken, and we were able to get only scant bucketfuls from pits dug in the ground. It was dirty and tainted, and even after boiling, not potable. We drew a bucket of it at night, and when the shooting died down for a little, carried it out to the shower room and bathed as best we could, usually rinsing out our clothes and towels in the same water. The result was that we were even filthier than before, and could scarcely bear ourselves. Few of us had more than one change of clothes left since the looting. After the years of wear, and the muddy water, washing didn't improve their appearance much—certainly not their cleanliness.

Over all hung the dust of battle, and the stench of death, and the heat of Manila's dry season. Flies descended upon us in relentless numbers, so that in the daytime, we almost gave up trying to eat. Between the plate and the mouth, the food could become contaminated, and the thought of where those flies were breeding was too disgusting to tolerate. Illness spread through the prison. Dengue fever laid low those who escaped dysentery; nausea and diarrhea exasperated us as we tried to accustom ourselves to protein again, and what they called protein poisoning added to the beri-beri swelling of not only body joints, but faces and bodies, giving people a deceptively plump appearance. There was no rest, any time, for twenty-four days, and we were terribly, deeply weary.

But all this was just an *obligato* accompaniment to the drama of our daily lives. The second day after our return from Ang Tibay, a jeep drove into the compound at Bilibid, and two fine-looking Red Cross men and a photographer sent word to the office that they had mail for us. They asked me to distribute it, and with Virginia, I handed out those hundreds of "Liberation Letters," written in November and December of 1944 and collected by the Red Cross for this day's delivery—uncensored, joyous, grateful messages from our families and friends all over the world, read with streaming eyes and bursting hearts, and answered at once from the fullness of that moment.

Then these messengers of mercy brought us the little things we needed so much—soap, toothpaste, magazines, cosmetics, sewing kits, candy, gum, cigarettes, tobacco and pipes for the smokers; even a small amount of clothing. The shipment of clothes sent out for the express purpose of delivery to us had met destruction somewhere in the early days of the invasion. Daily they dodged the snipers and unloaded for us their Santa Claus packs. Once their jeep was damaged by sniping gun fire, and they had to abandon it on the street, but found another and made their trip quite unperturbed.

Food poured in from the horn of plenty of the American Army faster than we could use it. Norman was delegated to make the morning coffee, and he used twenty pounds a morning; cups and buckets were filled with satisfaction, and no more did we "submarine."

As the battle moved toward the river and away from us, the gates were opened and, armed with passes, the internees ventured forth at last—first, to visit Santo Tomas, then for short explorations, and finally, all over the areas not off limits. We even were able to accept, with excitement, a short cruise on a crash boat out in the hulk-jammed Bay. We cared nothing that it still wasn't quite safe, nor for the dirt and heat and flies. To be out and free—to walk down a city street without surveillance—was ultimate adventure and satisfaction.

Norman and Walter came in one day very late, and looking a little white, but merely commented casually that they had been down in the business district, and among other things, they had found a white shoe "with a foot in it." Norman took me with him once for a walk through that area, and I could only "oh" and "ah" at what I saw—such devastation being almost incomprehensible. It has been said that only Warsaw or Dresden could compare in the completeness of damage with the city of Manila; seeing it then, we could scarcely believe that it could be equalled.

One sight I will ever recall: a tall, modern building, front shot completely away, floors hanging down like the pages of a book held open. The lovely Bay View Hotel seemed to be standing on one leg, with most of the ground floor shot away. Fire had gutted the business district. Our city was crumpled, her beauty gone, her bones stripped, barely alive, it seemed.

We returned from one of our visits to Santo Tomas late in the afternoon, and just as we entered our gates, heard a terrible sound that we had come to know and dread—shelling, very close, although the battle was entirely across the river now. And as we came into the building, we learned that once again, vicious mortar fire had been directed at the stricken prison camp where we had spent the day, and watchers from our roof had seen direct hits made again at least on the tower of the Main Building of Santo Tomas. A sick feeling always gripped us at this new terror for Santo Tomas, where so much suffering had already been experienced. My first "homecoming" there had broken my heart, as we learned how many of our friends had died—of starvation—even after liberation.

As we discussed the culmination of the three years with Santo Tomas people, and heard the story of the Japanese soldiers there taking refuge in the third floor of the men's building, so that they could not be extricated without endangering the lives of all the men whom they had trapped there, and enabling them to get a promise of safe-conduct from the prison, it dawned on us what the sinister meaning of that list of ten men of Camp Holmes was. We became convinced that the Japanese military had intended kidnaping the ten and holding them as hostages if a similar situation had occurred at Bilibid, and the prisoners had been rescued by force of arms. In their cultural reasoning, it was necessary that the men be prominent.

The vital statistics of the Bilibid internment Camp underwent some radical changes during the six weeks of our liberated prison life. Small Richard Patton waited his entry into the world obligingly for the few days necessary to see his mother safely into a field hospital. The old man who had lain paralyzed through most of his internment passed away without knowing that he died a free man. Several men were released to seek their families in Baguio; one family of mixed blood and four of the rescued military prisoners were admitted as members of our group, for various reasons. Our camp psychotic made the error of directing her monthly tantrum at an M.P., and was hustled home by plane. Carl stood admiringly by and said to the army doctor in charge of our Camp health, "Gosh, I wish I'd had you around for the last three years!" A few persons transferred to Santo Tomas to be with family or friends, and our Father Sheridan rejoined his fellow priests.

I descended to the office one day to find that I had acquired a neat Filipino office boy named Jesus, who gave his smiling all to please. We now shared our office with a C.O. and his aides, and I had a new volunteer assistant, frail, hardworking, beautiful Mrs. McDaniels, to help me with the increasing demands. And we had a telephone. I approached it almost gingerly the first few times, but felt smugly important even while struggling with the complexities of Army exchanges.

All the while, we waited and waited for our chance to go home. The former military Prisoners of War had been flown out immediately, to our deep satisfaction. But we were still in the very center of war, and ships and planes were busy with more important tasks, and we could recognize that. Nonetheless, we hinged every thought and hope and prayer on getting out of Manila, at least, and homesickness grew into almost a physical illness with us.

Then the first repatriation order did come through, and we were given a small quota, filled by lottery, chiefly men. Carl Eschbach was appointed to go with this group to give a first report at home and to prepare the way for the rest of us. How we would miss him! But we thought joyously of his not-distant reunion with his dear family, and sent him off with our love and deep, deep gratitude for all that he had done for us.

Two weeks later, a few more left, and this time we lost our Tong family, so that Norman and I felt bereft. We were trying to get as many of the larger families on their way as possible, but the allowances for women and children were always so small that it was awkward, and two of the quotas were not able to be filled.

The third time, a brusque colonel whose headquarters were at Santo Tomas, telephoned me, asking for a certain type of completely itemized listing of our people. I had classified them many times already in every way I could conceive—by sex, age, nationality, marital and family status—but the colonel had some slight new angle I had apparently overlooked, and delivered a scathing rebuke for my unpreparedness. This was too much. After a weak promise that I would take care of it immediately, I hung up, and dragged out my pages of careful statistics, to add one more category, but all my weariness, ragged nerves, and overwhelming emotion suddenly boiled up and spilled, blotting out the pages before me, and flooding my eyes with tears I was ashamed to shed. Phil, who was standing near me, gaped in astonishment, and when he had the story, raged that he'd "see about that," and away he went, with our C.O., over to Santo Tomas, before I could stop him. They indeed stalked into the colonel's office and told him in no gentle words what they thought of his scolding a civilian, particularly a prisoner, and one who was trying to help—not hired personnel. The colonel was taken aback and with the regulations against him, sent me a handsome apology, and offered me a job in his office!

But I was doomed to trouble in my dealing with the Army, and a major from the colonel's office was my next nemesis. On March 14, we were given our largest quota, and by careful figuring, we found that we could include all the rest of the families and married couples, leaving only the forty or so unattached women and the British, who hadn't received their clearance from their government. This meant that Norman and I could go, too, and my head was whirling—but still I had my office duties to perform until the end.

It was up to me to prepare the list for the Army, and with the copies necessary for our own records, that meant eight carbon copies! Word hadn't come to us until very late in the afternoon, and then individuals still had to be interviewed, some last minute changes made (when a man decided not to go, and a woman, listed as an American, revealed she was actually a citizen of Canada), and I finished the list by candle light. Just then the burly major, with four or five other officers, strode into the office to get it. He glanced at the pages critically, then with a snort of disapproval, said "This isn't right, and won't do. You can't use initials—we want the full names!"

So I plodded through those endless pages once more, putting Robert James and Ruth Mary as directed, and my sense of humor gave a last gasp and died. Dark, noisy, hot, with constant restless activity all around me, the flickering candlelight making shadows on the pages—what a scene to remember forever. But we were going home! Or at least we were leaving Bilibid, and Manila, and I was scarcely able to touch the floor.

It certainly was no large task to pack for the great trip. Our few small possessions, and the army blankets we had been given and were told to bring, fit neatly into my battered suitcase—so sleek and new on its first evacuation—and a small duffle bag of Norman's, with room to rustle around. We had a change of clothing for each, and a new bathrobe, the sterling teaspoons, three pairs of nylons, and three frameless paintings. Then we carried around the excess food that had accumulated, trying to give it away, and went to stand in line for our heavy army clothes (to wear when we arrived home).

There were olive drab trousers and shirts, a warm field jacket, and high, stout shoes for Norman. For me, there were the sturdy oxford-type shoes known by some of the Army women as "gruesome twosomes," and the smallest available WAC suit—both shoes and suit much too large, but we were elated. [Later, with my carefully hidden manicure scissors and some sewing thread, I put an eight-inch hem in the skirt, which helped, although it was a bit bunchy around the bottom. The thread had undoubtedly come from the Red Cross kit.]

Canteens and canteen cups were distributed to us, for from here on our civilian status was to be merely nominal. Until we arrived in San Francisco, Seattle or Los Angeles, wherever we were to go, we were "displaced personnel"—waifs, countrycousins and wards of the American Army.

On the morning of March 15, burdened by two large hands of bananas Jesus had emotionally presented to me with a vow of undying loyalty to my memory, we waited two hours for trucks, and two more hours for planes. At noon, we walked thankfully aboard a great silver C-47, soared over the wrecked, desolate "Pearl" and away to the South, with Norman eating happily all the way to the Philippine island of Leyte.

[I had worn my cherry red pants-suit, and when we disembarked on Leyte, a friend quickly stood behind me—and whispered that I had sat through my slacks. I wasn't surprised, but I was a bit chagrined at such an ignominious arrival to a place filled with young servicemen!]

GENERAL DOUGLAS MACARTHUR
SUPREME COMMANDER OF THE PACIFIC FORCES

~ PART FIVE ~
RESCUE

Chapter 37:
LEYTE

Leyte—the scene of a gigantic sea and air battle, with beaches and surrounding waters the graveyard of planes, landing craft, ships. Hot, steaming, filled with American GI's—this was a huge convalescent hospital, and there we stayed for another month in the Spring of 1945. The women and children were at one end of this island in the Philippine Sea, the men at another, and the military people were everywhere.

We were assigned to large tents for our sleeping quarters, and I believe that I had never felt more vulnerable than when we heard planes overhead—the tents didn't seem like very good air-raid shelters. I recall asking one of the GI's (maybe a paratrooper) what they did if there were an alarm, and his probably facetious reply was "dig a hole in the beach and hide."

On this tropical island, we swam, ate, and rested, always with the "boys," for the next month, still longing always to be on our way home, but gaining a bit of strength and incredible tans. The war was still very much in progress, and it was not easy to find transportation for us. The GI's wanted us to play, and we sat on logs for movies, danced in the makeshift canteen, lay on the beach, enjoying a whole new world of freedom and ease. We hated the big tents, so hot and crowded, so spent almost all of our time outside. Norman would hike over to see me whenever he could, but it was quite a distance. The water off the beach was warm, infested with jellyfish, but we swam there anyway. It was a health-restoring time for many of us, and as always, we were treated wonderfully.

At last a Dutch converted freighter, now a troop transport, was made available, and we boarded almost unbelieving. Once again, this was Army travel—I slept on the third bunk up! The ship Captain assigned us all duties, but our men protested that the women were not to be used in this manner. So once again, we spent our time in idle pursuit of pleasure: reading, visiting, walking the deck, talking to the boys. The food was Army rations, huge portions, with a handful of pills on every tray—for jaundice, malaria, and who knows what.

The trip took twenty-three days, zigzagging across the Pacific, under strict blackout, for the Japanese submarines were a constant possibility. We were grateful for calm seas, for this was no ocean liner. We were horrified to see great boxes and cartons of food tossed overboard—after years of near starvation, it was impossible to tolerate food waste.

Chapter 38:
SAN FRANCISCO

Glorious homeland—beautiful San Francisco—wonderful bridge. As we entered the Bay in May 1945, we were so cold that Norman wrapped an Army blanket around me. But on the dock, there was my brother Kent, tears streaming unheeded, and other dear ones. There was family and friends and the Red Cross with any help that was needed. There we all parted from our fellow-prisoners, some perhaps forever, with loving goodbyes. There was a noble city without war damage, cars in the streets, busy, hurrying healthy people. We were home. And free. Life would never be long enough to express our gratitude to God, and to those He sent to bring us out of prison.

SAN FRANCISCO CHAPTER
AMERICAN NATIONAL RED CROSS

TO Mrs. EVELYN WHITFIELD   DATE   March 8, 1945

FROM   MRS. THELMA WEINHEIMER   SUBJECT
        87 Seal Rock Drive
        San Francisco, California

        Telephone: SK 1088

Please contact me at the above address upon your arrival. I am an acquaintance of your sister and her husband, Major and Mrs. E. C. ALLWORTH of Corvallis, Oregon.

San Francisco Chapter
American Red Cross
2018 Steiner Street
San Francisco, Calif.

EVELYN AND NORMAN WHITFIELD
CORVALLIS, OREGON, MAY 1945

Chapter 39:
. . . AND HOME

The rest of the family was waiting for us at the train station in Albany, Oregon. They had not been able to get to San Francisco because of the gas rationing, but they were in Albany, ready to take us to nearby Corvallis and home. There was never a pause in conversation then, for they were as starved to know how it had been for us as we were to know about what was happening here. Private baths, soft, clean beds, bountiful food, clean clothes—all lovely—but loveliest of all, to be safe and free and home.

&

Some months after we came home, after a wonderful long rest at my sister's beautiful farm outside of Corvallis, Norman took a job in northern Washington State and was gone during the day, every day. We had a tiny apartment in a poor section of Everett, and of course I knew no one. I had long days and my typewriter and wrote of our experience, just as I remembered it so vividly. For whatever reason, which now escapes me, I still had many carbon-copy documents from our General Committee records to help me with names, dates and facts, so I just wrote and wrote. It was a release, and it helped my family to understand what we had endured without their feeling as if they were "opening old wounds" by inquiring. Then I put "my story" away for lots of years.

Washington, October 5, 1942.

Mrs. R. H. Whitfield,
    c/o Base Metals Mining Corporation,
        Field, British Columbia.

My dear Mrs. Whitfield:

    The Provost Marshal General directs me to inform you that the persons listed below have been reported to be interned by Japan in the Philippine Islands.

                    Mrs. Evelyn Whitfield

    While communication by mail is still difficult due to infrequency of transportation between the United States and the Philippines, you may direct letters to the persons mentioned using the following form on the envelope:

    Civilian Internee Mail   Postage Free

            (Name of internee),
            Interned by Japan,
                Santo Tomas Camp (other camp if indicated),
                Manila (other city if indicated),
                    Philippine Islands,
                    VIA: New York, New York.

On reverse of envelope: Your complete name and address.

    As all such mail will pass through American and foreign censors, you should be very careful not to mention any public matters, or any matters remotely concerning the armed forces of the United States or any other nation, or of the personnel thereof. Your letters should be short and limited to purely personal and family affairs. It is further deemed unwise to refer to any informal reports you may previously have received concerning the persons listed or others interned in Manila; to do so might endanger their welfare.

    All future official correspondence respecting the persons listed herein should be directed to The Chief, Information Bureau, Office of the Provost Marshal General, War Department, Washington, D. C.

                        Very truly yours,

                        E. D. Hester
                        Economic Adviser

~ PART SIX ~
POLLY'S SCRAPBOOK

Chapter 40:
RETURN TO SENDER

There was never a time during those long years that I was not poignantly aware of what my family was thinking—I knew their prayers, their daily anxious, loving thoughts. The little hint in my sister's letter received in the first mail about "Son's tip-toeing through the tulips" was a clue to me that my nephew was in the war in Europe—double weight on the hearts of the family. I sensed, though I couldn't picture the procedure, that they were moving heaven and earth to communicate with us, to receive something from us to confirm our very existence.

And so it was. Polly Whitfield (Norman's step-mother), and my two sisters, Norman's sister in Canada, and a friend of the family were in constant touch with the Red Cross and the United States War Department. They missed no possible opportunity to get news of us and to send messages. As I have said, few of those precious messages reached me. Each was dearly received and treasured.

After we were home, we read many letters that were stamped simply, "RETURN TO SENDER." Our families had kept them for us so we would know they tried—how they tried!

I was touched, too, to learn more about their first Christmas of our captivity. Shipping to and from the Philippine Islands in those pre-war days was pretty much by sea, and took about a month. So, by the first of December 1941, I had already sent my Christmas gifts home to Oregon, Washington, and British Columbia. My family waited until Christmas to open them—but found that they couldn't bear to use them then, having no idea where or how we were. My brother-in-law folded the linen handkerchiefs with the fine Chinese embroidered monogram in their tissue wrappings and put them in his drawer, and they did not come out until after we were home. Those who wait also serve!

Chapter 41:
IN THE NEWS

Our families had saved many magazines and newspapers from our time of captivity. For months after our return, Norman and I spent our evenings reading about what had been happening all over the world—even to us! *Life* magazine was endlessly fascinating, and we felt especially excited over Carl Mydan's pictures. We knew next to nothing about the European war, and certainly nothing about the stupendous war effort here on the home front—Rosie the Riveter, Red Points, sugar and gas rationing, tanks instead of cars, "mend it instead of throwing it away," short skirts and Glenn Miller, swing music and shortages. The newspaper clippings and magazine articles told us where we had been and what the world knew about our circumstances, bringing home the realization of our limbo experience for nearly four years.

WW II Captives Honor Boss of a POW Camp

It was a different kind of reunion last night at the Presidio Officers Club, where more than 120 World War II prisoners of war gathered to celebrate their liberation from the Japanese 32 years ago — and to toast one of their former captors.

There was plenty of back-slapping cameraderie and misty-eyed reminiscence by the former civilian POWs, who were taken captive in the Philippines during the early days of the war, when the Japanese juggernaut was rolling across the South Pacific.

The guest of honor was Rokuro Tomibe, who for more than a year was the commandant of their prison camp — Camp Holmes, 170 miles north of Manila.

"We all loved him because he was compassionate and understanding," said Edna Miller, a 75-year-old school teacher from Washington, D.C. "He acted like a Christian, even though he was a heathen by our standards. After him, the commandants were devils."

ROKURO ROMIBE
'I want to beg your pardon'

FROM THE SAN FRANCISCO CHRONICLE, FEBRUARY 14, 1977

EPILOGUE

More than fifty years after liberation from my internment camp experiences, when I read what I wrote then, I realize that my emotions were fragile, and I was writing as though I were telling a story. Many bittersweet memories, closer thoughts of the ones who shared this experience—now it becomes so poignant to me that I cannot yet re-read these pages without a lump in my throat, sometimes a tear, a longing to close that chapter in my life.

But I have come to believe that this story needs telling. The thirty-seven months of actual captivity, the long journey home, the healing years that followed, the understanding that there was no cause for bitterness nor a sense of loss, that material things are expendable—all are part of knowing that there is only one real power, and that is God. He never left us.

Many of the dear ones I have mentioned, either by name or incident, are gone, or forgotten, or long out of touch. Much water has "passed under the bridge," and the years have blurred details and faces. The feelings remain, and I am quite vulnerable to the theme music of "Schindler's List," a hostage's plight, the face of a displaced child.

Because I have had a fine life, a career I loved, a long and good marriage, a daughter and granddaughters, and still rejoice in every day, I recognize each day that my religion is my strength, and that the hand of God has been on my shoulder always.

Recently, I have been hearing from others who shared many of my same experiences—none who were in both Santo Tomas and Camp Holmes internment camps, as there were just the little handful of us who managed that. I have heard from some who were children or teenagers then; their memories are different, and many of them have kept in contact with each other. Their friendships bonded during the difficult years when nothing was there for a normal childhood. I have talked with friends who visited Santo Tomas as tourists. They could not visualize the campus and buildings of that ancient university as a prison camp. Bilibid Prison has long since been razed, and Manila is again a thriving, crowded city. Only memory tinges it with tragedy.

Dusting off the patina of half a century, I feel safe in recalling what it was really like to know imprisonment. I can face the realization that only by the grace of God did any of us survive at any time, and that we were aware of this. I know the sensation of a bayonet inches from one's body, the snarl of a displeased captor, the misery of hunger. It is possible, in the safety of my sheltered existence now, to feel again the shock of a bomb exploding just beyond where I was lying, to be aware again of suffering for others who were not "making it," no matter how they tried and tried.

Our first Thanksgiving dinner at home, with my beloved family around us, with sumptuous food in front of us, and the blessing that was said included heartfelt gratitude for our return, broke my husband, who left the table in tears for those who didn't make it back, and for his own problems of readjustment. There were people who said to us, "Why, you look fine. I guess it wasn't too bad where you were." There were people who didn't want to hear anything about it—who were either bored or just openly skeptical. This hurt Norman, who had lots of healing to do.

But there were all the dear ones, then and now, who were so interested, so compassionate, so empathetic. I was asked to "speak" dozens of time, at schools, clubs, private parties, or just to a friend sitting close by. I saw tears in eyes, heard spontaneous laughter or gasps, and felt the love that was there.

We then succeeded in separating ourselves from this part of our past, going on about our lives. We attended only one of the many reunions of the Baguio internees—the one in San Francisco when Commandant Tomibe was our guest of honor. It was good to see him, and our friends from those years, but we felt that we were healthier and happier to move forward without this weight of memory. I have been deeply grateful for this.

But when the 50th anniversary of that war was being celebrated, family and friends began urging me to bring "my story" out of retirement for sharing. I called it "Three Year Picnic," quoting my late husband at the height of our stress.

To all who do share these memories, my love to you. If your perception differs from mine, so be it. By pooling our memories, we offer hope and lend global perspective to all war-torn families, and provide new generations with first-hand lessons in American history.

EVELYN WHITFIELD, CORVALLIS, OREGON, 1998

ABOUT THE AUTHOR

The last of six children, Evelyn was born into the bookish, warm and stable family of Effie and Elias Henry Walker in Corvallis, Oregon. Her father was a long-time school teacher and administrator, and she grew up knowing she would also teach.

Her mother died when she was only seven years old. Three years later, she went to live with an older sister, staying with her and her family until she was 18. At age 22, following her studies in Business Education and Social Sciences at Oregon State College (now OSU), she lived in Portland, working for a year as a secretary.

Then she joined her fiancé Norman Whitfield, someone she had known most of her life, where he was working in the Philippines. Their young marriage was soon interrupted by the intrusion of the Japanese occupation of the Philippines during World War II, which is the subject of this book.

Later, they lived and worked in a number of places in Oregon and Washington, with Evelyn teaching whenever there was an opportunity, until their daughter Lauri was born. They returned to the Philippine Islands for a year when Lauri was 11, to fulfill a work contract for Norman. Then they returned to Corvallis, Oregon, to settle down for good. Evelyn completed an advanced degree at OSU, and continued to teach until retirement age.

Happily preoccupied with both family and church activities, Evelyn also keeps busy tending a lovely garden at her Corvallis home.

GLOSSARY
Dictionary of
Foreign Terms

Amah ~ (ä´mah) Nursemaid, babysitter, usually Chinese or
Filipina

Ang Tibay ~ (Öng Tee´buy) Former shoe factory a few
miles from Manila

Antimonan ~ (Anti mō´n ăn) Site of battle on Luzon

Aparri ~ (Ä par´ree) The northern most settlement of
Luzon, and the Philippine Islands, just across the straits
from Formosa

Bacolad ~ (Ba cō´låd) Large town in Ilo Ilo

Baguio ~ (Bä´ gh ee o) The 5,000-foot-high city in north-
central Luzon, a gold mining center among the mountain pines. Used before WWII for R&R for American
armed forces in the Philippines.

Balatoc ~ (Bal´ a toc) The largest gold mining camp in the
Baguio area.

Barrios ~ (Bar´ ee os) Native villages.

Batangas ~ (Ba tang´ as) Site of major battle.

Batong Buhay ~ (Ba tong´ Boo´ hī) The Baton Buhay Mining Company of Manila, a gold mining camp, was located in the northern part of Luzon, about 80 miles south of Aparri, the farthest point north of the Philippines.

Bay View Hotel ~ One of the largest and most modern tourist hotels near the Bay.

Bilibid ~ (Bil´ i bid) The ancient Spanish-build prison in Manila, partially razed at the time of our imprisonment there.

Binalonon ~ (Bin a lō´ nan) Provincial village.

Bodega ~ (Bō day´ ġa) Spanish for warehouse or storage place.

Bucacao ~ (Boo kå cow) Coarse grain useful for grinding into flour, or for cereal. Ours was imported from China.

Butbut ~ (Bůtbůt) An Igorot tribe, head hunters, very pagan.

Cabanatuan ~ (Ca ban´ a tu wan) Site of notorious P.O.W. camp. [see map]

Cargadors ~ (Kar ġa dors) Native carriers.

Cavite ~ (ca veet´ ā) Southern Luzon military establishment and city.

Centavo ~ (sen tä´ vō) Coin at that time worth half a penny.

Chayote ~ (shy ō´ tay) A type of cabbage grown in the Philippine Islands.

Chenala ~ (chen ā´ la) Backless straw slip-on sandals worn by everyone — men, women and children. They were cool, inexpensive and sometimes pretty.

Chow Line ~ Common name for queue for meals in the internment camps.

Cogon Grass ~ (kō´ ġun) Tall, coarse grass with barbed edges that grew in open areas of the mountains. The natives burned it off from land to be cultivated.

Davao ~ (Da vow´) Southern most point where Americans were held for awhile.

Dewey Boulevard ~ The beautiful boulevard that runs along the edge of Manila Bay, famed as a promenade.

Ducks ~ Amphibious landing craft during WWII.

Escolta ~ (Ess kōl´ ta) Commercial district near the Bay in Manila; chiefly native, Chinese and East Indian stores. Its hotels and apartments were glamorous before the war.

Fort Santiago ~ (Sän tee ä´ gō) Ancient Spanish fort in Manila, long a much-dreaded prison.

Gripsholm ~ (Grips home) Repatriation ship from Far East to USA.

Igorot ~ (ig´ ō rōt) Mostly pagan people of the northern mountains. They were known as head hunters, but were generally friendly to us. Many had been taught and/or converted by missionaries. They ate dogs and monkeys, and worked in the mines as cargadors.

Kapok ~ (kay´ pock) Tree native to the Philippine Islands

producing cottony substance used world-wide for furniture, pillows, etc.

Legaspi ~ (Le gasp´ ee) Site of major battle on Luzon.

Lingayen ~ (Ling guy´ en) Gulf where major landing was made.

*Los Baño*s ~ (Lōs Bäñ´ yōs) Smaller internment camp set up later in the hills of that province (rescued by paratroopers).

Lusod ~ (Loo sůd´) Mountain logging camp (we had lived there in 1936 and 1937) in the Mountain Province about 30 KM from Baguio (no roads).

Luzon ~ (Loo zon´) The northernmost and most settled island of the archipalago. Both Manila and Baguio are on Luzon.

Mayon ~ (My own´) Formerly a small, beautiful cruise ship. Used also to carry freight between the Islands. Norman and I took an inter-island cruise on this ship the spring before the war.

Mestizo ~ (mess tee´ sō) Person of mixed parentage, with one parent being a Filipino.

Medico ~ (med´ ee ko) Doctor or medical practitioner.

Mount Data ~ (Mount Dotta) A rest stop and inn on the Mountain Trail ~ 7,000 feet high.

Mountain Province ~ North Central Luzon, distinguished from the lowlands.

Nipa ~ (Nee´ på) Native material from palm trees, used for building houses .

Oura ~ (Ō oo rah) Japanese Lieutenant in charge of Camp Holmes and Bilibid, replacing Tomibe.

Pasig ~ (Pah sig) River running through Manila.

Pomelo ~ (pom´ å lō) Grapefruit-like fruit grown in the Philippine Islands; dry, but sweet, and easy to peel.

Petate ~ (pe ta´ tee) Woven mat used for everything.

Poro ~ (pōr´ ō) A town on Luzon. [see map]

Poto ~ (pō tō) Moist bread made from ground rice without leavening.

Quezon ~ (kay zone) First president of the Philippine Islands.

Sawali ~ (så wå´ lee) Materials woven from palm or bamboo.

Tagalog ~ (Ta ġäl´ oġ) Official language of the Philippine Islands, one of about 80 dialects.

Tao ~ (Tow) Filipino peasant.

Trinidad ~ (Trin´ i dad) Agricultural valley near Baguio in the Mountain Province.

Tarlac ~ (Tar´ lack) Town on Luzon. [see map]

Tondo ~ (Ton´ dō) Large slum area in Manila.

Zigzag ~ Only highway between the Lowlands and the Mountain Province. Descriptive name!

INDEX